lulu
in the
sky

Also by Loung Ung

Lucky Child
First They Killed My Father

lulu

in the

sky

a daughter of cambodia finds love,
healing, and double happiness

loung
ung

HARPER ◑ PERENNIAL

NEW YORK • LONDON • TORONTO • SYDNEY • NEW DELHI • AUCKLAND

HARPER ● PERENNIAL

HarperCollins books may be purchased for educational, business, or sales promotional use. For information please write: Special Markets Department, HarperCollins Publishers, 10 East 53rd Street, New York, NY 10022.

FIRST EDITION

Designed by Michael P. Correy

Illustrations by Loung Ung

Library of Congress Cataloging-in-Publication Data is available upon request.

ISBN 978-0-06-209191-8

12 13 14 15 16 OV/RRD 10 9 8 7 6 5 4 3 2 1

For my mother, Ung Chourng

contents

Part Three: Double Happiness

Author's Note

Lulu in the Sky is part memoir and part creative nonfiction. As such, this book is a culmination of research and of many formal and informal conversations, chats, and interviews with the people who touched me and the lives of my family—and hence, it serves also as a collection of their memories. I've translated my family's Khmer and Chinese words into English and my American friends' spoken English into a book narrative. To protect their privacy, I've taken the liberty of changing some of the names, characteristics, and current locations of many of the people in this book.

My family's story was gathered over a period of fifteen years and thirty-plus trips back to Cambodia. Many of the people I interviewed are well into their sunset years, and most live in worlds without journals, birth certificates, calendars, video cameras, photographs, and other forms of documentation we in the West use to mark the passage of time. In my family's village in Kompong Speu, time is not marked by year, month, or day, but by the celebrations of Buddhist festivals, weddings, and the births of new family members. As a result, my Cambodian family lives a communal life, and through time and space, we become one another's memory keepers. But memories are fallible, especially when combined with immense suffering, great love, and a desire to preserve the spirits of lost loved ones in the best possible light. In cases where I could fact-check, I have done so with research and field trips. When this was not possible, I chose to let my mind wander, my heart open, and my spirit roam without boundaries. In this way, I hope to capture the essence of my family's human stories. And, I hope, their humanity.

lulu
in the
sky

Prologue

Amah Chiem La Aw
(Grandmother Who Possessed Good Blood)

Kompong Speu, Cambodia, January 2000

"Daughter," my grandmother called me, her hand reaching out. "Did you bring me a grandchild?"

"Amah," *Grandmother*, I addressed her in Chinese, taking her hand.

At ninety-four, my maternal amah had lived to see five of her children bring thirty-one grandchildren into the world. But Amah was a greedy woman when it came to her family. Whenever I visited from America, she would pat and pinch my bottom, telling me it was plump enough to bear her seven great-grandchildren. Even though her grandchildren had already extended the family line with forty-two great-grandchildren, she wanted more. So on this visit, my tenth or so trip in five years, Amah again pressured me.

She giggled, rocking back and forth in her wheelchair. I took Amah's hands. Her skin was soft, cool. It was January in Cambodia, our cool season, when temperatures often wavered between sixty and eighty degrees Fahrenheit, perfect for my Cambodian-American skin. But for native Cambodians, the Khmers, sixty degrees was cold. Earlier that morning, I saw our neighbor leave his house, cursing the chill and morning dew. He wore two layers of sweaters, a red wool hat, and black socks under his open-toed sandals. A woman holding a toddler followed behind him, both bundled in scarves and heavy coats.

"A-moy," *little daughter*, Amah said, pulling me closer to her. In our family, we spoke both Khmer and Chinese, and often switched between the languages depending on with whom we were conversing. With Amah, who came from China, we spoke Chinese.

I leaned in, squeezing her hand lightly. "I'm here," I told her.

My family's village sits on the outskirts of Phnom Penh, Cambodia's capital and largest city, where over 1.5 million people make up the hustle and bustle of big-city life. Our village is a two hours' drive from the city and houses five hundred families, equaling around three thousand people. Only two hours away, but a life as different as day and night. In the city, they have electric lights, paved roads, cars, hospitals, high schools, movie theaters, tall buildings, and, in one shopping mall, mechanical moving stairs. My family told me this with the delight of rural people discovering their country for the first time, which in many ways, they were. For in the village, they lived by the light of the sun and the moon, grew their own food, slept in wood homes, and walked on winding, red dirt roads.

I turned my gaze from Amah to the small, wooden cow wagon pulling young students in white and blue uniforms on their way to school. They sat crouching, body to body, their eyes not yet alert. A row of boys sat in the front with their feet dangling in the air, their toes pinching their sandals tight on their feet. In the midst of the boys, a lone girl sat leaning against the edge, her white shirt tattered but clean, and her blue skirt falling past her shins. She turned to me and waved.

Probably to many in the world, this patch of earth was just another village among many small, dusty villages. And at first glance, like many small villages, it looked impoverished, crowded, and populated with thatched roof huts built on wooden stilts. But if visitors were to stay, if they learned to navigate around half-naked toddlers, squawking chickens, wandering pigs, and barking dogs to our *psah*, our outdoor market, and meet the people who called this place home, they would change their minds. In our *psah*, from 6 a.m. until 6 p.m., local Khmers shopped, bartered, argued, laughed, and ate. There you could still buy a bowl of steaming noodles for five hundred Khmer riels, twelve American cents, and have it served with a spoonful of local gossip or a ghost story. The vendors, farmers, butchers, fishermen, flower pickers, clockmakers, and motor repairers were sometimes friends, often family, a community of souls who had suffered together, and were now surviving and thriving.

For all these reasons, the village felt like home, even though I'd lived in America ten years longer than in Cambodia. I keep returning to this community, my roots, and the place of my birth. This land, measuring only 69,898 square miles, is roughly the size of Washington State in America, and small compared to other countries I've visited. But like its people, what it lacks in size, it more than makes up for in heart and rich history. In this nation of around fifteen million people, 90 percent are ethnic Cambodians—or Khmers, as they call themselves—with an assortment of other groups making up the rest of the population: Vietnamese, Thai, hill tribes, Chinese, and a mosaic of newly arrived Westerners. Cambodia's story is diverse and fascinating. With its first national election held in 1993, modern Cambodia, which had existed for two thousand years under royal rule, was by 2000 still in its infancy as a parliamentary democracy.

"Daughter . . ." Amah called me back.

I returned to my grandmother, stared at her transparent skin covering thin blue veins like dewy sheets of rice paper. Gently, I stroked her palm, her knuckles, the length of her fingers, the tips of her opaque nails. And as I gazed at Amah's face, I understood that for me, Cambodia would always be about family. For this reason I looked forward to coming home, despite the exhausting twenty-five-hour-plus flights, the jetlag, and the keeping up of dual lives as both a daughter and a human rights activist. It was all worth it for moments like this with my family, my sister, my amah.

"Where's my great-grandchild?" Amah prodded.

I laughed. It was due to such grandmotherly insistence that Cambodia had grown from five million people in 1975 to twelve million in 2000.

"How can I have children if I am not married?" I countered.

She sighed, making the sound of a small wispy willow rustling in the wind as she pondered this. "True," she said.

As much as Amah wanted to populate the world with her

family, she was still traditional and believed in marriage before children. I hoped this would end her "baby" talk—for the next hour anyway. Still, I waited; I knew my amah wasn't done yet. Eighty pounds, withered, and wrinkled, Amah was the matriarch of the Ung clan, and with this title she wielded the formidable power to coerce all her descendants to reproduce. A lot. Everywhere. The Ungs had already taken over the village, but if Amah had her way, next we would take over Cambodia. And then the world.

"Amah, I brought you a gift," I said, changing the subject.

Her face lit up. "Did you bring me what I asked for?" she asked, struggling to sit up straight.

"Of course!"

In a country where life expectancy is roughly sixty-one years for women and fifty-seven years for men, Amah had outlived all of her friends, many of her children, and a few of her grandchildren. In the village she was celebrated as *Amah chiem la-awe*, a grandmother who possessed good blood. Amah attributed her health to a shot of Hennessy a day. Whenever she had visitors, Amah didn't ask for gold bracelets, moon cakes, or ripe mangos, just a bottle of Hennessy. The *real* stuff, not the imitations. For a woman who could not speak, read, or write English, Amah knew how to draw the letter *H* perfectly.

I handed her the bottle I brought from America.

"Hennessy," Amah eyed the decorated *H* on the bottle, nodding her head in approval. "Hennessy keeps me warm and living a long time," she chuckled, her gnarled fingers working like claws to unscrew the bottle's top.

"Daughter," Amah said. "Pour your amah a drink?"

I took the bottle from her. My four aunties had given me strict instructions not to give Amah a drink. They had worked out a schedule to regulate Amah's shots to one for lunch, and, if she was having trouble sleeping at night, perhaps another before bedtime. I put the bottle on the table in the corner of the room—out of her reach and sight.

"Amah, how are you feeling?" I asked, hoping to deflect her question.

A light broke through her cataract-afflicted eyes. Amah sat up in her chair, raised her hands, and smacked her thighs with glee. "First, I find you a husband," she said. "After, you give me seven great-grandchildren."

My demanding amah was back.

I decided to play along. "All right," I said. "Here's what I want in a husband: tall, handsome, sweet-natured, young, funny, rich, educated, comes from a good family . . ."

"You are almost thirty years old," she told me, wagging her finger at me so fiercely her whole body followed the motion. "You are no longer a yellow chick."

"But," I began to argue, but Amah was not listening. Instead, she pointed to a framed black-and-white picture of her younger self hanging on the wooden wall.

"When I was young I was picky too," she said. "Now I am old. And old women cannot be so picky . . ." She broke into a smile, her leathery thin lips opening and exposing her few remaining teeth. Quickly, Amah covered her mouth with her hands. In that gesture, I saw her as a girl, and flashed through the years of training it took to transform herself into the ideal of her Chinese culture: a modest woman.

Amah asked, a mischievous glint lighting up her eyes as she looked at the picture, "Wasn't I pretty then?"

"Very pretty," I agreed, nodding my head.

I imagined she had just traveled back in time. Perhaps to a period when her hair was as lustrous as black silk and flowed past her waist, when her teeth were made of white pearls and her skin was as smooth and soft as a baby's bottom. Perhaps she was with grandfather now, reliving a private ribald moment. I was filled with admiration for the tiny woman beside me, a woman who had survived nine decades of poverty, war, and loss, and yet was still full of life.

Amah brought her cackles to a stop. "Daughter, you are pretty but you are old."

"But I'm no—" I stopped myself.

There was no use arguing with her. In Cambodia—where girls often marry at sixteen, seventeen, or eighteen—at thirty years old, I was old. It did not matter that I was educated, had a job, and looked young. In the village, it was all about numbers, and the number thirty was old, but old was bad only if you were unmarried. By my age, my sister Chou was not only married, but had given birth to five children. Now, at thirty-three, she was respected in the village as a woman, wife, and mother.

"You listen to your amah; you need to find a good husband," Amah warned. "And a good husband needs to be only two things: He needs to respect your family, and he needs to love you."

Suddenly, my boyfriend Mark's face floated before me, his eyes the color of a blue ocean, and all of a sudden, I was back in America with him.

Marry me . . .

In the moment of his proposal, I'd transformed into Rebecca of York, the beautiful healer in Sir Walter Scott's *Ivanhoe*. My first big book, I read it when I was a romantically impressionable fifteen-year-old. In the novel, Ivanhoe is torn between two women: the dark-haired, worldly Rebecca and the blond, chaste Lady Rowena. Ivanhoe's choice of the boring Rowena over the warrioress Rebecca tormented me for months. If a powerful, exotic woman skilled with a sword and healing couldn't win the man she desired, what chance did the rest of us brown, slightly height-challenged, double-jointed girls have of winning the man of our dreams?

But there I was, and my Ivanhoe had chosen Rebecca. I stood on my tiptoes and wrapped my arms around Mark's neck, my face resting above his heart. I could hear it beating.

You are so precious to me . . .

When my Ivanhoe raised my hands to his lips, my body lifted off the ground toward the sky. Soon, I was with the stars above the world. In the night sky, fireworks exploded into colorful bursts.

Yes! I wanted to tell him. *Yes, yes, yes!*

Mark held me tighter.

Yes . . .

But suddenly the fireworks stopped, and the sky split open. Like a curtain, cosmic particles that separated my worlds parted, and from behind them, the soldiers appeared. One by one, they amassed, their eyes gleaming. They did not stop arriving until they'd formed an army. Then as a black, swirling mass, they flew after me, their dark shirts and pants flapping in the wind like angels of death, leaving trails of horror, mass graves, and tears in their wake.

Slowly, I descended to earth, my elation infused with fear. When I landed, I was still with Mark, his arms encircling me. I struggled for my breath. In that moment, I knew I had to leave.

"I'm sorry," I told him.

A month later I'd come to Cambodia, to my village, my family, and my grandmother.

Next to me, Amah noticed my silence and touched my face, bringing me back to the village. "Daughter," she said. "Find a man who loves you."

"Amah, how do I know this in a man?" I asked, my voice barely a whisper.

She considered me for a moment, and then said, "You have to trust your heart."

Part One: Love

1

Born of Kambu

A long time ago, there was a girl who trusted her heart. It was as simple an act to her as catching raindrops with her tongue. She believed she was loved and wanted, even though she came into the world as the sixth of seven siblings, in the middle of a raging civil war. Until the age of five, the girl grew up oblivious to the firebombs or the "metal killing birds" that carried them to her land. Her parents, being good parents, had woven a protective spell around her. Thus, for a brief time, her life revolved around school, attending Buddhist festivals, and her family. Safe in this world, she looked up to a father whose gentle round face resembled the full moon, and a mother whose beauty was renowned throughout the city. The girl spied on three older brothers who wore trendy bell-bottom pants and listened to the Beatles, and played and fought with three sisters so frequently that their father threatened to replace them with monkeys. When the girl at first heard this threat, her face burned as if she had been bitten by a thousand mosquitoes, because she never wanted to be parted from her family. She clapped her hands with joy when she learned her father was just teasing.

The girl lived with her family in Phnom Penh, the capital city of Cambodia, along with two million other Khmers. In this city, there was electricity, paved roads, schools, buildings as high as three stories, radios, televisions, and movie theaters—all things to keep the girl's young mind busy, away from boredom. As if that weren't enough, the girl's father was a master storyteller who could weave epic tales of battles between gods and monsters, and the powerful kings and queens who defeated them.

"Pa, tell me a story," the girl would often ask him.

One day, they were visiting relatives in the country, something the family often did to escape the city during the dry-hot season when temperatures often climbed past 100 degrees Fahrenheit and the red earth cracked from lack of water. Still, the girl believed their land must be the most beautiful in the world because there were always pink bougainvilleas, yellow orchids, and red roses in bloom, no matter the season. There were also water lilies, lotuses, and jasmine flowers to give fragrance to the air, and palm trees stood like giant lollipops in the sky near the ponds where the girl and her family cooled themselves.

"Pa . . . one story!" the girl begged, clinging to his back as he walked deeper into the water. "Tell the one about how Cambodia was born. Pleeasssse . . ."

"All right," her father agreed. "One story, and then you let me swim."

"Yes!"

"Many years ago," he began, "there was no Cambodia, only a water world."

The girl kicked the water behind them in delight, making small splashes.

"And then a prince named Kambu sailed into this rich water world armed with a special magical bow. As soon as he arrived, the dragon princess—the daughter of the dragon king who ruled this water world—turned herself into a human girl and paddled to see him. But when she arrived, Kambu saw that she was beautiful and shot his magic arrow at her boat."

"He scared the princess into marrying him!" the girl piped in.

"Yes, and when her father, the dragon king, heard this—he swallowed up all the waters, turning the water world into land as a dowry gift for the prince. The prince and princess married and had many children who lived and grew on this new land, which they called Kambuja," her father said. "It means born of Kambu."

"Cambodia!" The girl bounced on her father's back.

"And once there was land, people soon appeared," her father whispered as he dove under water, taking the girl down with him.

FROM THAT LEGEND CAME CAMBODIA'S HISTORY, as Kambuja's early settlers, the Funans, Chenlas, and Indians, took root in the land, ruling over the collection of small states from the first to the eighth century. Then in 802, a mighty Khmer king proclaimed himself a universal monarch—a god-king. Through alliances and conquests he united the nation-states under his control, becoming the first king to rule Cambodia. He called himself Jayavarman II; *jaya* for victorious, and *varman* for protector. His reign ushered in a seven-hundred-year period that would see the rise and fall of the Khmer Empire, and leave behind a stunning legacy of art, architecture, bronze sculpture, massive irrigation works, and ancient temples. The most magnificent of these temples was Angkor Wat. It took thirty-seven years to build (1113–1150) and was widely viewed as the largest religious structure in the world.

Designed as a temple and a mausoleum for King Suryavarman II, Angkor Wat, or Temple City, sat protected by a 190-meter-wide moat surrounding an area that measured 1.5 by 1.3 kilometers. Inside, rising fifty-five meters above the ground, grand towers rose like majestic peaks toward the home of the gods, the mythical Mount Meru. The roads to the gods were guarded by stone *garudas*—half-man, half-bird creatures—as well as magical tigers, turtles, and crocodiles. Nearby, carved on the stone walls of this ancient temple, were three thousand dancing Apsara nymphs who swayed enchantingly while armies of gods and demons fought in a battle known as the Churning of the Ocean of Milk. In this epic struggle, eighty-eight Asuras, or devils, and ninety-two Devas, or gods, used a giant serpent to churn the seas to retrieve from its depths the elixir of immortality.

Alongside these gods and legends, the population expanded and grew. At the turn of the twelfth century, at the height of its power, over a million citizens lived in this temple city. But in the years that followed, careless kings and political infightings infected the land, and the people rebelled by leaving. Five hundred years later, the jungle had reclaimed Angkor Wat, but remnants of its magnificence still stand.

•   •   •

"CHILDREN . . ." THE GIRL'S MOTHER beckoned. "Come, it's time to go home."

As her father swam back to shore, the girl rode on his back and watched the sun lower into the Mekong River. In the water's reflection, the yellow ball burst like an egg yolk that had just been popped, spreading out all over the surface. The girl marveled at her charmed life.

But soon after the day at the river, the war came.

The soldiers called themselves Red Khmers, Khmer Krahom in the girl's native language. It was the name given to the followers of the Communist Party of Kampuchea, known later to the world by the French translation Khmer Rouge.

On April 17, 1975, Khmer Rouge soldiers stormed into Phnom Penh on muddy trucks with their guns, grenades, and a vision of a pure, utopian, agrarian society. The soldiers pulled out their bullhorns and began to scream for everyone to leave the city.

"Pack as little as you can to live on for three days!" the soldiers yelled as rounds of loud, crackling gunshots were fired into the air. "You can come back to your home after three days! But you must leave now! No one can stay! The Americans are coming to bomb the city! If you stay, you will die!"

The girl was afraid. She didn't know who the Americans were. She didn't know if the soldiers spoke truth or lies, but on that day, she and her family were among the two million Khmers forced to leave their homes and their belongings. They poured out of their buildings like colonies of black ants, filling the streets and marching into the countryside.

On that day, Kambuja became a prison. The girl and her family lived like prisoners in villages akin to labor camps, where every day was a workday, no matter if you were six or sixty. Every day, the girl and her people worked to build dams, dig trenches, and grow crops, helping to rebuild the country in the image the new communist government, the Angkar, forced upon them—a new world order they knew little about, didn't choose, and didn't want. And they couldn't leave. To prevent them from escaping, the Angkar had soldiers who patrolled the villages and borders, littering the ground with millions of what their leader called "silent sentinels of death": landmines. These soldiers needed no sleep, food, or pay, and once activated, they stayed active for decades.

In this new world, everything the girl had taken for granted in her old life—colorful clothes, books, movies, concerts, going to school, markets, and temples—was banned, destroyed, or abolished. New laws were enacted that dictated travel, work, relationships, and life. The soldiers told the girl and her family what to wear, when to sleep, eat, work, and what to say. There was no time for play.

Nine months into her new life, another group of soldiers arrived at her village. The girl had never seen them before.

"We need every teenage male and female to come with us," the new soldiers announced at the village square, their guns cradled in their arms. "They will go live in Kong Cha Lat, a teenage work camp."

Upon hearing this, the girl watched her fourteen-year-old sister Keav's eyes well up with tears.

"Anyone who refuses this order is an enemy of Angkar and will be destroyed!" the soldiers yelled.

The girl bit her lips in silence when Keav and her teenage brothers Meng and Khouy left with the soldiers. She watched them until she could no longer make out their figures in the road.

The girl's father walked up to her. "Come, children," he said. "It's time to go inside." Silently, the girl followed her remaining family—twelve-year-old brother Kim; sisters Chou, eight, and Geak, three; her parents—into the hut. In three months, she would turn six.

The days turned into weeks, months, and soon it had been one year of this new Cambodia. And in this new Cambodia, no matter how hard they worked, there was often a shortage of food. Especially during the months when the sky refused to open and drop down rain, causing the crops to shrivel. In those months, rumors of war hovered over the village like swarms of black flies.

Then one day, another group of soldiers came to the village. "We need everyone to harvest what crops there are and load them into the truck!" the soldiers ordered.

Without protest, the people did as they were told. When there was little left in their fields, the soldiers departed. As they drove away, the girl watched hungrily.

"Brother Kim, where are the soldiers taking all the food?" she asked.

Kim mulled over her question for a moment. "I don't know for certain," he said. "I heard that when the Angkar formed armies, there wasn't enough money to buy guns and supplies for the soldiers. The Angkar had to borrow money from China to buy guns and weapons. Now it has to pay China back."

The girl and brother were children and did not know if what they'd heard was truth or another lie. They had thought of asking an adult for confirmation, but it seemed the adults in the village were as afraid as they so they stayed silent. Instead, they watched the soldiers return often for the village's harvest, and the girl's stomach ballooned from hunger. She soon began to notice the flesh from Chou and Geak's bodies disappearing, leaving their faces hollow, and their eyes curving in like dark holes. Yet, from dawn until dusk they worked, harvesting rice and loading it into trucks that drove it away. To survive, the girl scoured the land and newly razed fields looking for something to eat. She ate roots, beetles, snakes, and rats. One day, she was so hungry she ate a piece of charcoal and dreamt that it was cake.

Six months after she left, the girl's fourteen-year-old sister, Keav, died from food poisoning. When the girl learned this, she hid in the woods and prayed to the gods to have mercy and end their suffering. But the fighting went on. Slowly, eventually, inside her body, hate grew like pebbles of black coal that fell in clumps to the bottom of her stomach. There, they smoldered and weighed her down.

Why? the girl kept asking. Why did the soldiers hurt her family when they looked just like them, spoke the same language, and sang the same songs? *Why?* When the majority of their countrymen and women followed Theravada Buddhism, which valued the principles of right thoughts, right living, and right deeds? Their religion taught that how you treat others in this life would affect your reincarnation in the next life. And if your karma—or life's actions—was bad, you risked returning as a snake or a slug instead of a human.

The girl did not understand. She could not imagine why the soldiers would hurt people who also were related to the great, ancient builders of Angkor Wat.

The new government, the Angkar, did not ask the same questions. Instead, they set their minds to ridding the country of threats and traitors. They sent their soldiers out to gather former civil servants, politicians, soldiers, and builders of the previous regime, and executed them en masse. Still, everywhere they looked, the Angkar saw more threats, more traitors. They sent out more soldiers, this time for the teachers, singers, dancers, musicians, writers, brothers, sisters, wives, husbands, and fathers. It had become evident that everyone was a suspect.

Then came the day when the soldiers came for her father.

The soldiers arrived at dusk and asked him to go with them to help remove an ox wagon that was stuck in the mud. Her father went inside their thatched roof hut to talk to her mother while the children waited outside. The girl could hear her mother sob, a sound so breaking that the girl's knees buckled, forcing her to sit on the ground. When her father came out of the hut, one by one he picked up her brother and sisters and held them in his arms. When it was the girl's turn, she wrapped her arms around his shoulders and rested her face at the nape of his neck. With her feet dangling in the air, she smelled him. He smelled of the Mekong River.

"Can I go with you, Pa?" the girl asked, her voice small.

"No . . ." her father replied. "You be good and take care of yourself and your brother and sisters. And be good to your mother . . ."

When he put her down, the girl did not cry. Instead, she watched him walk off into the sunset with the soldiers. That night the gods had painted the sky a majestic palette of gold, red, magenta, and orange. The girl cursed them for it. She was only seven years old.

In the months after her father was taken, the family began hearing another rumor. Brother Kim said the Angkar feared the survivors and children of the men they had killed would one day rise up and take their revenge. To eliminate this threat, soldiers were killing entire families of those they'd taken away, including young children. The girl didn't believe her brother. And yet, entire families were disappearing from their village.

Three months after the soldiers took her father, the girl's mother woke her and her siblings up early one morning. "We cannot stay together any longer," she said to the children. "If we stay together, we will die together, but if they cannot find us, they cannot kill us."

The girl shook her head.

"You three have to leave and go far away," her mother pointed to Kim, Chou, and the girl. "Geak is too young to go," she said, gathering the four-year-old into her arms. "She will stay with me."

"No!" the girl yelled.

Her mother looked at her sternly. "You have to," she said. "Your Pa is gone now, and I cannot take care of you kids. I don't want you here! You are too much work for me! I want you to leave!"

When the girl refused to move, her mother turned her by her shoulders and pushed her out the door. The girl left; filled with anger at the gods, the war, the world, and, now, her mother. This anger fed the girl, so much so that when she found her way to a children's work camp, she was placed in a child-soldier training program.

The next year, while children in other parts of the world went to school to learn and make friends, the girl was taught to hate and hurt. While other children were playing hide-and-seek, the girl was training with guns a third her body's weight and half her height. There, her rage was rewarded with food and praises.

"You are the children of the Angkar!" hollered the camp supervisor, a young woman in her early twenties. "In you lies our future. You are pure and uncorrupted."

"Angkar! Angkar! Angkar!" The girl pumped her fist to the sky and shouted with her comrades.

The camp supervisor paced around the circle of girls, her face contorted with fury. "Even if you are nothing, the Angkar still loves you!" she yelled. "Many people have hurt you, but the Angkar will protect you. However, you must give your complete loyalty to the Angkar!"

The girl knew the Angkar told many lies. Nevertheless, some of their messages were imprinted in the girl's mind: Love makes you vulnerable; hate makes you strong. And only the strong survive.

Those lies were cemented one year later when the girl learned the soldiers had traveled to her village and taken her mother and little sister. She screamed at her mother for leaving her, and as she shrieked, her mother began to shrivel in the girl's mind, until the image of her youthful mother was replaced by an old woman. A woman who abandoned her daughter. The girl's tears, like torrential rain on the Mekong, drowned her from the inside, a flood of hurt so vast and never-ending, the girl did not know if she could survive it. She began to hyperventilate, and mercifully, she blacked out.

Sixty days later, on January 7, 1979, Vietnam captured Phnom Penh. Nine years old, orphaned, and full of rage, the girl escaped the bombings and gunfire only to walk into the snare of a Vietnamese soldier. She was thirsty after a long day of collecting kindling in the forest, and when the soldier promised to give her water, she followed him into the woods.

"Nam soong! Nam soong!" The soldier ordered her in Vietnamese to lie down as he pushed her down on the ground.

The girl was too terrified to scream. In her culture, a woman learned the physical act of marriage the night of her wedding. She did not know exactly what the Vietnamese soldier intended, but she knew it was bad.

"Shhhh . . . shhh . . ." The Vietnamese soldier hissed, his hand covering her mouth, his nails digging into her cheeks. The girl moaned, her eyes wide with fright.

"Shhhh . . . shhh . . ." He warned, letting go of her mouth to tug at her pants.

A scream exploded out of the girl's mouth then. "Help! Help!" she shouted, but no one came. The Vietnamese soldier grabbed her leg, pulled her roughly to the ground. The girl fought and twisted out of his grasp, kicking him in his groin with all her hatred. As he doubled over in pain, she pushed her trembling body up and ran. She escaped. But in her heart, she would continue to fear him.

The girl's war ended when Vietnamese troops defeated the Khmer Rouge soldiers. Yet it came too late for 1.7 million of her people; over a quarter of the country's population died from hard labor, diseases, starvation, and executions. Among the victims were the girl's parents and two of her sisters. The girl had survived, but her anger grew. And now, there was something else growing alongside it—something dark and oppressive, cold and unforgiving. What exactly it was, the girl would not know for many years.

Still, the girl considered herself lucky, because four of her siblings survived. Eventually, they were reunited. Together they returned to their family village and began to rebuild their lives.

ONE YEAR AFTER HER RETURN TO her village, the girl sat on the top deck of a small fishing boat leaving Cambodia for another land. The sun hung low along the horizon, casting shadows on the group of refugees on the deck. They had been sailing on the sea for three days and nights, sitting in each other's sweat and vomit. The girl was with Eldest Brother Meng and Eldest Sister-in-Law Eang, who at twenty-one and twenty-two had aged beyond their years. They were with eighty-nine other displaced people who had left their families and homes, hoping to make their way to the refugee camps in Thailand.

When Eldest Brother had announced six months earlier that he was leaving Cambodia in search of a better life elsewhere, the whole family met to discuss the matter. In the village, they had heard of such attempts by people whose boats became lost at sea—captured by pirates who raped the women and children, or blown off course so far and wide that good people turned into cannibals. The children repeated these tales in gory detail, tormenting each other about who would be the first to get eaten and who would be the first to eat another.

"The journey is too dangerous and expensive; the risk too high," the aunties and uncles concluded. "So if you must go, you may only take one sibling with you."

Arguments erupted over who Eldest Brother should pick amongst the family. "Choose Khouy," a cousin suggested. "He is strong like a tiger and can fend for himself."

"Pick Kim," another chimed in. "He is fourteen, and quick as Bruce Lee."

"Take Chou," yet another recommended. "She is twelve and hard working."

The girl's thoughts jumped to their lost sisters, Keav and Geak. She saw Eldest Brother's face darken with weariness and remembered again that he was only twenty-one.

"I'll take Loung," Eldest Brother said softly.

The girl was suddenly cold, but on her skin, hot beads of sweat formed. "Koan Samnang," *Lucky Child*, the villagers called the girl when they heard of the decision. The girl was nine, chosen because as the youngest she would have the most years to receive an education, should they find a new home where such dreams were possible. But the girl didn't feel very lucky. She was scared to leave her village and her family, especially her sister.

The day they left, the family gathered in the middle of the

red, dusty road. The girl sat on the back of Eldest Brother's bicycle, on top of a small pile of clothing and a little bag of rice. She stared at her land. In her country, the weather consisted of only two seasons—dry and wet. From November to April, the dry season, water receded and green lands became red and brown. During these months, the temperature climbed so high that even the normally mud-loving crabs crawled out of their hiding holes to find shade. But come May, the southwest monsoon arrived and brought with it 75 percent of the country's rainfall. And for six months, the whole country was lush and green once more.

The girl took in the village—the green rice fields, the pink lotus blooms, the brown cows. Even with all that had happened, she loved this land. One by one, the aunts, uncles, and cousins came up to say their goodbyes. The last one to come up was her sister Chou.

"Don't forget us," Chou cried, her face wet with tears.

The girl was now ten, and Chou was twelve. Though they were children, they had supported each other over the deaths of their parents and sisters. All their lives, each had been the other's best friend and protector, and now they were to be separated.

Chou cried as Eldest Brother pedaled the girl away. "Don't forget me . . ." Chou held on to the girl and ran along with the bike until the moment she knew she had to let go or risk pulling her off the bike. She let go. As they pedaled away, the girl did not look back. Her last image of the village was of her sister crying.

ON THE SEA, THE GIRL WONDERED HOW it was that their rickety boat stayed afloat when their hearts were so heavy. The sun was high in the sky that day, and hot rays singed the oils on the girl's unwashed scalp and hair. The girl did not care. She poked at her swollen belly, made round by malnutrition, and slowly ate her rice gruel along with small bites of salted dried fish. In the reflection from her aluminum bowl, her face was distorted, her features twisted like a ghost, but her brown eyes still held specks of hope and dreams of another life.

Eldest Brother walked over to her and mussed up her hair on top of her head. "Little sister," he said. "When we get to our new home, what do you want?"

The girl thought the question over for a moment. *A shiny pink bicycle? A pretty red dress to wear? A life-sized doll?*

"I want a new life," she told him resolutely.

Then she returned to staring at the never-ending sea and dreaming up what that new life would look like.

2
Crush

Ten years, and many lifetimes later, I strolled down Church Street. Cambodia was a million miles away; it was as if the events there never happened to me at all, but rather to another little girl whose name happened to match mine. And yet, I couldn't escape the knowledge that they had. My proof came a few years after our arrival in America; Cambodia had reopened its borders to the outside world, and we were able to reconnect with the brothers and sister we left behind. Our guilt about leaving lifted with the knowledge that our family was alive and well in our native land. In Vermont we were similarly blessed. Shortly after our arrival, my brother Meng and sister-in-law Eang quickly found work and added two lovely daughters to our family, Maria and Tori—our first American Ungs.

On Church Street I slowed my pace and tilted my face toward the bright sun. It was a breezy summer day in Burlington. In the clear blue sky, wisps of white clouds expanded and changed shape, blown around by crisp, fresh air. Above me, lush green leaves danced on the trees that lined the paved walkway, cooling the land with their shade. I sauntered by, passing people whose arms were heavy with bags, their naked toes browning in Birkenstock sandals. In a state known for its long and frigid winter, days like these brought Vermonters out in droves. Especially on Church Street, a cobblestone historic market place with more than a hundred retail stores and restaurants, along with street artists and performers to entertain shoppers. I looked up and saw that the clouds were now forming triangle shapes that looked like corn chips. I hurried along to meet Beth, Christina, and Cassie at Sweetwaters for plates of the best nachos in town.

When I first came to America as a child, I would crawl into bed every night dreaming of new friends, clothes, and a normal day-to-day life, but I never really believed that any of it was possible for me—an orphan girl, a refugee, an awkward foreigner with the social skills of a Tasmanian she-devil. But I knocked on heaven's door and was let in; a decade later I was living my dream. I was a healthy second-year college student on a full scholarship, and I had thriving families growing on two continents. By day, I explored life with a group of fabulous girlfriends and ate all the delicious food my stomach could hold, and at night, I snuggled in the safe and warm dorm room I now called home. As I closed my eyes to sleep, the war—my war—flailed behind me like an old, decrepit despot.

I was glowing with this happiness when I saw Mark.

• • •

I'D SEEN HIM WALKING AROUND CAMPUS the week before at Saint Michael's College's orientation week. Instantly, I knew he was a new student. I would have noticed had he been at the school my freshman year. Tall, handsome, with long, blond hair that he wore in a ponytail, Mark would be hard to miss at our small, private Catholic college of 1,200 students. That week, more than a few girls noticed.

Like the others, I'd watched him from afar throughout that week, and when he walked into my political science class, I stared at him from a few rows behind, my eyes distinguishing the blend of blond, gold, and brown hair on the back of his head. A few days later, I found myself standing next to him in front of our professor's desk after class. We were briefly introduced by our professor then, but I, like many girls who grew up believing they were nerds, assumed Mark wouldn't remember me.

But there he was on Church Street. He walked with the long, easy strides of an athlete in his acid-washed blue jeans that were ripped at the thighs and knees. I stole glances at his face, his long hair pulled back into a ponytail, showing off his chiseled features. There was a wild and untamed quality about him that caused all other thoughts to flit out of my head like moths.

At twenty I'd only had three crushes. That not one of these crushes returned my feelings did not surprise me. In high school, I attributed this sad record to the environment in which I had come of age, one in which boys were more accustomed to blond girls with pale skin. My brown skin, black hair, and dark eyes must have seemed as alien to these boys as a bug-eyed, green-skinned Martian landing in rural Essex Junction. At least, I had hoped it was that, and not the alternative: that I was too weird and strange for someone to date.

I consoled myself with the thought that I wouldn't know what to do if my crushes had returned my feelings. Since the beginning of our family history, the Ungs had always believed in arranged marriages. My great-grandmother, grandmother, mother, brothers, sister, aunts, uncles, and cousins had all been set up in their marriages. In these unions, love often came after the firstborn child, if at all. Meng and Eang, whose marriage was arranged by my aunts the year before we left Cambodia, had brought their beliefs twelve thousand miles with them to America. When we arrived in Vermont, they worked hard to give me a safe life, a chance to better myself through education, secure in the hope that someday this would lead me to a stable job in accounting. Their vision of my new life did not involve me dating.

"No dating, no boys." Eang set down the rules when I was thirteen.

That was how she said it. Not "no dating until you turn sixteen," or "no dating until you're eighteen." Not "no dating anyone we don't approve of, anyone we don't know, not while you live under our roof." Nope, just "no dating, no boys."

"And no boys calling on phone, no boys visiting house, no go to boys' house."

Meng was nowhere to be seen when this conversation occurred. By this time I had learned to recognize their division of parental responsibilities. If our talks had anything to do with school, work, or money, Meng would speak to me. Everything else was Eang's domain.

"No friend boys, no boyfriends."

"But Saw," *Sister-in-Law*, I said in Chinese.

Like our family in Cambodia, we often switched between Chinese and Khmer, then later we added English to the mix. When we first arrived in Vermont, Meng made a point of speaking mostly Chinese, and Eang spoke Khmer to Maria, Tori, and me. As a result, the girls and I became proficient in all three languages. But it was not easy, considering that Khmer and Teochew, the Chinese dialect we speak, sound as different as day and night. When spoken together, they often made our tongues tired.

I stopped stirring the pot of curry to plead my case once more. "Saw, all my friends date!"

As usual, all our conversations happened in the kitchen, usually with me stirring something, and Eang sitting or squatting on the floor chopping or peeling something. On this day, she was quartering a white, featherless chicken on a big round chopping block with her sharp, shiny cleaver.

"Everyone dates in America," I said again when I got no response the first time. "That's how they fall in love, find a husband, and get married."

Eang looked at me, her face scrunching like she'd just eaten a sour apple. Then she put her cleaver down, got up off the floor, and walked over to me. "You too young to think such nonsense."

"But . . ."

"What in love?" Eang replied. "What girls know about love?"

"In America, that's what they do . . ."

"Pfftt . . ." Eang made a spitting sound. "Everywhere here, girls and boys hold hands and kiss for everyone to see. It's bad. Make girls not pure."

In our traditional culture, a girl's most valuable possession was her purity. And once tainted—by such things as going on dates, holding hands, and kissing—this purity was difficult to get back.

Eang washed her hands and held up a fruit as a demonstration. "See this? Girls are like plums. Everyone wants red, ripe plum. No one wants fruit everyone has tasted. If plum gets passed around too much, it becomes brown, bruised, and infected with diseases. It turns into ugly, dry, diseased prune. People throw away old prunes."

That was the end of my dating talk with my sister-in-law. But of course, I did not obey them. Instead, I did what all American teenagers did in my situation: I snuck out. In the guise of studying at a girlfriend's house, or researching at the library, I managed to go on a few dates and, for a short time, even had a boyfriend they knew nothing about. But still, my experiences with men were so limited that at twenty years old, I was as comfortable with them as E.T. was with humans on his first day of life on Earth. So on that September day, far away from Meng and Eang, I strolled down Church Street eyeing Mark as if he were a tasty bite of candy. When he paused in front of a shop, I ducked into a jewelry store. I ran to a mirror and examined my reflection. My hair was tied back, my face clean and clear. I smoothed my bright summer dress, and then, slowly, as nonchalantly as I could, released my hair so that it fell to the small of my back, all while spying on him in the glass.

Mark walked with a look of concentration on his face, an expression of bewilderment, as if he couldn't digest the fact that everything before him was real. I knew I needed to put myself in his path, so I slipped out of the store. We were about to pass each other on the crowded walkway when a gust of wind lifted my hair away from my face and fanned it to the side. In what seemed like slow motion, I caught his eye and gave a small smile. He stopped and turned. I held his gaze and, this time, grinned widely. He opened his mouth as if to say something, when, *Thwonk!* I slipped on the sidewalk, my iced coffee flying into the air.

"Oops!" I hollered as I fell backward.

If there were a competition for falling, I would win the gold medal. Years of high school soccer had killed the nerves in my ankles, so anytime my feet stepped on cracks, tree trunks, rocks, or pebbles, I would fall. Through practice, I'd learned to perfect my fall. No flailing arms, inappropriately splayed legs, awkwardly crossed feet.

"Are you all right?" Mark crouched down next to me, his hand resting lightly on my arm, and where his fingers touched my skin, a fire spread and burned.

I nodded. "Mmm-hmm . . ."

Against the backdrop of the bright afternoon sun, I saw strands of blond hair fly across his forehead like streaks of gold. His necklace, a piece of dark wood carved in the shape of an eagle, hung on a leather strap close to his throat. And just like a desert drought after the first rainfall, I was immediately flooded with lust. Somewhere in the Sahara, thunder and lightning split open the sky, pink cactus buds bloomed into luscious flowers, and frogs emerged from the mud like princes.

Seeing that I was all right, Mark stood up and offered me his hand. As I took it, a lifetime of adolescent romantic fantasies competed for attention in my imagination: somewhere in time, we were on our first date, having our first kiss under a tree.

I imagined my women ancestors grimacing at my wanton boldness. In their homelands in rural China and Cambodia, they scowled, their black eyes squinting, red lips pursed in disapproval. In a culture where proper girls would never flirt with a man in public, there I was, holding hands with a strange man who was not my betrothed, or even of my race. The shame of it all was enough to make the spirits of my relatives crawl out of their resting places to haunt me. But I was protected by vast open waters, safe from their wrath.

"Are you sure you're all right?" he asked again.

I nodded mutely. Somewhere on different parts of Church Street, I was sure my girlfriends could feel my shivers.

Don't worry, you look so cute, my friend Christina, the one who never left a nice thing unsaid, told me in my head.

Don't overdo it, just relax, sensitive Beth worried.

Nice work, bold Cassie confirmed. *Go ahead, cop a feel. You know you want to; it's the thing to do. You're an American girl now, and all American girls are corrupt.*

My American sisters, like three fairy godmothers, came into my life when we were schoolgirls. Beth, my oldest friend, I met in grade school, and Christina and Cassie I bonded with the first day of college. Together, they saved me from my teenage geekdom and brought me into a world of boys and parties. With my friends, I was an American girl, Lulu, with my big Cher hair, gypsy skirts, and boots. And as an American girl, I moved through life as if I did not have a worry in the world—beyond the constant stress of cramming for tests or the weekend plans of which movies to see and whose party I could get myself invited to. Of my Cambodian history, the girls only knew that my parents were deceased, that I lived with my brother, sister-in-law, and two nieces, and that I did not talk about my family. They didn't know about Cambodia, or the Khmer Rouge, or much about the brothers and sister I had left behind. As an American girl, I didn't need or want them to know all these things. What I wanted most from them was their help sneaking me out of the house without my brother's knowledge. With this, they gladly complied. On the floors of our bedrooms, in whispers, they shared with me all they knew about dating and boys. And what I didn't learn from my girlfriends I learned from television, movies, and books—my teachers, mentors, and friends. My shelves were full of them:

Frog Went A-Courtin', Sixteen Candles, the Nancy Drew books, *Forever . . . , The Kama Sutra.*

As I stood there next to Mark, lessons from my books and my friends flooded my mind. I ran my fingers through my hair.

"I'm Mark," he introduced himself.

"I know . . ." I said. "Lulu."

"Is that your real name?"

"Why?" I asked a decibel too loudly.

He shifted his weight from his right foot to his left. "No reason."

"Well, it's Loung . . . but . . . I go by Lulu or Lu."

"I like Loung. It's a nice name."

I frowned, realizing that perhaps I was being a bit too defensive. "Uh, thanks . . . Umm . . ."

"We met in Professor Grover's class . . ."

"Yeah . . . you . . . remembered?" I sounded too shocked, so I stopped myself from saying anymore, mentally shoving a fist in my mouth.

Froggy went a-courtin', uh-huh, uh-huh, the green Froggy hummed in my mind.

Please stop! I begged, but Froggy kept jumping from one lily pad to another and singing, *Uh-huh, uh-huh!*

"Hey, where are you headed?" Mark asked.

"To Sweetwaters."

"I'm going that way. I'll walk with you."

My lips stretched from ear to ear, any wider and my face would split. "Sure . . ." I said casually, but inside, I was leaping.

Froggy went a-courtin', and he did ride, uh huh.

Froggy went a-courtin', and he did ride, uh huh.

3

Fish Sauce and Prahok

Saint Michael's College is nestled on 440 acres of emerald green land with views of the Green Mountains of Vermont, the Adirondack Mountains in New York, and Lake Champlain. A small Catholic liberal arts college, Saint Michael's ranked as a top school for independent studies, English as a second language, and international programs. Every year, students from all over the world matriculated at Saint Michael's, a fact the school proudly observed in its hall of flags. During my senior year of high school, I toured the school and stood in awe under the rows of international flags. I could see into my college future: images of me eating handmade sushi rolls at a

Japanese party, me sopping up lamb curry with spongy Ethiopian bread during International Week, and me licking the bottom of a bowl of thick Russian beef stew at a yet-to-be-made Russian friend's house. I knew in that instant I had found my new home for the next four years. And it had the added bonus of being five miles from home.

Now a second-year student, my stomach growled at the memory of my food fantasies, a low grinding sound resembling a garbage disposal. On my bed of grass in front of St. Ed's Hall, I sat up and opened a bag of salt and vinegar chips, popping a handful into my mouth and wiping my greasy hand on my pants. The growling slowed as I inhaled the chips and studied the students around me. Many were lounging in groups, their heads immersed in their opened schoolbooks. I glanced at my own books and knew I should get back to them, but my head was in a pot, planning what I would eat for dinner even though I had just finished lunch. Cassie called me "the tiny bottomless pit." She was right. People wouldn't have known by looking at me how much and how often I ate—because at my heaviest, I was still only 110 pounds. But I loved to eat. It really didn't matter what; I adored food and all its colors, tastes, and smells. Eating together connected people and cultures. No matter where you went in the world, you were welcomed into a community with food. For some, it was a plate of sugar cookies, for others, a basket of seasonal fruits. In my mind, there was no better way to begin a friendship.

When I looked up from my bag of chips, I saw Mark walking across the campus lawn. "Hey, sista!" he called. I waved, watching him stroll toward me in his unhurried way.

Since the day of our Church Street meeting, Mark and I had met up many times for meals. Our first outing had been to the bagel shop across from campus. By the time I had finished my first cup of coffee, I'd told him about my interests in politics and that I was originally from Cambodia. In turn, he told me he had just returned from his year abroad, working as an English teacher at a refugee camp in the Philippines. There he'd witnessed firsthand the power of his passport and white skin, the desperation of poverty and hunger, and the trauma of war. He came home questioning many of his values and political beliefs. Two months later, he was walking down Church Street in Burlington when I fell onto his path.

Kismet! I thought as he talked. In that twist of fate, I, a brown girl living in the whitest state in America, met the only Caucasian person on campus who had been to my part of the world.

By the time our second cup of coffee arrived, we had already shared the history of our dating lives, and lack thereof at the moment. But bagels had been a month ago, and we were still strictly platonic friends. Even though we saw each other everywhere and practically every day. It turned out we were both sophomores and political science majors. Thus, we had classes together most days, and on the days we didn't, we met to study. As our friendship blossomed, we began to spend more and more time together outside of class. All the while, I longed for a tender, accidental touch; a mere fingertip on an elbow that might spark a hundred volts of electric shock.

How is it possible you don't know about my crush? I would ask him silently, especially since whenever I was in his presence, my cheeks turned pink.

Of course, I knew he was completely out of my league. He was handsome, easygoing, and could talk to anyone of any political leaning or religious background. Mark could make friends anywhere, and with anyone—the waiter at our favorite pizza joint, the checkout person at 7-Eleven, and even the professors at our school. In contrast, I was the foreigner in a land full of Jessica Rabbits. So I hid my adoration and gushed instead about the bottles of soy, fish, and oyster sauce in his cabinet. My palms slick with nervous sweat, I would touch him . . . a friendly punch on his back, a sisterly push on his shoulder, or a girlish slap to his arm.

We are just friends . . . I repeated to myself, over and over.

But lately, I was beginning to wonder. Especially when, out of the blue the week before, Mark suggested we make a trip to Montreal to seek out restaurants serving tasty Cambodian dishes. That was when I learned that he knew about *prahok* (a Cambodian fish paste) and *somlaw machou kreung* (spicy Cambodian sour soup). When he told me he enjoyed Cambodian cuisine, I felt as if he had touched a deep part of my being, a place where food and tenderness nestled side by side, kept warm by childhood memories of a time when I had family, safety, and acceptance. He did not know that his words made me feel as if he had looked inside my heart. He understood the complexity of Khmer curry, the heat of Southeast Asian chili peppers, the softness of jasmine rice, the freshness of lemongrass, the pungent sour of tamarind, and the sweetness of coconut juice. It was around then I began to suspect that the impossible might be possible, that Mark might actually have feelings for me beyond those of a mere friend. For weeks, I dissected with Beth, Christina, and Cassie the moments that led me to believe this. I relived the time he put his arm around my shoulder as we walked to class. I recounted the days when we didn't have classes together but he'd come to my work at the language lab anyway and wait for me to finish so we could eat lunch.

"He likes you!" Beth assured me after one such analyzing session.

Cassie rolled her eyes. "Duh!"

"You must let him know you like him, too!" Christina advised.

"Yes, yes, yes!" the girls agreed.

Thus, finally, I resolved to tell Mark my feelings and maybe even ask him out—if the signs were clear. Today was the day. I couldn't wait any longer; I was ready to take the bull by the horn, as the American saying goes. A journey of a thousand kisses must begin with this first step, Confucius might advise. Behind my dark sunglasses, I carefully rehearsed the words I wanted to say. But I was interrupted when a lilting female voice called out his name.

My face darkened as I watched a pretty brunette walk toward him. For a moment, my insecurities surfaced. I waited to see if he knew her, if he would stop to talk to her. But he did not stop to talk to her. Disappointed, the girl walked away, her grin gone.

In the sun, I rolled up my sleeves and pants to soak in more vitamin D, hoping the sunbeams would give me courage. I quietly psyched myself up by shouting *Carpe diem!* in my head. But as Mark neared, my fingers tap-tap-tapped the cover of my book with nervous energy, my courage ebbing. And when my courage went, so did my mind.

I cruuussshhh yooouuuuu . . . I framed his bobbing head between my thumb and index finger.

In my nervousness, I'd looked for comic relief and landed on a recent skit I had seen on *The Kids in the Hall* in which the Head Crusher, a geeky man, walked around framing people's heads between his index finger and thumb, then cruuussshhh-ing them. Using a funny accent, the Head Crusher crushed the heads of people he saw as snobby or trendy. It had made me laugh so hard Pepsi had spurted out of my mouth and nostrils.

The next day, I walked around campus crushing the heads of everyone I knew—with my added twist.

"I cccrrrush your head!" Gently I squished. "Your eyeballs just popped out, your brain is oozing out of your nose, shooting out of your ears, vomiting out of your mouth. Blood spewing everywhere . . ."

The more I focused on crushing Mark's head, the more my nerves calmed. "No matter how you run, you can't escape me. I'm crushing your head into itsy bitsy pieces. Your head is squeezing like a ripe watermelon, your brain cracking under all the pressure . . . crushingggg . . ."

He plopped himself next to me on the ground. Where the bend of his elbow nudged my arm, the skin warmed more than it had out in the sun. "You know, you're rather violent," he commented.

Oh, crap! Did I go too far? I worried. This was no way to start a conversation to make your crush fall for you.

He turned his face toward the sun. "But random. I like that."

"Lulu is my name, and random is my game," I said.

Mark looked confused. I had no idea what I'd meant, so I went back to tapping the cover of my magazine.

"What are you reading?" he asked, taking the magazine from my hand.

"*National Geographic*," I answered, grateful for the switch in topic.

Mark stared at the picture of the stone face sculpture on the cover. "'The Temples of Angkor,'" he said, reading the title of an article aloud. Quickly, he flipped through the magazine. "Wow, it's a whole issue on Cambodia!" he exclaimed. "Where did you get this? It's dated May 1982."

"I borrowed it from my brother for a research paper. He collects *National Geographic* magazines, and this issue is his pride and joy."

"Cambodia has an amazing history," he said, returning the magazine to me and lying down on the grass with his hands locked behind his head.

"Yeah," I said, lying down next to him, my face staring at the blue sky.

For a moment, I forgot about my anxiety. When the sun cast shadows over my face, images of my childhood flooded my retinas: my brothers' smiling faces as they danced to Elvis Presley songs in our living room, their hips twisting as if they'd been injured in a bike accident; my sisters and I jumping up and down on our bed, our bodies flying higher and higher toward the ceiling with each bounce, until our mother screamed for us to stop; my father sitting in his chair, a look of absorbed concentration on his face as he lost himself in one of his books.

Like my father, I loved books. Because my schooling had been cut short by the war, I started reading late, something I greatly regretted. The first moment I walked into a library, I knew I'd found a home where I would always feel welcomed. A place where, no matter what else was going on in my life or the outside world, I could always return to to get lost, grow, travel. When I walked out with my very first library card, I knew I would never be bored again. Still, as much as I enjoyed reading, I was discriminatory against my father's favorites—history books.

TO ME, HISTORY WAS MAINLY STORIES OF dead people I'd learned about in American classrooms—mostly white men whose tales had no relevance in my life. I did not see the circular thread of how their stories connected with mine, nor how knowing about them would make my acclimation into America easier. History was the past, and I was too busy living in the present. In high school, I took the prerequisite courses on U.S., Chinese, Japanese, and even Russian history, so I could get my diploma.

As a new American, I wanted to pretend my history started in Vermont with my new life. I would have been successful had it not been for Meng, who read and left newspaper articles about Cambodia on our kitchen table. We never discussed them, but in between reading cereal boxes and comic books, I read Meng's articles about Cambodia and the Khmer Rouge. In this way, through small doses, I learned that war had entered Cambodia long before I'd arrived.

Following its formation by King Jayavarman II in 802, Cambodia was a land of master builders. This made it one of the most powerful empires in Southeast Asia, with territories that included all of modern Cambodia and much of lower Thailand, Laos, and South Vietnam. But then it suffered from neglect under a succession of kings who waged wars and ignored the welfare of its people. After the death of its most powerful king, Jayavarman VII, in 1219, crops began to fail and people starved. In 1444, the king and his people left Angkor, the temple city that was the heart and soul of Cambodia, and moved its capital to Phnom Penh.

In 1863, fearful that Cambodia would soon be completely swallowed up by its neighbors, France made the state a protectorate. For almost a century, Cambodia was part of French Indochina, a group of nations that included present-day Vietnam and Laos. Then in 1953, a young Khmer king named Norodom Sihanouk fought and gained independence for his nation.

During the 1950s, communism swept through Vietnam and much of Indochina. That same year, the Cambodian communist movement joined Vietnam in the fight against French colonization, and among them was a group of leftist Khmer students, including Saloth Sar, who would later take the guerilla name Pol Pot and became Brother Number One in the regime. Like other communists of their era, these students considered rural people, the Khmer farmers, to be the true proletarians and representatives of the working class. The students based much of their philosophy on a form of Maoist and Marxist-Leninist ideologies that were anti-intellectual, anti-industrial, and anticolonial. The students formed and led clandestine communist cells, later naming their group the Communist Party of Kampuchea (CPK). In the decade that followed, CPK members fanned out into the country and recruited members as teachers, organizers, and revolutionaries. Amidst Cambodia's political upheavals and its leaders' preoccupations with the growing conflict in Vietnam, the CPK grew. Then in 1962, the CPK led several small-scale insurgencies against the government, prompting Prince Sihanouk to call the group the Khmer Rouge. In response, the government started targeting, arresting, and jailing suspected Khmer Rouge members. But the Khmer Rouge did not give up on their mission, and in 1967, they came back in force and launched a national insurgency across the country. The government countered with even more arrests, driving the Khmer Rouge deeper underground and into the countryside where they waited and plotted, waiting for an opportunity to fight back.

As a child, I was sheltered by my parents and did not know about the communists, the Khmer Rouge, or their fights to take over Cambodia. Then came April 17, the day Khmer Rouge soldiers stormed into my city. The next three years, eight months, and twenty-one days were the period I tried to forget.

Then there was Mark. Through his volunteer work at the refugee camps in the Philippines, he had met other Cambodians and learned a bit of our shared history. He'd made friends with people whose stories he wanted to know more about, but a language barrier kept them from fully conversing. In me, Mark felt he'd met the person to whom he could finally ask all his questions. But I wasn't ready to speak—at least not of my personal story about the war. It was a part of my life that still felt so raw that I feared if I spoke of it, I would open the floodgate of pain I had worked so hard to keep at bay. Still, Mark's interest was infectious, making me want to learn more about Cambodia's history.

"'Kampuchea Wakens from a Nightmare' . . ." Mark read the title of the article from the magazine.

I put the magazine in my bag. "I haven't read that article yet," I lied. It was easier than telling him I didn't want to talk about it.

"I can't believe something like that happened in my lifetime," he said. "I was the same age as you when the Khmer Rouge soldiers came to power in Cambodia. I was playing soccer and messing around with my brothers and sisters when other families were forced to separate. I was getting into food fights with my brothers when Cambodians were starving."

I looked away as he kept talking. I had shared little of my personal story in Cambodia with him but he knew that Meng, Eang, and I arrived in America as refugees in 1980. And that we came without the rest of our family.

"Do you remember it?" He asked.

I raised myself onto my elbows. "Enough," I whispered.

Mark looked up, waiting.

I considered what I was going to say next, which was not much. Once I'd made a mistake of talking about the Khmer Rouge at a party and was accused of being a "party pooper." I didn't want that to happen with Mark. With my face tilted up to the sky, I sighed. "I was there," I told him, making my voice unemotional. "It sucked. My parents and two sisters died. My brother, sister-in-law, and I migrated to America. We left two brothers and a sister behind."

"I'm sorry," he said.

I shrugged.

"You know," he continued. "I didn't know anything about Cambodia until I went to the Philippines."

"I think it was briefly mentioned in my class on the Vietnam War in high school. But I wasn't really paying attention . . ." I was too embarrassed to admit that until I came to college I couldn't even locate Cambodia on a map.

I let the silence drag, hoping this part of the conversation was over. I focused on the clouds changing shapes in the sky. It was a warm, sunny day, a gift to help us prepare for the oncoming long winter. I shivered at the thought. Although I had lived in Vermont for eleven years, my body still hadn't gotten used to the cold. Or the dark sky when the sun set at 3 p.m. Winter was still two months away, but I already dreaded it. I let the sun's warmth drench me until I found a rush of courage and quickly bolted up.

"Mark . . ." I began, but the words I had carefully chosen failed me. "I . . . I . . . I . . ."

He looked at me quizzically.

It seemed as if the world had quieted down all of a sudden. Amidst the green trees and blue sky, red robins sang their songs while white clouds formed puffy happy faces. They were all urging me on. I opened my mouth and took a deep breath.

"I was wondering . . ." but before I could say anything more, Jenny, our school's Betty Boop, came bouncing toward us. Or rather, her two oversized melon breasts came bounding toward us, obscuring all else from our view.

"Mark! Yoo-hoo!" Jenny called from afar, her voice as bouncy as she.

I watched Mark gawk at her, and my face darkened with jealousy. I couldn't believe any man would find Jenny attractive. To me, she was just a collection of pale flesh, anime features, and a huge chest that did not fit her tiny frame. But I thought I would test Mark's reaction.

"Isn't she pretty?" I asked, keeping my voice cool as she approached.

"Sure."

Instantly, I disliked pretty.

I stared at Jenny, my eyes squinting to focus. She had the whole pink thing going, from her brand-name shirt to her shoes and lipstick. Even her fingernails were a bubble-gum pink, the same color as her earrings. Jenny was so matchy-matchy I wanted to trip her, just to get some green grass stains on her clothes. I imagined tackling her to the ground, a handful of her hair in my hands. She was bigger and taller, but I knew I could take her. I started chortling.

Mark looked at me. "What?" he asked.

"Nothing," I said, smirking.

"Mark, you're just the big, strong man I'm looking for!" Jenny's words floated like bubbles, full of soapy fragrance and air. "I need help carrying my new TV to my room."

Jenny and I lived in the same dorm, and on moving-in day she alone had a whole team of boys helping.

"The TV is in my car . . ." Jenny cooed. "So, strong guy . . . can you help?"

"Sure," Mark replied.

I stood up abruptly, picking up my bag. "I've gotta go." In another realm, I was still overpowering Jenny, rolling her on the grass, sitting on her chest.

"Wait . . ." he called out.

But I took off.

4

A Good Aunt

After I left Mark with Jenny, I spent the next hour aimlessly circling the school library, trying to clear my head of visions of them together. Once back in my room, I dropped my book bag on the floor, flopped on top of my bed, and buried my head in the pillow.

Could I have been that wrong about the signs?

I blamed my girlfriends, of course. It was their fault for insisting I tell Mark about my feelings. My fairy godmothers, indeed! Thank goodness I didn't get the chance to make a complete fool of myself.

Ugh . . . I moaned.

Outside my dorm, the wind howled at the world, whipping branches around in its wake. And one by one, leaves, flowers, and buds were torn from their hosts; a never-ending game of he loves me, he loves me not. I stared at the ceiling, focusing on a brown stain in the midst of all the sterile white. I could not get Mark out of my mind.

Was this love? The swinging feeling in my heart as if it had gone through a round in a boxing ring? I had never been in love, and so had nothing in real life to compare this feeling with. I'd read my share of Harlequin romance novels in high school, but those stories often followed familiar arcs and all obstacles were resolved in 285 pages. I knew real life was more complicated and less predictable. But knowing the difference between fantasy and reality did not stop me from daydreaming about a glamorous dating life awaiting me in college. One in which handsome men with long, blond flowing locks and hairless, muscular chests showed up at my door to take me to romantic, candlelit dinners.

In preparation, Beth showed me how to properly hug a boy.

"No A-frame hugs!" she warned, standing up to demonstrate.

"What?" I asked, having never heard the term until then.

"This is how mothers hug their sons," Beth said, leaning her shoulders into me. "Shoulders to shoulders, arms extended straight out. Hands pat, pat, pat on his back."

"Oh!" my lips rounded in surprise.

"When it comes to boys," she said, pulling me into a close hug, "chest to chest is best."

Four years later, I was in college with all the freedom to press chest to chest with someone of the opposite sex, but no opportunities to do so.

"Why isn't anything happening?" I whined to Beth.

"Guys are just intimidated by you."

"Beth . . . I'm not—"

Beth interrupted me. "Lulu," she said. "You're pretty."

However, I was beginning to wonder. As a child in Cambodia, I was told I was brown and pretty, and people treated me as such, often giving me compliments and candies. Then in Vermont, my skin had turned yellow and my face suddenly prompted the other kids to burst into that nonsensical song that ended with the phrase *Chinese, Japanese, Indian Chief!* in a tone that rang like put-downs in my ears. At the same time, whenever I left the American town we lived in to visit Asian communities in Montreal or Boston, I was once again viewed as pretty. As I grew from a girl to a young woman, I was becoming ever more confused by these changing standards of beauty. And still fresh in my mind was a kid named Tim's comment to me in high school that I had meaty legs. Remembering this, I felt an old desire to kick Tim in the balls.

On my bed, I reached over for my journal and pen on my nightstand. I chewed the tip of my pen, telling myself that if Mark was the type to be impressed by the likes of Jenny, then I wanted no part of him.

When one door closes, another opens. I wrote Alexander Graham Bell's quote in my journal.

I stared at the phrase. Seven small words that, if you believed them, opened a whole chest of hope. I chose to believe. But I still pressed my pen onto the page and added a plea to the universe:

Please let this be true!

A FEW DAYS LATER, IT HAPPENED: I met someone. His name was Charles, and at twenty-five years old, he was a grown man. He was also a handsome, athletic, and professional man.

A lawyer by training and a Vermonter by birth, he had pedigree, class, and family ties. He was a friend of a friend, and he said I was exotic. He asked me out on a date only a few minutes after we'd met.

On the day of our arranged outing, I rushed out of my dorm to meet him. I wore my long hair up, hoping it made me seem older. In the breeze, my purple silk floral dress added an aura of elegance and sophistication.

"Hi," Charles greeted me, looking like a gentleman in his crisp white shirt and khaki pants. "You look very nice."

"Thank you," I replied shyly as he opened the door to his new black Audi for me.

"Ready?" he asked. I got into the car, admiring the leather interior and spotlessly cleaned floor.

As Charles drove, I watched his hands on the steering wheel—big, with long, delicate fingers that when laced together looked like a web. They appeared larger than life—strong and commanding—the hands of someone who would take good care of you if you fell. I smoothed my dress, hiding my small, unmanicured nails in the folds of my skirt.

"I've got a special evening planned for us," Charles said, breaking the silence.

I smiled. "Great."

The drive took us away from the city. Our conversation flowed easily, like a nice jog in the park on a fall day. It was neither hot nor cold, but pleasant and a bit breezy. There were a few bumps and potholes to avoid as we talked, but we learned that we held similar views on music, politics, and religion. Outside the window, I watched as farmland replaced the cityscape, and concrete parking lots became green fields.

Half an hour later, Charles pulled his Audi into a church parking lot.

"We're here?" I asked, surveying the fields and farms surrounding us.

Charles parked his Audi between two muddy trucks. "Yes," he answered.

"Oh," I said, trying to hide my surprise. "This was not what I expected . . ."

"I thought for our first date I'd take us to a strawberry church dinner. You've never been to one before, right?"

"No . . ."

"I thought it would be fun."

I could see Beth, Christina, and Cassie laughing hysterically as they enjoyed fancy, candlelit dinners with their dates at Leunig's, the Inn at Essex, and the Five Spice Cafe, while I was at a church supper.

Charles exited the car, walked to the passenger side, and opened the door for me. "Shall we?"

"Sure . . ." I said, climbing in. As I did so, I cheered myself silently. *It could be fun.*

I was wrong.

I knew it wasn't going to be fun when I walked through the door and saw that I was the only brown, Buddhist girl in a sea of churchgoers. As I crossed the threshold, my silk dress felt as light as chiffon, and just as see-through. I crossed my arms over my chest and hunched over.

"Isn't this an amazing church?" he asked, guiding me in.

I nodded, though inwardly I began to count down the minutes.

But time can be tricky, and knowing that I wanted the supper to be over with as soon as possible, it moved at a snail's pace. When Charles and I were seated on a wooden bench that snagged at my silk dress, the snail barely yawned. When the kindly church ladies brought out the meatloaf, mashed

potatoes, and their pièce de résistance and raison d'être—
strawberry pies—the snail slowly put on his glasses and slippers. By the time Charles and I left an hour and half later, the
snail was heading out the door to go to bed.

As we drove away, Charles turned to me. "Did you enjoy
yourself?" he asked.

"I'd never been to a church supper before . . . but that was
fun."

"I wanted our first date to be something you would remember."

"Yes. The people were super nice, the food was good,
especially the strawberry pies. Everything just had this nice
homey feel. And the church! It's breathtaking . . . so rustic
and historic . . ."

When I lied, I had a habit of overcompensating with details.

"I'm glad you had a good time." Charles said, taking my
hand.

My blood did not boil at his touch; fire didn't ignite where
his fingers entwined with mine.

"I was watching you," he said, looking at me. "You were
the prettiest girl there."

I liked Charles, but I wasn't sure I wanted to see him
again . . .

"I hope I can see you again," he said.

I exhaled, suddenly happy. Charles wanted to see me again!
Above me, the moon winked in and out from behind the
clouds, waiting for its turn to shine. As we pulled onto the
open road, I rolled down the window. I stuck my hand outside
and caught the wind with my fingers.

"That would be nice," I finally answered.

In front of us, the sky was a palette of shimmering red, orange, and gold.

• • •

I RETURNED FROM MY DATE GLIDING into my room to lie languidly on my bed. My body felt tall and light, my legs—no longer meaty—stretched miles long. True, I felt little passion for Charles, but he was very nice. And he fit my vision for a life partner—easy, gentle, a soft talker. There was no question he found me pretty, no doubt he liked me. He was full of compliments and praise, and was direct with giving them.

But what of the fire? I asked myself.

In my mother's Chinese cultures, love grew after the roots of a relationship had already been planted. Perhaps then the fire ignites. But that didn't really matter. According to this belief, a perfect pairing of mates should not possess too much of any one element; earth, water, wind, or fire. Too much wind created tornados that knock you off your feet. Too much fire burned quickly, leaving behind only ashes. Too much earth weighed you down, while metal made you rigid, and water cooled your spirit. If I was fire and Charles was water, we would be balanced.

But what of Mark? I wondered.

Mark would be the fifth element—wood, I giggled.

My room flooded with thoughts of him.

Ughh . . . I threw a pillow against the wall in frustration.

I WOKE UP THE NEXT MORNING WITH an extra spring in my step as I walked to the bus station. I was still grinning twenty minutes later when I arrived home to find Eang in the kitchen deep-frying a batch of egg rolls, a shower cap covering her hair and a pair of long, wooden chopsticks in her hand. A few feet from her, Meng was busy paying bills.

I greeted Meng and Eang, calling them by their Chinese titles of Eldest Brother and Eldest Sister-in-Law. "Toa Hare, Saw."

"Hi, Loung," they replied.

As always, they looked tired. And for a moment, I just stared at them.

Since I was eight, Meng and, later when they married, Eang had been my surrogate parents. As a child, I didn't always see eye to eye with them, or appreciate the way they parented me. They wanted me inside their house and under their constant watchful eyes, so I'd disappear for hours on my bike. They demanded that I be more studious; I wanted to play. Still, we managed to live together without any major blowouts for eight years until I moved out to college.

Now that I wasn't seeing Meng and Eang every day, I could view them with more objective eyes. I could see on their faces signs of twelve-hour work shifts, the difficulties of adjusting to their new lives in a foreign land, and the guilt over leaving family behind. Like Meng, whose heart was heavy from missing our sister and brothers in Cambodia, Eang's body twisted and turned in her sleep from worry, as she, too, had left a sister behind. The days they received letters from our families in Cambodia were always happy days in our home.

Despite these obstacles, Meng and Eang worked hard to achieve their American dream. It took them ten years to realize their goals of job security, citizenship, and owning their dream home. A house on a hill, built brand-new with plans drawn to their specifications and extra rooms to house our friends and family when they visited. Meng and Eang worked hard to fill this home with love. For Meng, this meant mowing the lawn, paying the bills, and making sure the car's windshield-wiper fluid was always full. For Eang, it meant cooking. In the process, they'd taught their daughters and me the importance of hard work, counting our pennies, and taking care of one another.

I walked over to Eang. "Saw," I said. "Can I help?

Eang pointed to a stack of dewy, soft egg roll wrappers on the kitchen table. "You can separate those."

"Okay." Slowly, I began to peel apart sheets of the doughy skin.

It was well known in our community that Eang was an exceptional cook. Each Christmas, she passed out egg rolls the way the other American women shared cookies. Because of this, Christmas week at the Ung house had a particular ritual: Eang would wake early to chop cabbage, carrots, scallions, and white onions by the bucketful. Then in large pots she would mix in ground pork, crushed peanuts, and her special ingredients—which consisted of a dash of this, a pinch of that, and a plop of her secret sauce. After the mixing, she donned her shower cap, rolled up her sleeves, and got ready to roll the stuffing into egg rolls, a process that would take several hours.

By the time Maria, Tori, and I were up, the stuffing was ready and waiting for us. My job was to unpeel the sticky, thin square dough wrappers from one another and hand Maria the sheets, in the middle of which she would place two tablespoons of stuffing. Then she would pass it to Eang, who would roll it into an egg roll. In this way, we moved like an assembly line, roll by roll, until the cookie sheet was full. As we worked, Tori would entertain us by singing songs she'd learned at school.

While the girls bonded over making food, Meng could be heard running through the house and pulling the doors closed to the bedrooms, bathrooms, and linen closets so our clothes and towels wouldn't smell like deep-fried egg rolls. But still, the aroma of fried egg rolls flowed under the doors and flooded the rooms.

Today, however, with Christmas still several months away, the egg rolls were just for us.

"Loung," Eang said, chuckling. "A woman called the house asking if you are ready to get married . . ."

Meng quickly gathered his papers and exited the room.

"Loung . . ." Eang continued.

Since the day I turned eighteen, a few Chinese and Cambodian mothers had visited Eang and Meng's house to drink tea, a guise to scout out my potential as a future daughter-in-law. Half a world away from their native lands, their tradition of arranged marriages was alive and well.

"Her son is a dentist," Eang said, sounding like an investigative reporter. "His mother said he is a very good son and will always take care of his family."

I rolled my eyes in exasperation. "That means she would always live with him," I told her.

"He's no leftover," Eang reassured me, as if that made a difference.

"Tell her no," I said. "And that when and if I ever decide to marry, I will find my own husband."

"But how would you know to find a good match?"

I didn't. For a moment, I wanted to tell Eang about Charles and his profession, nice house, and Audi. For a second, I believed the traditional Cambodian message that a woman was merely an extension of her provider—be it her father, brother, or husband. A girl was often raised to be obedient to her father, sweet to her brothers, and pretty for her husband. In exchange, they would take care of her. And if she was good and lucky, she would be gifted with many children and 24-karat gold jewelry. For a short breath, I wanted to praise Charles's attributes as if they added worth and value to mine. But that moment quickly passed.

"Girls are like plu—"

"Plums, I know," I interrupted. "I am not a diseased fruit yet, so I am okay."

Instantly, I regretted being short with her. I knew Eang only meant well. For ten years she had raised me as a daughter, and like many mothers, she wanted to see me taken care of and happy.

But 1990 was an eventful year in the world—one that started with the celebration of the release of Nelson Mandela, imprisoned for twenty-seven years, from Robben Island Prison in South Africa. But as one part of the world was heading toward a more peaceful future, another exploded in violence when Iraq invaded Kuwait on August 2. In response, the United Nations Security Council ordered a global trade embargo against Iraq, and the threat of another war hung in the air. In the midst of this, the Cold War slowly began to thaw across Europe, paving the way for the reunification of East Germany and West Germany. So as I looked out into the world, I was more worried about its state than my marriage prospects. But Eang didn't know that. In fact, she knew very little of my life as an American college girl. To them, I was a Cambodian daughter, a girl who spoke little of politics and rarely opined about the world. Thus, Eang did not know about Mark, Charles, and my classes on Christianity, feminist theology, and Plato's *Republic*.

I walked over to Eang. "Let me take over the frying," I said, offering myself up to the hot oven as a way of apologizing.

"No, you eat," Eang told me, pushing me away. This was her way of telling me that all was forgiven.

I took a plate of egg rolls to the table, on which there were plates of fresh green salad, mint, sweet basil, and sliced cucumbers. I made myself an egg-roll salad. As I was about to take my first bite, Maria and Tori walked into the room, their hair wet from fresh showers. "Hi, Kgo," they said, greeting me as Auntie.

I hugged them, wondering how they had grown into such big girls. I still remembered them as infants, smelling of tiger balm oil and baby powder. When they were little, I used to tuck them into bed with a ritual I made up only for us.

"I love you," I started.

"I love you millions," one girl would answer.

"I love you billions," the other would follow.

"I love you infinity," one of us would finish.

I never wanted them to feel unloved or unwanted. The girls were our first generation of American Ungs. Long before their parents or I could apply for citizenship, Maria and Tori were already Americans. As their young aunt, I was among the half-generation immigrants, those who arrived in America young enough to begin anew, but old enough to remember another life. Their foreign parents did not express love in the American way with kisses and hugs, so I offered the girls physical affection to bridge the gap.

The girls sat down next to me at the dining table.

"How was school this week?" I asked, handing them each a plate.

For the next few minutes, the girls took turns telling me about their week at school. Then, when our stomachs were full, we headed up to my old room for girl-bonding time. There we piled on my bed, and the girls brought out their stack of new library books to show me. I watched with pride.

"You are the smartest, prettiest girls in the world," I said as I flipped through the books with them. "You know that, right?"

"Uh-huh . . ." said Maria.

Tori seated herself next to me. "I'm very cute," she asserted nonchalantly.

"Yes, sweetie pie, you're very cute!" I agreed, marveling at her confidence in her own "cuteness" when I'd struggled so hard to believe the same of myself. For a moment I lit up with maternal awe. Tori had surpassed me in this area of her growth. But then, my empowered aunt gene kicked in, and with it my desire to teach the girls of their worth beyond physical appearances. The college student aunt wanted the girls to know the value of their intellect, something they would need to rely on if they didn't want to be forced into an arranged marriage or dependent on their husbands for support.

"Sweeties," I said gently. "I just want you to know that when you grow up, you can do anything and be anyone you want."

"Okay."

"So what do you want to be when you grow up?" I asked.

Maria shrugged. "I don't know . . . maybe a teacher . . ."

"I want to dance . . . draw . . ." Tori hollered, bouncing up and down on the bed.

"Whatever you do," I said, "always know that you're more than just pretty girls, okay?"

"Okay."

"But pretty is okay, too," I said quickly, backtracking. "You're both cute, but you're also more than that."

Tired of jumping, Tori plopped herself next to me on the bed. "This boy John in my class is pretty," she said very quickly. "All my friends think so too."

"Oh . . . okay."

"So is Alyssa," she went on. "I think Alyssa is prettier."

"Okay . . ." College student aunt sat up with attention. In my mind I scanned through my studies and life experiences in an attempt to make this a "teachable" moment for the girls. As if on queue, a song popped into my head and began to play.

Birds do it . . . Bees do it . . . Even educated fleas do it . . . Eartha Kitt crooned "Let's Fall in Love" in my head.

"The birds do it, bees do . . ." I told the girls, singing the melody in my head. "Okay, sometimes bees love bees, and sometimes birds date other birds. But sometimes a bee and bird can like each other, and that's okay. Whatever you girls choose, bees or birds, bees-bees, or birds-birds, I will love you no matter what. Okay?"

"Okay," the girls replied.

"I will always support you no matter if you want to love birds or bees," I said, hoping to impart another life lesson to them. "Do you understand?"

They looked at me, their brows knitting together. "Umm . . . no, not really," Maria answered. Tori looked at her and nodded.

In trying to be a good aunt, I had succeeded in thoroughly confusing them. And myself. "Hmm . . ." I hummed, back-pedaling. "Maybe we talk more about this later, when you're older."

"Okay," they said and started playing with their Barbie dolls.

"Now about Barbie . . ." I pressed on.

5

To Speak or Not to Speak?

Winooski Park, Equinox 1990

Twice a year, in late March and late September, the length of night almost equals the length of the day. This event is known as the equinox—from the Latin *aequus* (equal) and *nox* (night). The autumnal equinox in September also indicates the arrival of fall, when temperatures drop and nights grow cold. To keep warm, I dreamt of falling in love and bathing in the sun. It was in this mood that I found myself walking next to Mark to the school auditorium.

It had been a week since the whole "he went with Jenny" incident. Since then, I'd resolved to not ask him questions about Jenny, and to stop fantasizing about us sitting under the

tree. No K-I-S-S-I-N-G. But when Mark sidled up to me and
draped his arm over my shoulder, my resolve evaporated.

"So what happened with Jenny?" I blurted out.

"She was a nice enough girl," he said. "We went out for a
drink, but that's it."

"Oh," I said, trying to sound casual. But inside my head,
high pitched woo-hoos and yippees were exploding all over
the place. "So . . ." I inhaled, speaking in a lower register. "Did
you do anything fun over the weekend?"

"No, not really . . . nothing special. And you?"

"Nope," I told him. But on my shoulder, Jiminy Cricket
chided and chirped, pecking at my conscience for not telling Mark about my date with Charles. I ignored Jiminy and
looked up at Mark, wondering if he could hear the pounding
under my breastbone.

"Are you excited?" he probed.

I gulped. *Was my face scarlet?* I wondered. "What?" I asked,
my voice wheezing a bit.

"The lecture . . ."

"Oh . . . the lecture . . . ha, ha . . . Sure . . . who isn't? I
mean, he's a brilliant thinker and mind and he writes so well
. . ." I rambled on as we walked.

Mark and I were on our way to the main auditorium to
hear a well-known political activist and Vietnam War vet-
eran speak. In preparation for his visit, I scoured the library
to read more on the war in Vietnam and its connections to
Cambodia.

From these books, I learned that by the time I arrived in the
world in 1970, much of it was already embroiled in proxy wars
fought in Afghanistan, Angola, Ethiopia, Mozambique, and
other countries. In Southeast Asia, the Cold War had spread
to Indochina, and the Soviet Union, China, and the United

States began fighting in Laos and Vietnam. Each superpower fought to make sure the dominos fell in the direction of their sphere of influence.

In the 1960s, fearing the U.S.-Vietnam war would soon cross into his country, Cambodia's Prince Sihanouk declared Cambodia neutral in the ongoing conflicts. But that was not enough to stop North Vietnamese troops from entering Cambodia, or the U.S. from following them. In 1969, when the Vietcong hid in the jungle borders of Cambodia, the U.S. began a secret fourteen-month-long campaign in which the tonnage of bombs dropped on Cambodia exceeded that of all the conventional explosives dropped on Japan during World War II. Many Cambodian scholars believed the bombings—which included operations codenamed Supper, Lunch, Dinner, Dessert, and Snack— would eventually leave an estimated 250,000 to 500,000 Cambodians dead and contribute to the destabilization of the country.

When Prince Sihanouk protested the bombings, his U.S.-backed general, Lon Nol, removed him in a military coup many—particularly the prince himself—believed was supported by the CIA, and seized power. On March 18, 1970, Lon Nol declared himself president and head of state of the new Khmer Republic. Shortly after that, Lon Nol opened Cambodia's borders for U.S. troops to enter and embroiled Cambodia ever deeper in the U.S.–Vietnam conflict. Now no longer a secret, over the next five years, B-52s openly chased after the Vietcong believed to still be hiding in Cambodia's villages and rice fields. This phase of the bombings left as many as a half million Khmer dead, produced an estimated two million refugees and internally displaced people, and made Cambodia one of the most heavily bombed countries in history.

The bombings also provided the Khmer Rouge with their two best recruitment tools. The first came in the person of Prince Sihanouk, who after being ousted from power, joined them to fight against the Lon Nol regime. Sihanouk's title as Father of the Nation, the figure who fought and gained Cambodia's independence from the French in 1953, gave the group the legitimacy it had been seeking. And Sihanouk's bloodline as prince gave the Khmer Rouge a way to reach the historically monarch-ruled people.

The Khmer Rouge's second best recruitment tool was the bombings. After each raid, Khmer Rouge soldiers descended upon the devastated village, promising to drive out the invaders and end the indiscriminate death caused by the "metal killing birds." The farmers, wearied from the fighting and eager for a ceasefire, were slow to join at first. But then they heard Sihanouk's voice on the radio, telling them he had joined the nationalist Khmer Rouge and urging them to follow him. And they did. From 1969 to 1973, the Khmer Rouge—formerly a small militia with little money or support—grew from ten thousand to two hundred thousand troops. By 1975, as man after man fell in the battlefields, and resources and support dried up at home, U.S. troops retreated. Weak, bloated by corruption, and now without its main allies, the Lon Nol regime was ripe for toppling by the Khmer Rouge, and that's exactly what they did on April 17, 1975. I was playing hopscotch with Chou on the sidewalk in front of our house in Phnom Penh when the soldiers arrived. Fifteen years later, I still remembered that day.

In America, I read these bits of history with my dispassionate college-student mind, the cerebral part that took in information and filed it away. But the other part of me, the Cambodian girl who connected this history to her life—wanted to throw the books against the wall.

When we arrived at the college's auditorium in Winooski Park, I was glad to see a large crowd had already formed.

"This is so cool . . ." I whispered to Mark, grinning widely.

The crowd was made up of community members and students, all of them bundled in layers of clothes against the cold wind. To keep warm, some younger couples huddled close together, hugging and kissing as they waited in line.

"My brother and sister-in-law would be so appalled at all these public displays of affection," I said, giggling.

"My parents, too," he agreed.

"In our culture, affection is not a matter for show and tell. It is a private bond between a man and his wife."

"Mmm . . . Catholics and Cambodians are closer than they think."

In the years I'd lived with them, I had never once seen Meng reach for Eang's hand, seen Eang lay her head on Meng's shoulder, or seen them hug or kiss each other. Not once had I heard them say "I love you" to each other or, for that matter, to me. They had raised me the only way they knew how, silencing my affection and keeping my emotions in check.

Once in college, my arms—as if animated by Dr. Frankenstein himself—sprung to life. They pulled everyone into an embrace, caressed everyone's arm, and massaged everyone's shoulders. I became one of those people who hugs everyone, whether they are strangers or old friends, boys or girls. But the people I hugged most were women. With my women friends, I felt safe, supported, and accepted. My girls were my best friends, classmates, sisters, aunties, and teachers.

As we walked to the back of the line, Mark wrapped his arm around my neck, pulling me along playfully. "Come on, slowpoke."

"Stop!" I hollered, struggling against his grip.

He ignored me and continued to pull me along.

"I said STOP!" I yelped, pushing him away. When I looked around, I saw that people were watching us. Mark noticed this too and let go of me quickly, walking away. "Crap . . ." I said under my breath.

It dawned on me then that in my life, I'd only known two models for men: fathers and soldiers. My father, brothers, and uncles were all fathers. They cared and provided for me. Then there were the soldiers, particularly the one who still haunted me at night.

But Mark was not the soldier. He didn't even know about the soldier or his existence in my life. He was a nice guy who would go out of his way to help people. He was a good brother to his three sisters, a good son to his mother. He would never do anything to harm anyone. Quickly, I banished the soldier from my thoughts and ran after Mark.

"Hey," I said, pulling his arm. "I'm sorry."

He did not slow his step.

"I feel really stupid," I said. "I overreact sometimes."

Finally, Mark turned around, his palms up in a surrendering gesture. "Wow, you can get angry fast."

"I know—I'm quick to explode," I offered as an explanation. "I'm sorry."

"Okay," he said. "But next time, give me a little warning."

"I'll try," I told him, smiling sheepishly. "Eang always says I burn hot, like oil in a hot wok. I'm a flash in the pants."

Mark guffawed loudly then, his shoulders shaking. I slapped a hand over my face and groaned. I sometimes got confused and mixed two familiar sounding expressions together.

"Flash in the pan?" I asked.

"No . . ." He continued to laugh at me. "Flash in the pants is the right expression."

"Whatever!" I stood with my arms on my hips, mocking anger at his teasing. "Hey! I may get quick-flash mad, but at least when it's over, I cool fast."

"Unless you catch on fire," Mark said, beaming.

I ran up and punched him on the arm.

WHEN WE FINALLY MADE OUR WAY INTO the auditorium, it was already filled to capacity. Around the room, many familiar faces popped out. Many of them I knew as a member of the Hunger Garden, the International Student Association, and the Multicultural Club. Others I had met at rallies against the invasion of Wal-Mart in Burlington, in support of a woman's right to choose, and to end apartheid in South Africa. Present was a who's who of student activists and leaders, my rock stars. I came to Saint Michael's in large part because of its commitment to civic and social causes.

As Mark and I took our seats, I looked around at the audience; everyone was talking and the room filled up with noise. Everyone was wound up about hearing the speaker, and completely fearless about voicing their approval or disapproval of him.

Mark knocked my shoulder with his arm. "Are you going to ask a question during the Q&A?"

"I don't know . . ."

I told myself it wouldn't be a big deal if I were to ask a question. I would be one of many in the crowded auditorium to do so. There was nothing special about that. There were no secret soldiers in the room spying on me, no one was keeping track of my whereabouts, no one waiting to take me away.

Angkar possesses more eyes than pineapples. A Khmer Rouge government slogan echoed in my mind.

Under the Angkar, we lived under such fear that on the few occasions I heard people speak, as soon as they were aware their voices were being heard, they silenced themselves. To survive, we all became mutes.

As I sat absorbed in my thoughts, the voices in the room got louder and louder. Competing with them was another Angkar slogan: *He who protests is an enemy; he who opposes is a corpse.*

You're in America now, I told myself silently. *We have the freedom to speak our mind here. You don't have to be afraid.*

Nonetheless, I was terrified.

"Do not speak," my father told me a week after the Khmer Rouge took over our country. "If you say the wrong thing, we could all be hurt. They may take your brothers and sisters away."

In America, my voice had started to return. At first, it came back small and high-pitched. When I read of the cruelties and injustices committed in different parts of our world, I wanted to rage up against them, but I could only whisper. For right there, next to my anger, lay the fear. Fear of being seen, heard, and made a target of violence if I dared to speak up. Fear not only for myself but for my family in Cambodia who did not have passports, or a way out should war break out again there. Fear that if somehow the Khmer Rouge should come back to power, and my family was once again caught behind enemy lines, my words could cause their persecutions. Or executions. I could not live with that. Thus, at school rallies and protests, more often than not, I did not raise my voice. Most of the time, I showed up and kept my face hidden behind bandanas, hats, or trees. In this small way, I felt a part of something.

The auditorium hushed, breaking my revelry. The moderator walked across the stage and stepped up to the podium.

"Welcome, ladies and gentlemen," he greeted the audience, and then went into his introduction of the speaker.

I nudged Mark. "There he is!"

The speaker stood on the stage as stately and distinguished as I'd imagined him. And when he spoke, his voice took on the resonance of a wise teacher, a brilliant academic, and a passionate activist. For the next half hour, I listened to him as a student eager to find someone to follow. I sat at the edge of my seat, my hands gripping the chair, listening in awe. The speaker's words took me from the auditorium to Congress in Washington, D.C., the cities in Vietnam, and, briefly, the rice fields in Cambodia. And then his talk was over.

During the Q&A session, I sat back in my seat and pulled a pen and notebook from my backpack. I scribbled down my question. Unsteadily, I rose to my feet and raised my hand high. For a moment, I hoped the moderator would bypass me, but instead he pointed right at me. My stomach fluttered like the wings of a hundred hummingbirds. I stilled myself against my chair.

"Sir," I began.

The words trickled out at first as if from an old, rusty faucet. The pressure of many years of unspoken thoughts bubbled forth and my words began to gush out in a steady torrent. In a long, drawn-out half statement, half question, I asked the speaker to comment on the U.S. invasion of Cambodia, to explain the Khmer Rouge's politics, to share the stories of the survivors he met. Only when I had finished was I aware that I needed to breathe.

"Your question requires much time to answer," the speaker commented. "I encourage you to read more on your own . . ."

He briefly answered my question, but I only heard some of his words. The rest were lost as my knees began to knock.

Mark put his hand on my knees, stilling them. "You okay?" he asked.

I said nothing. Slowly, a storm of anger began to swirl around me, creating an electrical storm that hummed in my ears. I got up and left the auditorium.

Once outside, I sat under a tree and tried to calm myself. Spinning around in the dark tornado inside my head were these thoughts: I wanted the speaker to shine a light on Cambodia, to cut the Khmer Rouge down to the cowards they were, and tell the audience about their victims.

In my mind's eyes, I saw my father again. His eyes blindfolded by a dirty piece of black cloth, his hands tied behind his back. He stood with a group of other men next to a mass grave filled with bodies sprawled on top of one another. A soldier approached him, a rusty hammer swinging in one hand, a lit cigarette in the other. I blinked the image away.

Mark found me moments later, still under the tree.

"Are you okay?" he asked, sitting down next to me.

"Yeah, I was just thinking . . ."

"About what?"

"That perhaps if people knew . . ." I said quietly.

If people knew, I wouldn't be the only one who remembered. I couldn't explain why I felt bitterly betrayed and disappointed. I knew none of it was the speaker's fault. I wanted it to be, but it wasn't. He wasn't responsible for my history or feelings of invisibility. I wanted something from him that he couldn't give. I wanted him to tell Cambodia's stories not as a scholar or an intellectual, but as a father, brother, and son. I wanted him to put a human face on the war and bear witness to our lives. I wanted him to speak for me. But he was a scholar, not my rescuer.

As these thoughts spun in my head, I knew I couldn't speak my thoughts to Mark. I was afraid that if I did my composure would break. I turned to him. "I was just thinking about what the speaker said," I told him, hugging my knees. "About how all of us need to learn more about our own history."

"Yeah." He put his arm around my shoulder.

And slowly, the storm settled. The speaker's challenge planted a seed; I would learn more about Cambodia and its place in the world. I didn't yet know how I would do it, but one day, I would learn to speak for myself.

6

Of Worms and Walls

Battery Park, October 1990

I couldn't talk. My voice, like spittle, flew out of my mouth as a gasp. The air conditioner that had been humming quietly in the St. Ed's classroom while Mark and I studied had stopped. In fact, the whole building fell silent. In this vacuum, time paused. Waiting.

Slowly, I sucked in my breath, dragging my voice back with it. "What?" I asked him, praying that I'd heard him right.

"Want to go to dinner tonight?"

"Dinner? Umm . . . who else is coming?"

"Just us."

Mark and I had had many lunches together, and a few dinners. But always with other friends, never alone just the two of us. Dinner. Alone. The two of us. A DATE!

Don't lose it, I warned myself. *Stop grinning like a baboon.*

"Sure, why not?" The words came out slow and casual, but microbeads of sweat collected in the bends of my armpits and on my palms. Quickly, I wiped my palms on my pants.

After we'd arranged a meeting time, Mark went back to his studies. I sat back in my chair and stared at the clock. A large white circle with black sundial hands and numbers, hanging on the wall like a full moon. I willed the clock to move faster, but the cheery face refused. I turned to look at Mark, who was bent over his books. I returned to my stack of books on the desk but was too distracted to read. *I've got four hours until our date!* my girl-self yelled to the student-self in my head. *How could you expect me to study? We've got much to do to get ready!*

I hurriedly packed my books. "I've gotta to go . . ." I mumbled, and left. I ran all the way from the study room to my dorm. In my throat, a big yippee crouched, waiting for the opportunity to spring forth and explode. "Yipppeeee!" I shouted, my feet skipping like a happy hobbit.

When I got back to my room, I called Cassie.

"Do you think he could like me?"

"Honey, he'd be stupid not to."

"No, but really, do you think he likes me?"

"Of course!"

"But what about Charles?" I panted into the phone.

"You aren't committed to him," Cassie told me.

"I'm not?"

"You've been on a few dates. You're not exclusive."

"Okay."

I was silent, feeling a bit guilty for being this excited to go out with Mark.

"Any other dating questions?" Cassie asked.

"No."

"Good. Go out with Mark."

After I hung up the phone with Cassie, I called Beth. For an hour we mulled over how the impossible had become possible.

"Remember that time when he swept my hair off my face?"

"Yes, you told me."

All of a sudden, I adored every single stray hair on my head.

After I hung up the phone with Beth, I dialed Christina. I recounted the days when Mark and I didn't have classes together, but he still came to my workplace at the language lab to visit me.

"Wear your hair up to show your slender neck," Beth advised.

"Wear your hair down; men like women with long hair," Christina said with confidence.

"Don't wear black."

"Wear black."

"Put on lipstick."

"Keep your lips clean and kissable."

I hung up the phone with the girls still fighting in my head.

Four hours and thirty minutes later, Mark picked me up for dinner in his brown Jeep. Its beat-up rusty body chugged and clunked reluctantly as he pushed it forward. He brought it to a noisy, screeching stop in front of me.

"Hi!" I waved, walking out of the dorm to meet him.

He wore the same beige T-shirt and ripped blue jeans I'd seen him in earlier. I stared at the blond streaks in his sun-kissed hair, wishing I could run my fingers through it.

"Hi," he said, grinning.

I wanted to run over and throw myself into his arms. Instead, as elegantly as I could, I gathered my flowing skirt in one hand and my jean jacket in the other, and climbed in. My feet bumped up against crackling paper bags on the car floor.

"Careful, don't step on the food," he warned.

And then I saw our dinner: two Chinese takeout containers and a bottle of white wine in a brown paper bag. He reached for the brown bags and moved them to the backseat.

"Dinner?" I asked, my face falling.

What was it about me? I harrumphed. First a church supper, and now takeout? Would I ever make it to a nice restaurant?

Mark shifted his Jeep into gear. The engine roared loudly. "A picnic, for our Indian summer day!"

I looked up at the dark clouds gathering like clusters of burnt popcorn on top of one another in the sky.

"It'll be fine!" He said, stepping on the gas, and we were off on our romantic date.

Thirty minutes later, we were running out of Battery Park to escape the rain. My flowing skirt was wet, my hair damp and limp, and my freshly made-up face was melting and smudging everywhere. We found shelter under the awning of an old church and ate our dinner on the steps. I watched him pick up lo mein with his chopsticks, amazed he knew how to use them correctly. Not to be outdone, I balanced my chopsticks in my fingers and tentatively picked up a piece of chicken. It almost reached my lips when—*plop*—it dropped and landed on my chest. It rolled down my shirt and got lost in the folds of my skirt.

Mark grinned, watching me searching my skirt for the meat. "You don't know how to use chopsticks?"

"What about it?" I challenged.

"Nothing," he said, his voice teasing. "Just . . . wow. You don't know how to use chopsticks, and I do."

"What's that supposed to mean?"

"You're half Chinese. Doesn't that mean you automatically know how to use chopsticks?"

I stared at him, my mouth half opened from shock. "I'm going to let that remark go," I told him.

Mark nipped at my nose and ears with his chopsticks. "I'm like Mr. Miyagi in *The Karate Kid*," he said. "I can catch flies with these." He twirled his chopsticks and then, using them like swords, jabbed at the air around me. He tossed his sticks into the air and caught them like batons. "They're nunchucks in my hands, weapons of destruction. Able to take people down with one single stick."

I'd had enough. Slowly, I looked right into his eyes. "I know how to shoot an AK-47."

That silenced him.

"Really?"

I picked through the noodles, looking for chunks of meat. "Mmm-hmm."

"Are you going to explain?" Mark asked.

"Then I'll have to kill you."

"Okay, you have me beat."

"Don't you ever forget it," I hissed.

I tossed my chopsticks on the ground and dug my fork into the box. I twirled the noodles like spaghetti and shoved them into my mouth. As I did this, it started to rain harder.

"I can't believe it rained," Mark said, looking up at the black sky. "I really thought the storm would pass us."

I looked at him and thought, *This is what absence of war looks like in a person. A perpetual optimist, nothing dampens his spirit.*

"Mark?"

"Hmm?" He turned to me, a mouthful of noodles hanging from his mouth like a long, greasy beard.

I suppressed a laugh and asked, "Why do you like spending time with me?"

"You're like no one else I've ever met," he answered, looking at me. "I don't know anyone else who gets so excited over a warm bagel, a hot cup of coffee, or a nice sunny day. You act as if you're experiencing everything for the first time, every time."

I found myself blushing. I'd never had anyone say such nice things about me before, and thus, I was at a loss for words.

He smiled. "You are someone who doesn't seem afraid to experience all that life has to offer . . ."

The wind picked up a little and pushed a wisp of hair across my cheek.

"It's never boring with you," he said, reaching out to pluck a strand of hair off my face. His knuckles caressed my forehead as he did so.

The rain was coming down like a monsoon now, splattering loudly on the concrete sidewalk. Mark extended his hand and caught raindrops in his palm. "I love the sound and smell of rain," he said.

I did not like rain. The water forced earthworms up to the surface, and I feared worms the way some people fear snakes. After a heavy rain in Cambodia, I had to hop from one foot to another like a crazy person to avoid stepping on worms. My eyes now followed the raindrops to a long, gray, wrinkled worm on the sidewalk. It was the size of a hot dog, and it wasn't alone. A group of its friends writhed beside it, making big, slow, slithering S's as they moved toward me.

In my mind, I pictured a decomposed body left lying out in the sun. The stench burned my eyes and nose. Still, I walked up to it, my fingers pinching my nostrils closed. When I poked the corpse with a stick, maggots and worms spilled out of its black sleeves. I shuddered, ending the image.

"Mark, could you just flick those worms out of sight or something?"

"What?"

I pointed to the writhing worms. "Earthworms. They gross me out."

He looked at me for a moment, as if he was going to ask something but then thought better of it. "Oh . . . okay," he said. He got up and moved the worms using a spare chopstick. When he returned, he sat up a step above me.

"You're all tense," Mark said softly.

Slowly, he slipped his fingers into my hair, and began to slide them across my scalp, massaging my head. My breath stopped. His fingers began to rub the base of my neck, and then moved to the top of my forehead, the side of my temples, across my skull, warmth spreading where his fingers traveled. It was the first time he had touched me this way, and soon I was relaxed enough to close my eyes. Soon, the ridges of my brain smoothed, spilling out twenty-one years of facts and information, until only his face remained. I pictured our lips connecting, warm and soft as we explored each other's mouths.

"Tell me about how your parents met," Mark inquired casually.

I froze. And just like that, the worms returned. The spell was broken. Then, it was as if the ground opened and thin slabs of earth jutted out, forming four walls around me.

"I have to go," I said, standing up to leave.

Mark touched my arm. "Wait, what's wrong?" he asked.

"Nothing . . ." I said. "I'm tired, I've got homework to finish, and . . . and . . . and it's raining cats and dogs out here."

Without waiting for his response, I packed up our wet picnic and ran to the Jeep. Mark followed wordlessly behind me, still wearing a confused look on his face. Once on the road, after ten minutes or so of silence, he finally turned to me. "I didn't mean to upset you," he said. "I just wanted to know more about you and your family."

"I don't like to talk about my family," I told him, looking away. "And there's not much more to know besides what I've already told you."

"I know that's not true . . . because you haven't really told me anything."

I stared out the window. The rain was coming down harder, creating large pools of puddles on the side of the road. "Should there be more stuff to tell some day, I'll bring it up—okay?" I said, leaning into my seat.

"Okay," he answered, but the edge in his voice cut me.

Instantly, I bristled. "I don't like being pushed," I told him, crossing my arms in front of my chest.

"I wasn't pushing." He returned his eyes to the road.

It was our first spat. For the duration of the short ride home, we were quiet. *Swish-swish-swish*. I focused on the windshield wipers as rain continued to wash over the earth. The walls closed tighter around me. When I got back to my room, I locked myself in.

THAT NIGHT, I DREAMT I WAS in a womb.

I crouched, hugging my knees tight to my chest. I was inside a round space barely large enough to fit my frame. It was red, warm, and peaceful. I stuck out my hands, felt the soft elastic cloth wall give against my palms. Somewhere outside, someone was humming a lullaby. I looked up and saw that I was sitting in the middle of some kind of tunnel. There were stairlike rungs stacked up on top of one another like the inside of a water well. I began to crawl on my hands and knees up the tunnel. When I arrived at the last rung, I climbed out.

I was standing on top of some kind of black pillar, a vast, never-ending darkness above me. I looked out. Below me was the sparkling, shimmering universe. It was flat and spread out as wide and far as my eyes could see. In this dark axis, a million stars, planets, and galaxies swirled and gleamed; falling and shooting stars flew amidst the white-fire tails of flying comets.

Jump! a gentle female voice urged me.

I wanted to. I knew if I jumped I would understand.

Jump.

But I couldn't.

I woke up.

7

No Rapunzel

Snow has a way of cleaning the earth by covering up all the ugly patches of dead grass and bald trees. Even when the mountains stand bare, shivering like old souls as the skies cast dark shadows over them, one good snowfall makes them majestic again. One good snowfall—that's all it takes for the world to shine anew, and for people to rediscover their smiles, even as their faces freeze from the frigid cold.

I stared out the window, marveling at the white snowflakes falling softly to the ground. It was only late November, and winter had already arrived. When I turned toward the full-length mirror on my wall, I saw an elegant woman with a long braid hanging down her back. A few minutes later, Charles arrived. I rushed downstairs to meet him, waving. In his gray Hugo Boss suit, Charles looked as if he had just stepped out of a men's fashion catalog. I'd never felt so grown up. Moments later, we pulled into the parking lot of Sirloin Saloon in Shelburne, which advertised itself as a "fine dining establishment since 1963." Once inside, I slid into my seat and saw an engraved menu. Fortunately, our church supper had not been repeated.

"You look very nice," Charles said.

"Thank you."

After my embarrassing picnic with Mark, I'd held Charles off, waiting for Mark to propose another outing. He didn't, and we never spoke of my strangeness that night. We continued to have lunch and study together, but it was different now. He was careful and cautious with me. And when we spoke of politics, he measured his words. I began to worry that he now saw me as this fragile breakable thing. When I told Beth this, she disagreed.

"Maybe you're transferring your own feelings onto Mark?" Beth was deep into her Psychology 201 class. "Sigmund Freud discovered transfer—"

"Beth," I interjected. "I took the same class. I know what transference is; the unconscious redirection of your feelings onto another."

"Well, then, isn't it possible that you're the one feeling unsure, fragile, and scared?"

I shrugged. "It's more likely that he realized I was too strange for him," I said. "If I were him, I wouldn't bother with me. Why would he when he could be with a normal girl?"

"You're that girl," Beth said, trying to make me feel better.

But it didn't matter. Mark and I went back to being friends, and I started to see Charles again. It was easier that way.

"Mmm . . . great menu," I told Charles, eyeing the menu approvingly.

Two months into dating, Charles gave me a friendship ring—a blue gemstone. He said he could see us spending our lives together. In his imagination, we would move in together after my graduation, get married, and raise a family in Vermont. And I had to admit, there was a part of me that found the thought of being taken care of appealing.

This was the part of me that wanted my life to fit together like a jigsaw puzzle, like the ones many of my friends had already pieced together. They'd come into the world with sections mapped out and shaped by their parents, family, community, and country. But my puzzle was different. There was not a set template for me.

The good thing was that I could choose any shapes and pieces I wanted. White house and picket fences? Abracadabra—gone! Two kids, a dog, and two cats? Presto—disappeared! Without a specific template, I had the freedom to pray to Mary and Buddha, eat rice or bread, live local and think global. I could create any kind of me I wanted.

But my puzzle pieces were often made with unsure hands, resulting in jagged, mishmash blocks. And when Charles showed up with the promise of a ready-made life, I was attracted to it. When I told Charles I wanted to live overseas, travel, and see the world, he assured me we would do that together in time. He said he would take care of all the arrangements; he would take care of me. There was a part of me that liked this option. The same part that also liked lobsters and steaks.

I closed the menu. "I think I'm going to have the surf and turf tonight," I said, grinning at Charles.

"That does look good," he agreed. "You know what Doug

said to me?" He brought up his friend's comment out of the blue as he continued examining his menu.

"Mmm?"

"Doug said you speak English very well." Charles answered without looking up, referring to the cocktail hour we attended on our last date.

"Why wouldn't I?"

"He was just surprised, that's all. You're a smart girl; you know I know that. But sometimes, I think, with your accent, when you use incorrect grammar, other people might wrongly assume you're not—"

He stopped himself when he saw my face.

Until I came to America, I thought my language—a mixture of Cambodian, Chinese, and French—was special. And whenever I was stuck on a word, all I had to do was reach into my brain and pick out another in a different tongue. In this way, the words flowed and comingled in a melting pot of cultures and translations in my mind. Like the Three Tenors, each language complemented the other, adding vibrancy, meaning, fullness, and music to a phrase in ways that one language could never do alone. But this was before one of my English tutors told me my English was broken. And with that, my language fractured, splintered, and snapped into pieces like an old tree felled in a lush forest. I became paralyzed, my ears deafened and my voice muted. I felt the sudden urge to apologize for all the broken words coming out of my mouth. Suddenly, I sounded out of tune. The Three Tenors had developed laryngitis and stopped singing in my head.

After that, everywhere I went in our Asian communities, I heard only broken words. Gone were the songs that sang of their triumphs and victories, gone were the mysteries and joys in the cracks of their lilted words and accents. And I began to see why our Asian friends became deaf and mute whenever we were out of the safe compounds of our homes. I grew more cautious with my words until I tried one day to teach the tutor a few words in Khmer. She couldn't even make the sound. After that, I began again to celebrate my many languages.

I looked at Charles. "What do people assume from my sometimes incorrect grammar?" I asked, gritting my teeth.

"Not important," he said, smiling. "That was a great party we went to."

"What do they assume, Charles?" I pressed.

Charles put his menu down and looked at me. He knew I would not let it go until he told me. "Well, when some people hear someone speak with an accent, sometimes they view that person as not as intelligent . . ."

"Do you know what you say to those people?"

"What?"

"You tell them that until they can communicate in four languages, they can go screw themselves."

Charles stared at me, his face still. "Now, that's a bit crass."

"Go to hell." I slapped the menu down on the table and stormed out of the restaurant.

BACK AT MY DORM, I TRIED TO study, but I couldn't concentrate. My thoughts kept returning to another recent conversation Charles and I had had that still angered me, adding fuel to the rage I felt from our dinner. I had shared the news that Meng was planning to go to Cambodia to visit our family. But because the U.S. did not yet have a diplomatic relationship with Cambodia, he would have to fly to Thailand and then apply for a visa from the Thai embassy to enter Cambodia. I explained to Charles that the political situation in Cambodia was not yet stable, and due to the years of war and poverty, bandits and kidnappers roamed the streets looking for victims to grab for ransom money.

"Don't worry," Charles assured me. "He has an American passport. He'll be perfectly safe."

"No, he won't," I argued. "If he gets kidnapped, the bandits can take his passport and sell it for a lot of money on the black market. Or, if they want to be cruel, they could flush it down the toilet, and my brother would be stuck."

"Don't be silly," Charles told me. "He's an American. Worse comes to worse, we—our government—would go into Cambodia and snatch him out."

For several minutes I argued with Charles, sharing with him the news we had received from our siblings in their letters. Our siblings, who actually *lived* there. But Charles was adamant, convinced that he was right and I was wrong.

That incident was the first clear red flag in our relationship. After that argument ended, I still couldn't get over the fact that he didn't, wouldn't believe me. I began to simmer with anger. Who was he to contradict our family? Who was he to say what was true or not in Cambodia, a country he had never visited and knew little about? But most of all, my anger was with Charles for telling me what to think, what to believe. I resented this.

Time ticked by on my dorm clock. Pages from Plato's *Republic* turned slowly, with tiny undecipherable notes scrawled in the margins as I tried to return to my studies. Thirty minutes later, I still couldn't get Charles out of my head. Something was amiss in our relationship. Charles was tall, handsome, and successful. Sure, sometimes he was paternal, but most of the time he was polite and kind. He was everything I had been taught to dream of in a prospective mate. Shouldn't that be enough? Charles's ring was burning the skin on my finger. In our few months together, we had rarely fought. When we did, he was always patient and willing to talk through the issues with me. I replayed the scene from the restaurant and tried to let go of my anger, make amends for my outbursts. Still, the ring burned. I took it off and tossed it onto my desk. And in that instant, I knew what was wrong.

When we first met, I admired Charles because he was established and rooted in his community. He was looking for a kindred spirit who wanted the same thing, and deep down inside, I knew I was not this person. And yet, in him, I saw a foundation on which to build my self-worth, someone to tell me I was pretty, to value me. But I realized now that a foundation not of my own creation was not the foundation for me.

I understood now that with Charles, I was asking for someone to rescue me, to tell me how to live my life. If I stayed with Charles, he would become that man. And if this happened, I would stay small, needing repair and help in his eyes. I did not want to live down to his expectations. I saw a life with Charles flash before my eyes: married, a full-time wife and mother, never leaving Vermont. I knew it was not the right path for me. I wanted something different. I wanted to eat Peking roast duck in Beijing, watch water puppet shows in Vietnam, and trek through the mountains in Nepal. I wanted to travel Europe, see Table Mountain in South Africa, and swim in the Mediterranean Sea. I wanted to live free, to be independent, to answer to no one. And I wanted someone to value me for being a solid rock—then let me go to cut, chisel, and polish the rock myself as I saw fit.

I rushed to the open window and stuck my head out. It had begun to snow. A cold gust of wind blew on my face and my long hair fell and flowed past the windowsill. I looked out into the open world below and knew that I was no Rapunzel.

I wasn't trapped in a tower, and I didn't need to be rescued. I walked over to the hall phone, dialed Charles's number, and broke up with him on his answering machine.

Then I went outside and made angels in the snow.

THE NEXT DAY, I CAME HOME from class to find a bouquet of long-stemmed red roses at my door. I picked up the bouquet, and one by one, left them at the doors of my dorm-mates. Without reading Charles's note, I crumpled it and tossed it into the trash can. Moments later, he arrived at my door.

"Did you get the roses?" he asked, a sheepish smile on his face, but underneath that, I sensed his anger.

"Yes."

"Where are they?"

"They were signs of your love and I didn't want them anymore, so I gave them away."

As soon as the words left my mouth, I regretted them. I was young and inexperienced in the ways of breaking up, but this did not negate the fact that I was mean. Deliberately mean. My Asian ancestors would be ashamed if they knew. I had broken one of the commandments for Asian girls: Be nice.

"I'm sorry," I offered.

Charles ground his teeth, his fists clenched by his side, and stared at me.

"Charles, it's over between us. We're not getting back together. Not now, not ever. Please, I told you that yesterday. I don't know how to make it any clearer to you."

His face was red then, his hands forming fists in his pants pockets. "You're a hard, cold bitch," he spat.

I slammed the door in his face, weighed down with guilt. I wished I could have found kinder words to end things with Charles. But when Charles showed up at my door, and then blocked it, I felt cornered. And instead of taking flight, my instinct was to come out swinging.

Charles's accusation hung in the air.

The image of Charles's ice blue eyes continued to burn through me; the heat of his anger clung to my skin. Five seconds passed. Charles was still out there. Fuming. Waiting. The wall stood between us. I pressed my ear against the door. Ten seconds. Charles huffed and puffed, but the door stood. Fifteen seconds passed before I heard Charles's footsteps walking away.

I moved back to my bed, knocking over the pile of books and papers awaiting my attention. As I stared at the white ceiling, I wished Charles the best with finding the woman who was right for him. She was out there, and in a way, I was getting out of the way for her.

Suddenly, my terror turned to excitement at a new realization: I was not at all afraid of the fact that I'd just cut Charles out of my life. In fact, I was rather happy to be finished with the fantasy that I had to attach myself to a man who would take care of me and provide for me. But now I was facing a new unwritten reality, one in which I would build the life I wanted for myself. And I did not want any man to tell me how to do it.

8

Klutz and Misdirection

Manchester, December 1990

After I broke up with Charles, I lost my balance. For days I walked into desks, chairs, and doors. I started each day with new bruises. I became convinced that the Shoemaker's two helper elves had turned evil. At night, they hopped out of my Brothers Grimm fairy-tale book on my shelf and onto my floor. While I slept fitfully in my bed, they scurried around my room, working their evil elfin magic on my shoes, slippers, and boots.

"Teeheehee . . . teehee . . ." they snickered maniacally as they inserted pebbles in my soles, sawed micro-inches off my heels, and sprinkled drunken pixie dust into my slippers.

"You're off balance because you're learning to walk on your own two feet," Beth empathized over the phone.

Cassie got straight to the point: "You're a klutz."

I was accident-prone. Cassie was right about that. In addition to the dead nerves in my ankles, I possessed little depth perception. When I sat down for dinner, one or more of my friends or family members would move the glasses of wine, the jar of raspberry sauce, or the tub of butter out of my reach, keeping me, the table, and their laps safe from spills. But this time, I had knocked over my happily-ever-after fantasy. I did not know where to go from there.

"Everyone falls down sometimes; that's life," Christina reassured me. "The important thing is to get back up."

Get up! I would tell myself after yet another tumble.

I looked down, and there, on my ankle, an egg-sized bump was bulging out of my skin. The pain throbbed, making my face sweat. I massaged my ankle and stared at my insanely small feet, the real reason for my falls. Barely a size five, they rarely allowed for the correct fitting of shoes. Had I been born in China in 1900, my small feet would have made me an ideal beauty. But in America, they were more like hooves; too tiny to carry the whole of my body. My remedy for this was to wear big, clunky shoes, and so began my extravagant purchases of Doc Martens boots.

When Monday came, I put on my Doc Martens and stomped my way to class. With each step, I felt somehow more solid, more present in the world, like I was taking up more space. With my big shoes, my steps sunk firmly into the ground, leaving a full mark. Nice girls didn't do that. Nice girls walked gracefully through the world and didn't disturb anyone. I'd had enough of nice girls.

I marched into class with my nostrils flaring, visualizing myself sucking in all the oxygen and air around me. With each powerful breath, my chest expanded, and I felt myself growing bigger in stature and physicality. When I settled noisily into my seat, I believed no amount of puffing and blowing from another person would topple me. Not ever again. But then Mark sat down next to me. "Haven't seen you in a while," he said, leaning back into his chair, his elbow touching mine.

I looked at him and felt air hissing out of me, as if a pin had pierced my arm where our skin touched, and now I was slowly inflating like a balloon.

"Hi," I said, averting my eyes from his stare because I'd been avoiding him since Charles and I broke up.

"I saw Suzie at the cafeteria," he said, looking at me. "She told me about you and Charles . . ."

I silently fumed at my hall-mate for being such a blabber-mouth. "It didn't work out . . ." I told him.

"You're okay?"

I shifted away from him, opening my book. "Yeah."

"If you're not doing anything this weekend, want to go hiking?" Mark said tentatively.

"I don't think so." I paused, trying to think up an excuse. "I have to study."

"Okay . . ." He slowly turned from me. "If you change your mind, call me."

I began reading my book. I was thankful when the professor entered the room and ended my awkward silence with Mark. Still, I stole glances at his long legs stretching into the aisle and stared at his long pointed cowboy boots.

Cassie called me when I got back to the dorm. "What are you doing?"

"Reading, homework."

"What are your plans for the weekend?"

"Umm . . . more reading . . ."

"That's it!" Cassie fired back. "We're going shopping."

• • •

CASSIE PICKED ME UP IN HER beat-up Honda Saturday morning. The trip should have taken two hours, but it would be three before we reached the Manchester Designer Outlets. My job was to help navigate, which was perhaps the worst job in the world for me as I possessed no internal compass whatsoever. If you set me in a field at 3 p.m. and asked me to look at my shadow, I still could not tell where east was. And before we knew it, we were twenty-five miles out of the way and very lost. An hour later, with an added stop at a gas station to buy a new map, we were still lost.

"Why can't they make road signs that are easy to read in Vermont?" I asked, exasperated.

"Easy wouldn't be any fun, just like you and Mark," Cassie teased.

"There's no me and Mark," I said.

"I don't understand why not," she said, her face contorted in confusion. "He's cute, you're cute. He's available, you're available. He likes to eat rice, you have a rice pot."

"Oh, if only it were that easy."

"It's not that complicated. Do you like this boy or not?"

"I do," I admitted.

"Well, go out with him," Cassie said. "Don't just sit there being a scaredy cat."

I sighed, my shoulders slumping into the seat. "Things have been strange between us since the night of the wet picnic," I told her. "He probably thinks I'm unhinged or something."

"Has he said that?"

"No . . ."

"Then why are you putting words in his mouth?"

"Doesn't matter," I muttered. "He probably likes Jenny anyway . . ."

Word had traveled to me recently that Jenny was gossiping about my breakup with Charles. My brain pulsed: *Jenny . . . Jenny . . . Jenny.* I knew I was spending way too much time focusing on Jenny. Maybe I should stop, make her as insignificant as a black fly, something annoying that I could swat away. *Or . . .* I grinned, I could pretend to be her friend and bide my time. To do this, I would have to restrain myself and become a sleeping volcano, simmering on the inside without exploding. I would gain her friendship, and when she trusted me with her secrets, I would erupt and tell everyone. A small curve pulled up the edge of my lips.

Yeah, I could do that.

I knew I was being childish and felt slightly ashamed. *Ugh.* I was taking classes in feminist theology and women's studies so I could be a better woman. I wouldn't accomplish that goal by daydreaming about stepping on Jenny like she was a gnat, or by belittling her. No matter how she bugged me.

My epiphany was interrupted when David Bowie came on the radio and sang, *Ground control to Major Tom . . .* I leaned my head against the window.

"That's my favorite song of all time," I told Cassie. "I don't know why it speaks to me so much."

Cassie paused, staring at me. "It's a song about homelessness and powerlessness," she said.

It seemed as if the sky opened and recognition rained down on me. *I am totally Major Tom! Floating in a tin can, trying to call home, looking for a place to land.*

"You're not homeless and powerless anymore, Lulu," Cassie pointed out.

"I know . . ."

But Cassie didn't know that the fear was always there. Had Cassie found me as a child, sleeping on the streets, eating out of garbage cans, hating the world and wondering why the world hated me, and told me that someday I would get to be a healthy, happy college student in the U.S., I would not have believed her. But had she told me I would still be on the street—a drug addict or a prostitute, and still homeless—*that* I would have believed. The way my life turned out seemed almost like a fluke; the other path still plagued my sleep. This fear permeated my entire being, and whispered for me to keep my heart and world small.

"Look," Cassie said, her voice gentle. "I don't know much about where you came from. But this much I know is true: You've been through some heavy shit. But you know what? You're not there anymore. So you don't have to live like you're still there. Live the life you have now."

I looked out the window and stared at my reflection on the glass surface.

"We're young, Lulu," Cassie said. "We're supposed to do crazy things, have mad affairs, eat too much, drink a little. Make mistakes, lose control."

"You know I only hear 'crazy' in your speech . . ."

"If you do go there, I'll still be your friend."

SIX HOURS LATER, AFTER HOURS OF window-shopping at the outlet, I returned to my dorm. And with a new clarity of mind, I made my way to the hall phone and dialed Mark's number.

The next day, we climbed Mount Mansfield.

"What a view . . ." Mark's voice echoed from his perch in a treetop.

I gazed up at him, and fear set in again. I worried the mountain would collapse from underneath us. I willed the thought away and let the fire burning deep inside me ignite. I wanted to grab hold of the world and swallow it whole. To taste its dirt, swim its oceans, climb its mountains. To gulp down its molten core, feel the lava smolder in my stomach. I stood at the mountain peak, arms spread like wings. The cold wind lifted my parka, pushed into my nostrils, and expanded my lungs. I opened my mouth and gulped it all down—the fears, the fires, and the mountains. Then I closed my eyes and let go.

I turned to Mark. Before me, the wind grew still, the sky opened with columns of light, and the world became magnificently bright.

ONCE I OPENED THE DOOR, LOVE SWOOPED in.

A week after our hike, Mark asked me to the winter dance. After I said yes, I ran to my room and circled the date on my calendar with a red felt-tip pen. Then I waited and counted the days.

When the night finally arrived, he showed up in a shiny black limo. I walked out the door to meet him, my hair flowing down my back and my feet click-clacking in high heels. In the dark sky, bright stars twinkled and a silver moon cast a spotlight on us. I moved toward him slowly.

"Wow!" he exclaimed loudly when he saw me.

I smiled. A week of my student budget went into my little black, backless dress. I looked admiringly at him. He had on a crisp, white shirt with his black suit and tie, and under his jacket, brown suspenders never looked sexier.

"Ready to dance the night away?" Mark asked, helping me into the limo.

"Yes," I answered, feeling like Cinderella on her way to a ball.

We arrived at the Burlington Marriott Courtyard, where the dance was held, to find the ballroom already crowded. Mark took my hand and led me to the dance floor. Under the refracted lights of the disco ball, we danced to pulsating music, my skin glowing red, silver, and blue. When a slow song came on, he pulled me closer to him. We swayed to the music, oblivious of other students around us, my arms around his neck. I did not notice when the song ended, only that Mark's arms tightened around my waist as he picked me up off my feet. His face was close to mine, and just like that, the butterflies animated to life in my stomach.

In that moment, I knew I was in love.

And suddenly the world was painted in brilliant new colors. The tree outside my bedroom window that had been mere green before was now the color of emeralds. The red roses on the school lawn were scarlet. How had I not noticed that an orange sunrise was really burnt sienna? How had I not seen the cerulean blue of the sky?

The next few weeks, Mark and I spent every waking moment together. At school, we sat next to each other in classes, perched like two birds in our own private nest. After classes, I joined him on his pizza-delivering job, giggling when he handed me his tips. On weekends, we'd lose ourselves in double-feature movies, hiking trips, or socializing with friends.

After every outing, I returned to my room and stared at my calendar. And for the first time, I dreaded the ending of the school semester, when I knew Mark would have to return to Cleveland to spend Christmas break with his family. My stomach knotted at the thought. I sated it with sizzling grilled burgers and steaming bowls of noodles, and by the time he got into his Jeep to leave Vermont, I was five pounds fatter.

9

Lulu in the Sky

Champlain Mill, April 1991

Whenever someone left me, the days and weeks waiting for their return were always excruciating. No matter how much they assured me they would be back, a part of me never expected to see them again. Thus, when Christmas break ended and Mark showed up at my dorm, I was shocked.

"You came back!" I squealed, jumping into his arms.

"I told you I would . . ." he said, a little confused at my surprise.

The next three months flew by so fast I barely noticed the cold winter that my Southeast Asian blood normally dreaded. Instead, I watched the sun melt the snow and ice, leaving the ground soft and fertile. Soon new green shrubs pushed out of the once frozen land, and bare trees and shrubs sprouted baby yellow buds. And in the blush of this spring, Mark and I snuggled our days away and only separated to attend school or for me to visit my family.

"It's strange that I haven't met your family," Mark said one day. "They're five miles away."

"They're old-school, even for my culture," I told him. "They believe a girl is supposed to stay pure and untainted until she gets married."

"Don't you think they know you're dating?"

"They're no fools," I said, chuckling. "They'd just rather not know so they don't ask." I did not tell my family about Mark. No matter how deliriously happy I was in my new romance, I still kept my head. And my head knew that Meng and Eang would not approve.

"Hi!" I called out, walking into Mark's apartment.

He lived in the poorest part of South Burlington, in a small, one-bedroom apartment that smelled slightly of mildew. Still, I could see our future selves in this very same room, see myself returning home from work to find him bent over a stove with very little on.

I followed the sound of metal utensils clanging against a pot. "In here," he called out from the kitchen.

As a couple, we were compatible in many ways—our beliefs, politics, principles, and values. We both liked the outdoors, liked to be active and strong. I did aerobics, and Mark practiced kung fu. He found me funny, although a little dark. I was crazy about his sunny personality, even if it was perhaps a little too much sunshine at times. And then there was that certain something, a spark between us that couldn't be explained, something that heated my face and body and made my glands sweat. But in spite of all that, there was one thing about which we could not agree: time. He could not keep it, and I could not ignore it. To him, fifteen minutes late was considered "being on time." In that fifteen minutes, my mind had chased after ambulances, police cars, and fire trucks, searched the trauma center in the hospital, the emergency room, the morgue.

"How was your day with the girls?" Mark asked.

"Good."

"What did you guys do?"

I hugged his waist from behind. "Shopping," I murmured. He stood more than a foot taller than me, and smelled faintly of Drakkar cologne. I pressed my body close to his, felt his back muscles expand and contract as he inhaled and exhaled. I rested my face on the space between his shoulder blades.

I love you . . . I wanted to tell him.

I was ready to take our relationship to the next intimate level, and spent the afternoon with the girls at an undergarment boutique preparing for it.

"Lulu, you need sexy undies." Christina nudged me into the store, followed by Beth.

"And nice undies don't come in a three-pack for three ninety-nine," said Cassie, closing the door behind us.

An older, elegantly dressed saleswoman approached us when we walked in. "Can I help you?" she asked.

"She needs some sexy bras," Beth giddily told her, pushing me forward.

"Okay, follow me," the saleswoman whispered in a conspiratorial tone.

In the pink dressing room, she showed me an armful of padded and very pushed-up bras. I looked at the price tags and gasped audibly.

"It's an investment for your breasts," she said. "As we age, some breasts sag, some spread sideways, and some can't make up their minds. So we need to keep them reined in."

I continued to stare at the prices.

"Yours look like they may both spread and sag," she warned.

I left the boutique with a pink bra that not only reined in my breasts, but also promised to double their size.

"Ready for our East meets West picnic?" Mark asked, loading our basket with bread, cheese, fried rice, and two bottles of wine.

"Yep."

Moments later, we arrived at the Champlain Mill in Winooski. Built to take advantage of the powerful falls of the Winooski River, the Champlain Mill was once an operating mill that employed more than three thousand people during World War II. Since then, this vast industrial building had been transformed into charming boutiques, galleries, and restaurants—and, for a few area students, a place to take their dates on a romantic picnic.

Mark took my hand and led me on a path that guided us to the falls. It was April, and the evening was unseasonably warm, almost as if spring had arrived in earnest. In front of us, the Winooski falls rushed water down a concrete dam into the gorge and the river. In the clear sky, stars sparkled like diamonds as we drank wine.

Lulu in the sky with diamonds . . . I sang in my head.

"Mark, even with everything you saw and heard in the Philippines refugee camp, do you still think the world is a beautiful place?" I asked, taking another drink from the bottle hidden in the paper bag.

"Yeah," he mused. "Don't get me wrong—there are corrupt parts, diseased areas, and bad people everywhere. But overall, it's a good place."

I wanted to learn to see the world his way. To see it for all its infinite good, its youthful wisdom and exuberance. As water flowed around us, Mark talked about his mother, father, and six siblings. A surge of memory surfaced, and I thought about *my* six siblings, mother, and father. I was grateful for my new life in America, but still, a part of me would always long for that former life. I drank from the wine bottle again. Was I being sent what I had been looking for? I wondered. Was it possible that my prayers were heard, and that I was being given a second chance to live out my dream of being part of a large family again? One filled with loving parents, raucous brothers, and gentle sisters? One just like the one I'd lost? Celestial music seemed to fill the space between us. I was smiling when Mark put his arm around my shoulders and pulled me in, bringing his lips closer to mine. I closed my eyes and felt his breath on my cheek. His lips touched mine, soft and warm, tasting like fried rice and chardonnay.

Mark pulled back, took another drink, and broke into a rendition of "Cat's in the Cradle."

I joined him, giggling. Under the starry moonlight, he leaned in and kissed me again. My skin danced, the hair on my body stood up and swayed. Our laughter sang with the rushing water as Mark picked me up and carried me over his shoulders. I felt like a bird in his arms when we returned to his apartment that night, my heart full of love, my head overflowing with wine. Outside the window, rain fell lightly on the ground.

"Tell me you love me," I whispered, my body entwined with his on the couch.

"I love you," he returned.

I had waited to say those three words to him, and to hear them from him. I wanted our moment to be special. And now it was.

Outside, thunder rumbled and rolled in the night sky. Time seemed to slow as heavy rain splashed against the window. A lightning bolt crashed, and the explosion tore into the wall, causing the room to feel as if it were vibrating. Then another bolt slashed through the darkness, illuminating monstrous storm clouds. A memory, a thing I couldn't control, sprung forth, and its tangled ropes fell on me. It caught my leg, pulled at my arms, wrapped around my neck, and cut off oxygen to my head. I felt myself falling, crashing.

The ground shook as another thunderbolt struck. In that blinding flash, I fell back into the rabbit hole. The tunnel was dark, heavy breathing echoed in its chamber. My hands grasped for any kind of vine, root, or tree to slow my fall. But nothing caught. I landed on my bottom, as I did when I was a child. The Vietnamese soldier hovered over me.

"Nam soong! Nam soong!" he ordered me.

I scurried away on my hands and knees, turned to run. He grabbed my ankle and pulled me down. "Nam Soong!" He yelled for me to lie down.

Time slowed as he unbuttoned his pants, dropped them to his ankles. His red underwear stood stark against his white skin. He pulled off his underwear and came at me. He covered my mouth with the whole of his hand, his fingers digging into my cheeks.

"No . . . please . . ." I whimpered.

"Shh . . . shh . . ."

A scream crawled its way out of my throat.

"Shh . . . shhh . . ."

I twisted myself out of his grasp.

"Get off me!" I yelled, slamming my palms into his chest.

Mark sat up in shock.

"Are you okay? I'm sorry."

I ran into the bathroom and locked myself inside. I slid onto the floor, hugging my knees to my chest. I grabbed my head and closed my eyes. The soldier hovered. "I'm in America," I whispered. "I have nothing to fear."

"Loung," Mark called me from the other side of the door, his fingers rapping on the wood. "Please tell me you're okay . . ."

I sat on the floor, my knees pressed up against my chest.

"I'm okay," I whispered, crouching between the toilet and the tub, the smallest space I could fit into. "I'm sorry . . . I'm really sorry."

"Please open the door and tell me you're okay . . ."

"I need a minute . . . I'm okay . . ."

I listened to the rain ease. Light drops pitter-pattered on the roof, dripping from the gutter onto the ground. The water washed away the soldier and his red underwear. I stood up, walked to the sink, and cleaned my face. When I emerged from the bathroom, Mark tucked me into his bed and went to sleep on the couch.

The next morning I woke up and went to class. I left Mark still sleeping on the couch, undisturbed. The clouds were dark, foreboding another storm. I sat in class, the feeling of *ting-tong* in my head, a Cambodian term to describe the sound an empty metal barrel makes when you knock on it. I felt hollow inside, my heart so overwhelmed it felt separated from my head.

On my way back from class, I stared at the new spring lawn on both sides of the pristine sidewalk. Firm young grass stood everywhere, waiting to grow into a never-ending field of green. I wanted to run over and dig my heels into the ground to make two imperfect holes in the perfect lawn. But then I saw Mark sitting on a bench. I sat down next to him, feeling shy and unsure.

He looked up. "How are you?" he asked.

"Okay."

A silence engulfed us.

"I want to explain about last night . . ." I said, averting my eyes from his probing gaze; my mind filled with words I wanted to say but couldn't get out.

"What happened?" he asked gently.

"I . . . um . . . I had a bad memory . . . of something that happened a long time ago . . ."

Mark waited.

"I've never told anyone about it . . ." I wanted to tell him about the Vietnamese soldier but feared it would change his opinion of me. I hated the thought of him feeling sorry for me or looking at me with pity. I didn't want that from anyone. "It . . . I . . ." I began again.

"It's okay . . ." he offered. "It's going to be okay."

My inner volcano erupted, burning my lungs with its smoke and ashes.

"How the hell would you know?" I demanded. "What do you know?"

The smoke surrounded Mark, covering him with black soot. His blue eyes softened, his face remained still. "You're right. I don't know. I'm sorry."

The cloud of ashes cleared, leaving him unstained. But it did not leave me, hovering over my head like a mushroom cloud. Instantly, I felt bad.

"No, I'm sorry," I said. "I shouldn't have yelled. And that night, I just had a freaky experience. I'm sorry. It was weird, and it didn't help that I was drunk."

"You don't have to explain."

I breathed a sigh of relief, thankful I didn't have to say any more in that moment.

•   •   •

A FRIEND ONCE TOLD ME THAT perhaps because my heart had been so irrevocably broken, it would never heal. And as I continued to push Mark away in the days follow-ing our big fight, I wondered if my friend was right. He attempted to connect with me, bringing me boxes of pizza, bagels, doughnuts, and Chinese takeout. But the nicer he became, the more insecure I grew, and my embarrassment, shame, and anger intensified. Since I did not know how to fight my demons, I fought Mark. And I ate. I filled my stomach, hoping to bury the darkness that was growing ever larger at my center. But no matter how much I fed the void, the darkness grew.

I WAS IN A HAZE WHEN MARK caught my arm a few weeks later. I flinched and pulled it out of his grasp. I didn't want to be touched by him, or any other man. I was embarrassed by what had happened and was afraid it could happen again.

"Can we talk?" he asked me.

Classes had just let out. Mark and I sat down on the bench in St. Edmund's Hall. All around us, students milled around and darted to their next class.

"Look, you've been acting like you don't want to see me for weeks, and now you won't take my calls. I don't know what's going on with you . . ."

I gripped my hands together between my thighs. "Noth-ing's going on," I said.

"You're acting very cold—"

"Men always say things like that when things don't go their way," I interrupted.

"I meant—"

"A woman is always a cold bitch when she isn't doing what

the guy wants," I said. My voice was even, monotone. "It's never the guy; it's always the woman this or that . . . They never think that maybe it's them."

Mark looked at me. "You can be very mean," he said quietly.

"Mean?" I hissed, and involuntarily, my knees began to knock together. "Just because I don't go around with sunshine up my ass every day? It's easy to be nice when you grew up choking on piles of silver spoons."

"Don't." His voice was low, his eyes bright with hurt.

I had succeeded in pushing him to anger.

"I know you've always wanted nice girls," I said coldly. "Nice, blond, unbroken, boring girls. Why don't you go date one of them?"

"Why are you acting like this? As if any of this is my fault, when it isn't?"

It was all his fault. Being with him made my anger soften, took away my power of self-control. My face started to quiver, my eyes misted over. To stop from crying, I lashed out.

"We should nip this in the bud," I told him.

Mark didn't say anything back.

"Go back to your nice girls; I don't really care," I said, looking up at the ceiling.

"Loung . . ."

"Go ahead . . ." I stilled my body and hardened my face. "Say it."

"What?"

"Say I'm a hard, cold bitch."

"I don't want to fight."

I glared at him. "That's just too bad," I said. "But it's not always about what you want."

"Maybe it's best if we go our separate ways . . ." he began, avoiding my eyes. His gaze moved to a flyer on the wall advertising for "roommates wanted" and posters announcing upcoming concerts at the college.

"Whatever . . ." I whispered under my breath.

"I guess we've already gone our separate ways . . ." he said.

The hall was quiet again. I raised my head and looked at Mark. The sun shone through the window, landing directly on his face. It made his eyes that much bluer.

Love me, love me, love me! I cried at him in my head.

When our eyes met, I held his gaze.

In movies, this was the part where the camera zooms in on the girl's eyes. Her pupils are enlarged, dilated, telling him silently of her feelings. The man reads her thoughts, leans in, and kisses her. The camera moves in on her crumbling face, full of sorrow and joy.

But real life was another story. As my knees knocked harder and harder, I told Mark I loved him in my head but could not make the words reach my lips or eyes. In real life, my eyes darkened with anger.

"I guess your silence says it all . . ." he paused. Slowly, he bent down and picked his school bag up off the floor, his thigh brushing against mine. He moved away, as if the touch had burnt him somehow. Then he stood up and walked away.

I was alone.

10

A Message in Ma Po Tofu

Chapel of Saint Michael's, Spring 1991

I submerged my body and head under water, my hands gripping the sides of the tub. The water soothed, relaxed my breathing, and helped to shut out the world. But then loneliness set in. I opened my eyes and watched small bubbles escape my nostrils and float to the surface. One by one, they burst. With each burst, my body grew colder. I turned the faucet back on and let more hot water in.

"Loung," Eang called from the other side of the door.

I'd been soaking in her tub for thirty minutes.

"You sick?"

"No . . ."

"Then come out, no more waste hot water."

I got out of the tub and made my way to the kitchen. Eang was already there, making me a bowl of steaming wonton soup. After she made herself a bowl, she sat down with me. I looked down at my soup, hiding my eyes. After I'd had my fill of wontons, I returned to campus with fresh laundry, a pot of soup, and a bag of chive pancakes.

The next few weeks, I went to school, ate, and went about doing my daily activities. It was not easy, as Mark was everywhere—in my classes, in the cafeteria, in the hall, and in my mind. Each time I saw him, I turned away. Then I would empty my mind of him, exhaling thoughts of him. Gradually, I arrived at the place where there was nothing.

THEN UNCLE LEE DIED.

Like us, Uncle Lee was a Cambodian genocide survivor of Chinese descent. In 1980, he left Cambodia with his family for the refugee camps in Thailand. From there, Uncle Lee and his family went to Montreal, Canada. It was in Montreal that we met him through family friends, and I took an instant liking to him. When he was alive, Uncle Lee was jovial, funny, always had a paternal pat for everyone's back. In our community of refugees and immigrants, he became everyone's uncle. He was fifty-four years old when he died, and left behind his wife and eight sons.

"What's wrong, Lulu?" my friend Suzie asked when she found me pacing the hall after I got off the phone with Meng and Eang.

I was all of a sudden exhausted.

"Lulu, are you okay?" Suzie asked.

When I tried to not think about Uncle Lee, my thoughts landed on the war in Iraq. In January and February, I'd watched as Iraq's dark sky blazed with explosions and bombs on TV. Every night I sent silent prayers to the Iraqi people, but still it felt somewhat sacrilegious to go on with my merry life when so many were suffering. I told myself I had to turn my attention to the finals and essays I had to take and write. I was at Saint Michael's mostly due to the generosity of the school and an organization called the Turrell Fund, and in order to keep my scholarships, I had to have good grades. So I turned off the TV, and for a while, I succeeded in shutting myself off.

But I could not close myself off from Uncle Lee's death.

The news cracked something inside me, slowly splitting my hard shell, and soon I was certain that all that I cared about would one day leave me.

"Lulu?"

I left Suzie. I was raised as a Buddhist, and as such, I was permitted, even encouraged, to find serenity wherever I could. And since there was no temple on campus, I headed for the chapel.

I'd always found it comforting that Saint Michael's was founded by priests from the Society of Saint Edmund who had fled France in 1889 to escape anti-clericalism. It made me feel connected to the school knowing that its founders also had to leave their home to rebuild their lives in another land. But these priests did more than that; they contributed to their new country. In 1904, they opened Saint Michael's Institute, and later they built the Chapel of Saint Michael the Archangel as a place for people to celebrate their spiritual and religious lives. Since then, the chapel had become not only a place to worship, but had also hosted volunteer programs, weddings, and prayer reflections.

Inside the chapel, I sat in a pew with my head bowed. Since I was in a house of God, I asked Him to take care of Uncle Lee. I wished Uncle Lee a safe journey to wherever he was going.

I was so deep in my meditation that I didn't notice my class-mate Julie had come in until she knelt down next to me. I looked up to see Julie smiling at me.

"Lulu, I'm so glad you know that you can always talk to Jesus," she said. "If you ever want to say something and share feelings you cannot tell anyone, you can always talk to Jesus. He is always there. He is a forgiving Christ. He loves you. He will never abandon you."

I stared at the wooden crucifix on the wall long after Julie left me. It showed a Jesus in agony and pain. On the same wall was a framed photograph of a serene-looking Jesus. I won-dered which Son of God I should talk to. In the end, my fear was so great I decided to ask everyone for help.

"Dear Lord, Jesus Christ, Mary, Buddha, Allah, Krishna, please take care of Uncle Lee." I whispered my prayers and hoped they all heard me. I closed my eyes and repeated my prayers. Between prayers, I breathed.

THE NEXT DAY, MENG, EANG, AND I traveled to Montreal to attend Uncle Lee's funeral. The hour-and-a-half car ride was quiet as each of us replayed our memories of Uncle Lee in our heads.

At the wake, I stood in line waiting for my turn to wish him a safe journey into the netherworld. As I neared, I saw the tip of Uncle Lee's nose peeking out of the open casket. A school of minnows, cold and slippery, rushed down my spine. I steeled myself, willing my feet to inch forward to pay my respect to Uncle Lee's body. But my feet refused to move. I turned and ran out of the room. On my way out, I saw Uncle Lee's widow, Aunt Lee, her gray hair blending in with her white mourning veil, sobbing into her white handkerchief. Her eight grown sons sat next to her, all dressed in white shirts and pants, looking down at their shoes. Raindrop tears dotted the floor.

For the next hour, I moved between the bathroom, lobby, and car, clutching a book to my chest. I was pacing outside the funeral home when Meng and Eang found me to take me to Aunt Lee's house. There, I stood mutely by the door as Aunt Lee held court in her living room.

"People in our lives will always leave us," Aunt Lee said to her sons and the family friends gathering around her. As she talked, a community of women scattered about in her kitchen cleaning and cooking. The clangs of pots and pans could be heard as the aroma of chicken rice congee and fried ginger spread throughout the house.

"Often, it's the men who go first." Aunt Lee started to list all the fathers and uncles lost in the family.

"Women, we are strong. We give birth, watch our children die, raise those that live, say goodbyes to our husbands, and survive to raise our grandchildren. You boys have to be more like women. You have to be strong."

Aunt Lee looked at her eight sons.

"People will always die, but we have to continue to live," Aunt Lee said. "Live, eat, and love."

I RETURNED TO SAINT MICHAEL'S WITH my head still in a fog. To clear my mind, I headed out for a walk in the wooded trail behind the campus. It was the end of April but it had begun to snow again. The early spring weather Mark and I had enjoyed a few weeks before had disappeared, much like our relationship. I wondered where he was, what he was doing, and who he was with. It had been three weeks since our breakup. And although I continued to see him in classes, we had not spoken to each other. Instead, we sat in seats far from each other, and headed in opposite directions when we saw each other approaching. I told myself I was better for it. Still, I felt a sharp pain in my gut as if I'd been hit by a fast-flying soccer ball.

A layer of freshly fallen snow muted the world so that the only sounds were the inhaling and exhaling of my breath. I shook my head to erase Mark from my mind and continued my walk. I did not stop until I'd reached the middle of nowhere. There, I stretched out on the snow and stared at the yellow sun trying to peek through the clouds, wondering what it would be like to be dead.

I'd always believed I would die young. Perhaps it was a lonely child's fantasy of death as a way to receive more attention. Or maybe I was just vengeful, wanting the chance to come back as a ghost so I could haunt all those who had wronged me in some way. But mostly, I did not speak these thoughts to anyone. I held them in my body until the feelings built up and formed knots in my stomach and shoulder muscles, and pains in my head. I tried to exorcise thoughts of death with good cheer, good food, and good friends. But death was everywhere. It came at the fairground, in the form of a monster truck I was convinced would lose control and plow into the stand where I sat. Death was in the lake, longing to pull me under in a mass of haunted, tangled seaweed. As I got older, I came to realize that fantasy deaths were the only deaths I could bear; they were a way to avoid thinking about the deaths of real people who would never come back.

I opened my eyes and saw that the sliver of yellow sun was no more. For a moment, I was again a girl waiting for my mother and father to return; the hurt of that wait rushed at me all at once.

Women are strong. Aunt Lee said the words like a mantra in my mind.

I am not a child anymore, I told myself. *I do not have to live in fear. I am a strong woman. And when a woman falls, she gets up.*

Get up, I told myself. I wiggled my fingers in my mittens and watched snowflakes landing on my eyelashes.

People will always die, but we have to continue to live. Aunt Lee's words echoed. *Live. Eat. Love.* As fresh snow continued to cover me, I thought of the aromas of Eang's Phnom Penh noodle soup and Aunt Lee's stir-fried crabs. I savored the deliciousness of Ben & Jerry's ice cream and melting mozzarella on Papa Frank's pizzas. Then I started to remember all the times Mark had brought me food. The hot-and-sour soup he delivered when I was sick, the bratwurst sandwiches he fed me on our hiking trips, and the pints of Chunky Monkey he offered to help me study. He even learned to make eggplant parmesan, *ma po* tofu, hot-and-sour chicken, and Thai basil curry, and he grilled chili dogs to their decadent best. All of them were my favorite dishes, and all of them he cooked for me. Slowly, and with my mouth watering, I began to see that written somewhere in the *ma po* tofu was Mark's love message to me.

A flicker of light warmed from the inside. I looked up at the gray sky, saw the world was not that dark after all. Slowly, I rose like a mummy, shook off the snow, and went home.

11

Cupid's Evil Twin

Fort Ethan Allen, May 1991

Once I knew I wanted to be back with Mark, I had to think up a plan to get us back together again. I was mulling over this in St. Ed's Hall when I was interrupted by Jenny.

"Hi, Lulu." Jenny sat down next to me.

"Jenny." I acknowledged her, opening a text book.

Without my asking, she launched into a story of the hot-tub party she'd attended the night before. "Mark was there! And we somehow ended up in the hot tub next to each other. And I had on this bathing suit that slit from here"—she pointed a finger to her neck—"to here." Her finger made a line to end at her navel.

I glared at her.

"It was so sexy it should have been illegal!" Jenny purred.

"You're a bitch," I growled, and walked out on her. I'd never wanted to beat up anybody more than at that moment.

Jenny ran after me.

"Lulu," she said, stopping me. "What's wrong?"

I was incredulous. "Jenny," I answered, my hands curled into fists. "You know Mark is, was, my boyfriend. Why would you say those things to me?"

"I'm sorry . . . I-I-I don't know . . ."

I marched away.

Back at the dorm, I put out three SOS calls. Like the fairy godmothers they were, Beth, Christina, and Cassie flew over and wrapped their wings over me. They let me vent and cuss. They also brought Papa Frank's pizza and pork rinds.

"Sweetie, there's plenty more fish in the sea." Christina stroked my back.

"I don't want another fish," I grumped, crunching on pork rinds. I wanted Mark. But the realization came too late because he had moved on to another girl. I buried my face in my pillow. All these years I'd told myself to never be ruled by fear, and now I had let fear rule me.

"Jenny's a slut!" Cassie declared.

Hearing Cassie's vehement announcement, I had another moment of clarity.

When I escaped the Khmer Rouge and came to Vermont, I vowed to live life with decency, integrity, and grace. I wanted to be a good person. This meant I supported not just human rights but also women's rights. I called myself a feminist. I read *Ms.* magazine and Gloria Steinem's work. I believed in being a friend to women and lifting them up. Yet I wanted to step on Jenny, to smash her like a bug beneath my Doc Martens.

Wherever you are, Gloria Steinem, I whispered in my head, *I could really use your advice.*

I began to channel the spirit of Ms. Steinem and tried to think of Jenny as a woman, not as my enemy. It was well-known gossip on campus that Jenny suffered from an eating disorder and mental-health problems. This gossip followed her everywhere she went. When she entered a room, people made judgments about her body and wrote their own stories about who she was. But what did we all really know about Jenny? I sometimes wondered if our possibly misguided assumptions affected the way she acted.

As a girl, I was used to people writing their own stories about me, and I did not like it one bit. A memory of this surfaced; I was nine, jostled by a woman on a crowded path as we each tried to squeeze through the entrance to a tented market in Cambodia. The crowd surged forward, and the woman elbowed me in my ribs.

"Stop!" I shouted.

The woman halted in surprise.

I'd been told there were eighteen levels of Chinese Buddhist hell. Level One was the Chamber of Wind and Thunder, for people who killed and committed heinous crimes out of greed; Two was the Chamber of Grinding, where wealthy men who did bad things and wasted food were ground into powder; Three was the Chamber of Flames, reserved for people who stole, plundered, and cheated. Level Four, the Chamber of Ice, was where children who mistreated their parents and elders were sent. I shivered at the thought of being frozen in ice for all eternity.

The woman loomed in my mind, her thoughts clicking so loudly I could hear her writing her version of me. I saw myself in her eyes: a rude disrespectful girl, an uncultured daughter who would amount to nothing. I should have been more used to it, people telling my tale as if they knew me.

"You dare to scream at me?" the woman challenged.

"You pushed me first!" I yelled back, standing my ground.

The woman's face abruptly softened. She stepped back. I thanked her and passed by.

Back in my dorm, I sat up in my bed. And in that kind-woman frame of mind, I began to change my story of Jenny. I wondered if Jenny had been misunderstood, or perhaps if she truly was ill and didn't have full control over her actions.

"Oh, that Jenny!" Cassie said crossly. "She's a bit—"

I cut her off. "Stop. Jenny may be mean, but she's no more than that."

"But—" Christina stammered.

"Listen," I told them. "Jenny has her own problems, and calling her names won't make me feel any better. If we don't like her, we can peel her off like a leech and toss her somewhere else, let her shrivel up in another place far from us."

I was trying to be compassionate, but I was no Mother Teresa.

"Let's leave her alone," I sighed to the girls. "It's not like she's our friend or anything."

"Well said, Lulu." Beth came and sat by my side.

For a moment, I felt almost like a mature adult. I was proud of myself.

Cassie downed her beer and tossed the can into the basket. "Enough of this sitting inside," she said. "Let's go find a party."

Thirty minutes later we found one at a friend's place at Fort Ethan Allen. The party was going full swing, noisy and crowded with college girls in sports jerseys and boys in baseball caps. In the middle of the room, a group of sweaty young bodies was gyrating to '80s music. I headed for the food table while the girls headed for the bar. I was making my way through my tenth cheese ball when Mark walked in. I watched him make his way across the room. When he turned, our eyes met. I raised an unsure hand.

"Opposites Attract," Paula Abdul's famous song, played as I moved closer to Mark. But then I stopped in my tracks. Mark wasn't alone. He was chatting with a girl named Tiffany.

On the ceiling in the corner where Mark stood, a winged cherub hovered. Only he wasn't adorable, and he was a little more than pudgy. *Gotcha!* Cupid's Evil Twin pierced me with his poisonous arrow. Purple jealousy smudged my cheeks, and now Tiffany, a girl I did not know, became someone I wanted to harm. Tiffany rested her hand on Mark's arm, threw back her head, and laughed. In another world, I turned into a rabid wolf and bit off her arm. Tiffany leaned into Mark, pulling him in closer as she whispered something into his ear. Mark backed away, gently shook her off, and walked toward me.

"Hi," he said.

"Ahoy," I replied, my greeting as awkward as the word I used. My eyes looked right and left, searching the crowd for my friends, but they were nowhere to be seen. "So, are you with Tiffany now?" I asked, focusing on the cheese balls.

"No," he answered. "We're just friends."

"What about Jenny?" I asked, my palms sweating.

"We're just friends."

In my chest, my heart was jumping double dutch. "I heard about the hot-tub party," I said.

"Everyone was there," Mark said, naming many of our mutual guy- and girlfriends. "The water was disgusting so I got out as fast as I could."

Jenny didn't mention the other people! I hollered with relief in my head.

"So there's nothing going on with Jenny?"

"I don't like Jenny . . ." He paused. "But I'm glad you thought we were together."

"Why?"

"Otherwise, I wouldn't have known that you still care."

I turned to him, my eyes staring into his. "Do you . . . still . . . care too?" I asked haltingly.

"Yes . . ."

I jumped then. Feetfirst, hands high in the air, hair flowing over my eyes so that I could not see into the future. I leapt into life, into love, into the unknown. And when Mark took me into his arms, I yielded. My lips were still smiling when he brought his down on mine. The fire reignited in my core. But this time, the red amber did not glow softly, it exploded, a supernova combustion all over my body, reducing the soldiers, their guns, and my fears into ashes.

But wait . . . a small voice interrupted my euphoria. *Meng and Eang are not going to like this. They don't approve of dating, of becoming tainted . . .*

Well, what they don't know won't hurt them, I told my critical self. *We'll just have to continue to keep Mark a secret.*

Part Two: Healing

12

The Long and Winding Road

Vermont, Maine, and Washington, D.C., 1993–1997

The class of 1993 tossed its hats into the air as our college president pronounced us graduates. I watched my hat fly high above the crowd, the tassels swishing and swaying like the tails of a golden phoenix. When they had reached their maximum height, they paused and hung briefly in midair before quickly beginning their descent. One by one, my friends' futures were projected on their caps: Cassie teaching students in an inner-city school, Beth examining a child in a white room, and Christina overworked as a public defender in some big city. Before any picture could form on my hat, it crashed onto the floor.

After college, Mark and I decided to stay together but in a long-distance relationship. He returned to Cleveland to join his father in the family's real estate firm while I stayed in Vermont. I had seventy-five dollars in my pocket, enough to rent a room in a friend's farmhouse in South Burlington. With my diploma in hand, I made my way to Saint Michael's international students' commons area, a well-kept secret among scavengers like me. It was where rich international students—after many years of buying all their necessities—threw away their stuff before they headed back to their home countries.

Half an hour later, I'd packed up my 1984 Nissan Stanza, "Little Red"—a graduation gift from Meng and Eang—with a new TV, microwave, and coffeemaker. My luck would continue the next day when I landed a job.

My nieces hugged me when I told my family the news. "Congrats, Kgo!"

"What is your job?" Meng asked.

"I am in the Executive Management Training Program at Kinney Shoes," I announced, putting as much excitement in my voice as I could.

Meng glowed with paternal pride, looking as if he'd stashed two bright red bulbs inside his cheeks. "Executive . . ." he repeated.

"Good . . . good . . ." Eang patted my arm.

Meng and Eang were hardworking people who held the immigrant mentality that no work was too small or low, except perhaps—*perhaps*—selling shoes. Or really anything that required one to touch other people's feet. According to their Buddhist belief, this was a sacrilegious act, because the feet were the lowest part of the human body. I conveniently left that part out of my job description. For three months, I touched people's feet and sold shoes. That was as long as I lasted at Kinney Shoes, because that's when Mark called and invited me to move in with him in Cleveland.

I hesitated before answering. "I don't know . . ."

"At least come for Thanksgiving."

"I'll think about it . . ."

When November came, I told my family I was visiting a girlfriend in Ohio, packed up Little Red, and headed west. When I arrived, Mark met me on his front steps and moved me into his one-bedroom apartment.

For a few weeks, living on love was all I had imagined it would be. We played mud football with his friends, hiked the Cuyahoga trails, and went on date nights to the movies. But only on Mondays, when tickets were discounted.

Soon Thanksgiving came and went, and I stayed. I found two part-time restaurant jobs. And instead of going to work for his father, Mark switched to construction contracting. We didn't have a lot of money, but we were in love. We went to sleep each night staring into each other's eyes. When snow fell, we made snow angels and a snow family with snow pets. We gave them piles of giant snow burgers and hot dogs. Then we went tobogganing, sledding, and caught snowflakes with our tongues.

In Cleveland, I felt safe and hidden from the world. I stopped reading the newspaper, listening to NPR, and watching the evening news. In our little cove of an apartment, everything felt very far away. And Cambodia was the farthest. I was living the fantasy of my happy middle-class American life. If I'd dyed my hair blond, I could have been Marcia Brady.

There were also days when this isolation bothered me, days when I felt a void, a restlessness and desire to be more involved in the world. Days when my mind felt numb, as if the months of newsless days had melted my brain. On these days, I toddled around Mark's apartment like a zombie, my arms arrow-straight in front of me, my tongue lolling outside my mouth.

Still, I had love.

But as December turned into January, love began to stink. Outside, the weather became frigid, the sky grew gray. Mark no longer worked outdoors or came home smelling of sunshine and fresh grass. When he did work, Mark was doing interior renovations, and he reeked of chemicals and butane gas. But more often than not, he was waking up every morning and staggering to his Nintendo console to play *Zelda*.

Then, in February, a burger set off our first unraveling.

Lumpy, gray, and dried, I pulled the burnt patty out of the microwave at eight in the morning. The stink of old meat flooded our small home, stirring Mark out of bed.

"Is that what you're eating for breakfast?" He grunted in disgust.

"Yes," I replied tersely. "Because no one shopped."

I plopped a spoonful of mayo on top of the blackened meat and ate it with my bowl of rice. "I've got to go to work," I told him.

Mark poured himself a cup of coffee. "Bye . . ." he mumbled, walking into the bathroom.

"Okay," I harrumphed, and left.

Mark and I did not fight the first few months we lived together. It was too cold for that. I was too cold to do anything but sit on the couch and read books. His parents, who lived in Cleveland, began to wonder when I would leave. Meng still believed I was living with a girlfriend, and Maria and Tori were missing me. Every week or so, Eang would call to report news of our family in Cambodia: of sister Chou, who had given birth to her third child, of Khouy's promotion to deputy police chief, and of Kim's move from Cambodia to Paris to live with our aunt.

What of sister Loung? they asked. What big life is she living? What big achievements and dreams? In their letters, they sent their joy and well-wishes. Through Meng, I sent them my greetings and best wishes. But still, each phone call filled me with guilt. Meng and Eang brought me to America to give me the whole wide world, and I knew I was not living up to their expectations. So when Heidi, a college friend living in Maine, called to say there was a position open at the domestic women's shelter where she worked, I went.

Once again, I packed up Little Red.

Mark wrapped his arms around my waist and pulled me toward him. "Maine is close to Vermont," he said. "Maybe when I visit you, we can go see your family."

I gave him no answer and hugged him tighter.

"If the job doesn't work out," he said, "you can always come back to Cleveland."

I buried my face in the warmth of his neck, thanking him for the stability he offered me.

"You are the salt of my earth, you know . . ." I whispered.

I also knew I had to leave for that same reason. I got into the car and drove away. As I merged onto the highway, I knew I would get lost before I reached my destination. But I was excited to begin my journey.

THE NEXT WEEK I STARTED MY new position as the community educator at the Abused Women's Advocacy Project in Auburn, Maine. I joined a team of ten women and one man, and my primary job was to teach police officers, nurses, clergy members, and others in the community about domestic violence laws, and to staff the hotlines.

After a month of training, I picked up the phone when a woman named Sara called, crying.

"Are you in danger right now?" I asked, my voice shaking as much as hers. "Do you need to call the police?"

"No . . ."

"Are you safe to talk?"

"Yes."

For an hour, I listened as she told me her story. We could not see each other's faces, but we were connected by our war stories, only hers was fought in her home. After our talk, she never called back, but I continued to think of Sara often. I wondered if she ever learned to trust again. In some way, the scars of my war were easier to identify, because the soldiers were the enemies, not my parents. And if the day ever came for me to face my family's killers in a court of law, I wouldn't walk in wondering if I still harbored love for them.

As the sun rose and lowered behind Maine's pristine mountains each day, I became more and more at ease with talking to women. And yet, it never ceased to enrage me each time I encountered a victim who described herself as "nothing."

Nothing. This identity was a dictum of war. To survive, you learned to see nothing, hear nothing, be nothing. I knew it all too well as a child. I listened to women like Sara and learned, and gradually I began to share their stories in my training sessions with police officers, doctors, students, and teachers. I enjoyed this part of my work, sustained by the hope that I was making a difference for the women and the little girls who came into the shelter. Some of the children were so scared that if you raised your hand too quickly around them, they crawled under the table. But every four to five weeks, I left work behind, when I visited Mark in Cleveland or he came to see me in Maine. With our busy schedules and lack of funds, we began to save all vacation days and pool our money to extend our otherwise short weekends into sometimes longer ones. During these few days, we visited museums in Cleveland, or swam in Maine's many pristine lakes and ate lobsters caught fresh from the sea. In this bliss, I told him I thought I'd found my place.

A year after my arrival in Maine, I met the person who would challenge that belief.

Dith Pran was world famous by the time I met him at Bates College in Lewiston, Maine. His story of surviving the Khmer Rouge regime, chronicled in a series of *New York Times* articles by reporter Sydney Schanberg, had been turned into the movie *The Killing Fields* in 1984. When Pou Pran, or Uncle Pran, as I called him—a Khmer custom of showing respect when speaking to an elder—walked onto the stage, I was mesmerized.

Pou Pran explained that before the Khmer Rouge takeover, he'd been a photographer, interpreter, and stringer for many foreign reporters covering the war in Cambodia. This, in the eyes of the Khmer Rouge regime, made him a traitor. And the Khmer Rouge solution for traitors was to purge them. Thus, when they took over the country on April 17, 1975, Uncle Pran knew he was marked. For the next three years, eight months, and twenty-one days, he had to hide his identity to survive. His voice rising up and down, he recounted the horrors of life under the Khmer Rouge as the audience gasped in disbelief. For an hour, I sat rigid in my seat, my body leaning forward to catch his every word.

After his talk, I approached him as a nervous schoolgirl might. "Pou," I said. "I am Khmer, and I just wanted to say thank you."

"Kmoy," *Niece,* he answered. "Did you live through the killing fields, too?"

I looked around before answering, as if to make sure no one was spying on me. "Yes," I said quietly.

"What do you do?"

I told him.

"So you do a lot of speaking for a living?"

"Yes . . . sometimes . . ." but I was unsure of myself. Where was he going with this?

"Kmoy," Pou Pran said kindly. "We need more voices out there. If you can, speak up. Tell your story. Help Cambodia."

But was my story worth telling? Five million Cambodian Khmer Rouge survivors had similar stories to tell and, I was convinced, many could tell it better than me. And yet, my wavering was stilled at once when Uncle Pran gave a name to it: Help Cambodia. I wanted to help, but I did not know what to do, or how to do it. I also realized that if Uncle Pran stepped away from his work as an activist helping Cambodia, there would be few who would step in to take over. If I stepped away from my domestic violence work, there would be tens of thousands of women around the world who would continue to fight. I came to realize where I would be most needed.

Several months later, when Meng told me he and some of our family were going back to Cambodia together for the first time, I decided to go with them, although I had to fly separately. I was vibrating with fear after I hung up the phone with Meng. My last images of my home country were of garbage-filled broken roads, fallen-down buildings, and villages filled with hungry people. And of my sister Chou.

When I closed my eyes, I could still see Chou's face on the day we were separated.

"Don't forget me," Chou cried.

Fifteen years later, I was excited to return to Cambodia and to the sister I had not seen since we were children. But as the date of our trip neared, my anxiety increased. For many weeks, I packed and repacked my backpack, sustained by the dream of being reunited with Chou.

•   •   •

ON THE DAY OF MY DEPARTURE, MARK called me. I held the phone close to my ear, trying to remember the sound and tone of his voice. In my mind, a small fear snaked to the surface. It slithered in the thought that should something happened to me in Cambodia, Mark and I would be halfway around the world from each other.

"I could still buy an airplane ticket and meet you there," he said.

"Funny," I told him, but I was not laughing. He was teasing me, of course, but as always, I felt guilty because after five years together, I'd yet to tell my family about him. As far as they were concerned, he did not exist and that hurt him.

"One of these days," he said, "I'm going to have to meet them."

"I'm going to miss you," I said, changing the subject.

"You'll be back before you know it," he told me.

I took a deep breath and righted my head. "I know," I said. "But if I don't make it back, I want you to mourn me for a year. Anything less than that and I will come back to haunt you."

"You are odd," he said tenderly. "But I adore that about you."

After I hung up the phone with Mark, I headed for the airport. An hour later, I boarded the plane with only my small backpack, wearing a pair of black pants, a brown shirt, and my Teva sandals. Twenty-five hours after that, the plane screeched to a stop at Pochengtong Airport in Phnom Penh. From there, each minute felt like an eternity as I inched through customs to exit the airport.

I saw my family at the arrival gate. There were twenty or thirty in total, all of them craning their necks to get their first glimpses of me. I walked slowly toward them, my fists clenched to my side. In the middle of the group, Meng, Eang, Maria, and Tori waved. Beside them, my brother Khouy, wearing a T-shirt with "I Love Vermont" printed on it. When I saw Chou, my throat tightened. When we parted, we were twelve- and ten-year-old girls. Now I was twenty-five, and she was a twenty-seven-year-old wife and mother of three. But despite our separate life experiences, our size, shape, and height remained equal.

"You look like a Khmer Rouge," a cousin announced, pointing at my dark shirt and pants.

The family laughed at me. I smiled even as the muscles in my cheeks shook.

"That's how she dresses when she travels," Eang explained to the family. "They're her comfortable clothes."

As I shifted my weight from foot to foot, Chou quickly walked over and took my hand. She was crying and laughing as our fingers clasped. "I can't believe you're here," she said.

"Don't cry," I told her.

Khouy walked up to us. "Loung, don't worry about Chou," he said, chuckling. "She cries all the time."

Chou let go of my hands to dry her tears. "Come," she said. "Let's go see the city."

My family and I spent the first week of our reunion visiting our village by day and returning to the city to spend our nights. But wherever we went, we were always together. And we ate. A lot. We sat on floor mats in circles, sharing sumptuous Cambodian meals of grilled eels, fried pork, sautéed gizzards, beef skewers, steamed fish, and morning glory sour soups. After we ate, we walked and talked. And so Chou was with me when I passed an ice cream cart in a crowded street that reminded me of my childhood. She was with me when we stopped at a row of vendors selling baskets of fried grasshoppers, tarantulas, and other bugs.

"Loung . . . you remember? It's your favorite food." Chou bought a bag for me.

I chomped down on one. It tasted salty, with a nutty flavor. *This would go really good with margaritas!* I thought.

"Delicious, just like I remember," I told Chou, smirking. "It would go well with a cold beer."

"Khmer women don't drink alcohol."

"This Khmer woman does," I said, grinning.

When we were not walking, talking, or eating, the family toured the city, taking in sights of the Silver Palace, markets, and temples. They were magical, but many times I also had to hide my eyes behind my dark sunglasses. Everywhere we went, there were signs of poverty: street kids digging through garbage mounds, elderly homeless people sleeping on the streets, disabled people selling gum and books. And there were many amputees—people with resilient souls and strong spirits—holding their hats in their hands, begging. Many were former soldiers.

"Where did they all come from?" I asked.

"War made them," Chou replied.

I found it hard to walk by the beggars without giving them money, and they sensed this in my lingering stares and pauses in their direction. Thus, they swarmed me. And after an hour of walking around the city, I had run out of money.

At the end of one such day, I was exhausted and decided to stay at the hotel by myself while my family went out to eat. But as soon as they'd left, I became restless and went out for a walk. I'd just stepped out of the hotel when a girl approached. She looked about seven years old and so emaciated I could count the bones in her hands. She wore a stained, tattered shirt, and pants that hung loose around her small body. In her arms, she cradled a sleeping infant with a round, bloated belly.

"Please, sister," she begged. "Give me one hundred riel. We are hungry."

In my eyes, the girl looked like my little sister Geak when she was lost and hungry during the war.

"Where are your parents?" I asked.

"My mother is sick," the girl said, her voice so small I could barely hear her. "My father died when he stepped on a landmine."

A moment passed before I could take the information in. "A landmine? Where?"

"In my village."

I swallowed, unable to speak. I looked at the baby; her ribs protruded from her chest, and flies circled her half-opened mouth as she slept. I dug into my pocket but found no money.

"I don't have my money on me," I told the girl. "Wait here. I'll get it."

I ran back into the hotel, but when I came back out, the girl was gone. I walked over to the hotel attendant standing by the door. "Did you see the little beggar girl with a small child?" I asked.

"I'm sorry she bothered you," he said. "I chased her away. Don't worry, she won't be back here again."

I shook my head. "No, no, she wasn't bothering me. She wasn't . . ."

The attendant looked confused.

"Which way did she go?"

He looked right, then left. "That way, I think. I wasn't watching."

Before he could say more, I took off. I searched up and down the streets, but the girl was nowhere to be found. It was as if she had just vanished.

I returned to my room and curled up on my bed, wishing I

could speak to Mark. The last time we talked was over a week ago, when I was still in Maine. I'd promised to call when I arrived safe and sound in Cambodia, but there was no telephone in my room. And the one telephone in the hotel office could not make international calls. Thus, it would be another two weeks before I would hear his voice.

Slowly, I pulled the covers over me and turned off the desk lamp. "Good night, Mark," I said, missing him terribly as I closed my eyes to sleep.

THE NEXT MORNING, MY FAMILY AND I drove two hours from Phnom Penh to a different village where more family lived. On the way, I noticed numerous red signposts staked to the ground. The signs had crude drawings of human skulls and crossbones over explosions.

"Chou, are those landmine warnings?" I asked, pointing to the signs.

"Yes," she replied. "There are minefields all over Cambodia, and some are near our village."

I stared at the lush patches of green, fertile land inhabited by children herding their cows and flying their makeshift kites.

"It's not safe for them to be on that land," I said softly. "They shouldn't be walking on it."

"But this is their home," Chou said. "If they don't live on it, where would they go?"

Chou went on to explain that there were minefields all over Cambodia, and some near our village. To keep her children safe, she taught them not to walk off the beaten path. Not even to pick pretty flowers in the fields. She warned them their curiosity could get them killed.

"We are fortunate," Chou told me. "Our family has a small fruit and vegetable shop, so we don't have to work in the fields."

I breathed a grateful sigh that my family was "safe." But my relief turned to sadness when I counted five more minefields before we reached our family's village. "This is our land, our home," I whispered.

WHEN OUR FAMILY VACATION ENDED TWO weeks later, I returned to Maine emotionally exhausted and spent. A few days after my arrival, Mark came to visit. I burst into tears as soon as I saw him at the airport.

"Sweetie," he whispered into my hair, holding me tight.

"I'm just so glad to see you," I said, suddenly aware we were being watched by other travelers. I wiped my face quickly. "Let's get out of here."

We drove to Old Orchard Beach, a popular summer destination known for its seven miles of beaches and amusement park attractions that in the summer drew large crowds. In the fall, it was quiet and calm. And there, watching the waves crashing in the distance, I told Mark about my Cambodia trip and the reunions with my family and the sister I'd left behind. As he held my hand, I began to share the details about my life under the Khmer Rouge.

"I was so starving that I could see my ribs," I said, my feet sinking into the sand. "But my stomach bulged like a ball . . . I remember thinking . . . if I prick it with a pin, I would pop and become . . . nothing."

Mark was quiet, giving me time to continue.

"Being in Cambodia brought back so many memories. Many I wished I could forget . . ."

I told Mark about my sisters Keav and Geak, and how the soldiers came for my father and mother. But I couldn't describe the scenarios of my parents' deaths, of how I believed they may have died. And I couldn't tell him about the Vietnamese soldier.

When I stopped talking, Mark put his arms around me. We stood together in silence, feeling the cool waves washing over our feet, cleaning them.

AFTER MARK LEFT, I BEGAN MY research of landmines. The more I learned, the more enraged I became that fifteen years after the Khmer Rouge soldiers had stopped turning children into orphans, landmines were still doing the job for them. Every month, eighty to one hundred Cambodians continued to be injured, maimed, or killed by these relic weapons of war. One in 252 Cambodians was an amputee, compared to one in 22,000 in the U.S., resulting in a population of 45,000 amputees in that small country. A poor man's munitions, landmines cost no more than three dollars to purchase, but once in the ground, each took five hundred to a thousand dollars to remove. In a poor country like Cambodia, this was a price few Khmers or even the government could afford. Because of this, Cambodia remained one of the most landmine-affected countries in the world.

As I read these reports, I was reminded of Elie Wiesel's words: "There may be times when we are powerless to prevent injustice, but there must never be a time when we fail to protest."

I decided to join the protest. I also knew how I would accept Uncle Pran's challenge. I was going to join the effort to eradicate landmines in Cambodia. I wanted to redeem myself for leaving Cambodia; I wanted to help that beggar girl. But to do this, I had to leave Maine, where I'd learned to live on my own, and leave my community of women warriors. I wasn't sure I was ready.

Mark and I were still going strong after five years together. We had stayed true to each other in a monogamous relationship and were best friends. And although there were days and weeks when I wished we lived closer to each other, I also liked being on my own. I had learned to take care of myself, enjoy eating at restaurants by myself, watch movies alone in the dark, change my car tires, and pay my bills. I was passionate about my job, which married my intellect and my convictions about women's rights. I was good at it. Did I want to leave my friends and start anew at something else? Someplace else? Especially when I did not know what that something else would be?

I decided yes.

It would be another six months before I took the next step, the only next step I knew to take—applying to graduate school. When I was accepted into Columbia University's School for International and Public Affairs with a fellowship offer, I jumped with joy. Then I followed up my lucky streak with an application to intern at Peace Action, a nongovernmental organization working to ban landmines based in D.C. One month later, I received an acceptance letter. My path was set.

I called Mark to tell him I was moving to D.C.

"The plan is," I said rapidly in my excitement, "I'll work six months in D.C. on Peace Action's Ban Landmines Campaign, then move to New York City in the fall to start at Columbia."

Three months later, I was in Washington, D.C., one step closer to Cambodia.

13

The Girl in the Mirror

Washington, D.C., May 1997

I waited for Mark at his gate at Washington National Airport, my eyes on the book on my lap. I had been in Washington, D.C., for five weeks and this was his first visit to see me. As I tried to concentrate on my book, the seconds ticked away slowly on my wristwatch. I checked it against the airport clock on the wall, saw that they were in sync.

Being in a long-distance relationship, I had become good at waiting. Or at least, at waiting out the long stretches of time before we saw each other. Our five weeks apart were both excruciatingly long and short this way. In those weeks, I'd missed Mark, and yet, I had also been too busy for him to visit.

My days felt like they had neither beginning nor end, but instead were a series of short vignettes, strung together by work, museum visits, happy hours, and new friends. It seemed as though the minute I opened my eyes in the morning, the day was already over. In this way, the days came and went quickly. But now that he was almost there, the last few minutes felt like many hours.

When the airline attendant announced the arrival of his flight, I stood up from my seat, straining my neck to see if Mark would be the first one to exit. Even after six years together, I was still excited to see him.

Finally, the door opened and the passengers came out. One by one, grandparents, mothers, fathers, and lovers greeted each other. Behind the group, Mark sauntered out of the gate, unhurried as usual. At the sight of him, my heart skipped a beat. When he reached me, he wrapped his arms around my waist and lifted me off the ground. "Missed me?" he asked.

"Who are you again?" I pushed him away. "You'd better let me go. I'm waiting for my boyfriend, who is big and surly and will kick your butt when he sees you."

"I don't think he's coming," Mark teased, and held me tighter.

"Well, then, I'll have to do it myself."

"Okay, Minnie Mouse," he said, putting me on the ground and kissing me. Instantly, my face warmed.

"Ready to see D.C.?" I asked when our lips parted.

Mark draped his arm over my shoulders as we walked out. Before we reached the exit, a television report caught my eyes.

"Today, President Clinton met with Rwandan genocide survivors," the anchor read.

I stopped and watched.

". . . eight hundred thousand macheted to death in a hundred days . . ."

On the screen, images of dead bodies, burning homes, and catatonic people with glassy eyes stared at the camera. A wounded skeletal child whimpered.

"Where are we going?" he asked.

"Huh?"

"I asked where we're going."

"Oh." I came back to the present. "I thought we'd go hiking along Skyline Drive, and then to Cassie's—she's hosting a small party." I spoke loudly, attempting to inject cheer into my voice.

Mark put his arm around my shoulder and pulled me away.

A FEW HOURS LATER, I LED THE way through a trail brimming with lush leaves and tall, old-growth trees. I stopped at a scenic point and waited for Mark. From where I stood, the sky was clear blue, and Shenandoah National Park spread out as far as our eyes could see. Somewhere a bird squawked. A sound resembling a human wail echoed in the woods. I tensed and quickly scanned the woods for movement. Mark came up behind me.

"Do we have to stop at every scenic point?" I huffed. "We'll never reach the top at this rate."

"What's your rush?"

"I just like to get to where I'm going, that's all."

Mark walked over to the lookout spot. "It's so tranquil up here," he said, exhaling slowly.

"Fine," I harrumphed, taking off my backpack. "Snack break it is."

I unzipped the backpack and pulled out half a roast beef sandwich. It was an awesome sandwich, packed full of juicy red meat and dripping with yellow mustard. Slowly, I took a big bite out of it.

"You call that a snack?"

"Uh-huh . . ." I answered with my mouth full.

Mark fished a granola bar from his pocket and offered me a bite.

"No thanks. If it ain't bleeding, I ain't eating."

For a few minutes, we ate our snacks and stared at the scenery. When he was done with his itty-bitty snack, Mark waited for me as I savored every bite of my sandwich. When I was finally done, I rubbed my belly in happy satisfaction.

"Mmm-mmm good," I murmured. "Now that's big people's food."

Mark moved menacingly toward me.

I stood my ground and took a karate kick stance. "Don't you dare!" I warned. "I may be small but I am mighty!"

He advanced.

"I am going to Hong Kong Phooey you to bits!" I chopped my arms through the air, imitating the movements I'd seen in kung fu movies. "Say goodbye to your ass!"

I moved in, flapping my arms rapidly, emitting the high-pitched grunts of Bruce Lee in *Fists of Fury*. With three quick moves, I rushed in and chopped Mark's arm, legs, and back. Mark avoided a punch to the stomach with a rapid sidestep, but not my kick to the butt.

"Ooooaaaahhhh!" I flicked my nose with my thumb like Bruce, hopping from one foot to the other.

"That's it," Mark sneered, lunging at me. This time, he caught my waist, lifting me up onto his shoulders.

"NO . . . NO . . . stop!" I squealed. "You can't use your size in this fight. That's not fair!"

Mark put me down, and as soon as my feet touched ground,

I escaped, kicked him in the butt again, and ran up the path. Mark picked up my bag and chased me all the way up the mountain.

"I won!" I pumped my arms in victory.

The sun was beginning to set in front of us. Mark walked over to the cliff's edge. "What a view," he said, beckoning me over.

As I made my way toward him, a familiar pang of hurt began to gnaw at my stomach. I stopped. In my head, I saw Mark fall off the cliff. I turned away and walked down the hill.

"Hey," he called after me. "Let's stay for the sunset."

"You know I don't like to walk in the dark," I said. "With my ankles, I'm bound to flip over a rock and break my neck."

"You can hold on to me."

"Then we'll both get hurt. Let's just go."

I started down the hill by myself. Mark hesitated and then followed.

BY THE TIME WE ARRIVED AT CASSIE'S, a small crowd of trendy people in their mid-twenties and thirties had already gathered. Music pulsed loudly. I spotted Cassie and waved. Cassie, the first of our friends to leave Vermont, was now a teacher in D.C. But once that 3 p.m. school bell rang, Cassie shed her teacher skin and transformed back into her old self— blond, sassy, and fun.

"How's the building business?" Cassie asked, hugging Mark.

"Booming," he replied. "What's up, Lu?"

"Nothing," I told her. "Just tired."

Cassie squinted her eyes in suspicion, but did not push.

For the rest of the night, I sat in the corner and sipped my drinks. As the alcohol worked its magic, I watched people

without recognition. It seemed they'd all turned into cock-
roaches with skin so thick they could not feel the cuts the
Rwandans suffered. As I watched, my face darkened with anger and sadness.

It was late into the night before Mark and I made it back to
my studio. I stumbled, a bit drunk, into the room on Mark's
arm. When he let go, I fell backward onto the bed.

"Loung, I was thinking," he said, lying down next to me.
"Maybe you need to talk to somebody."

"I don't need to talk to anybody," I told him.

But Mark was undeterred. "Sweetie, you have done a ton
of healing through the years on your own in a lot of different
ways and experiences. You've done an amazing job—everyone
can see that. In fact, I think in many ways you are probably
better adjusted than many people I know." He paused. "But at
the same time, it's okay that you get upset over the reports of
the atrocities in Rwanda."

I tried to turn my back to him, but he stopped me and held
on to my shoulder.

"I wish you would talk to me," he said, taking my hand.
"But you don't feel you can."

"I do—"

"Let me finish." He stopped me. "What you and your family went through in Cambodia was horrifying and traumatic. I
imagine all the news about Rwanda is dredging up memories.
I think maybe it's too hard to handle sometimes. It's . . . I think
it's hurting you."

"It should. It should hurt everyone. People should be
screaming. But obviously, they're not."

"I love how much you care about the world, but that in-
tensity must be exhausting," he said, caressing my arm. "And
when you're tired, you can be grumpy and a pain. And I don't

want you to become an alcoholic." He tried to make light of his words by laughing.

"Thanks for the support." I snorted. "I feel much better now."

"You make me want to do more with my life," he said, his eyes serious now. "When you're happy, you're overjoyed. But when you're down, you are in deep sadness. Not many people in our world feel things so strongly."

I pulled my hand away. "Are you saying I'm manic?" I asked, my face turning red.

"No, I don't know. You are very high and low. Maybe it's your past, maybe it's your nature. But I don't think many people out there understand what you've gone through—"

"One point seven million." I told him, sitting up abruptly.

"One point seven million what?"

I turned to face him. "One point seven million people out there feel as I do," I said, my voice icy. "I imagine maybe some of them can understand me."

I got up, walked over the sink, and poured myself a glass of water. I was angry at the world, mad at war, and furious at the insanity of it all. I thought about how my grandparents packed up my five-year-old mother and left China to escape the emerging wars there sixty-six years ago. Little did they know that they would land in Cambodia, and that years later, they would all be trapped in Cambodia's own revolution. My grandparents did not know the communist Khmer Rouge leaders were students of Mao Tse-tung, or that when they took power in Cambodia, they would implement the same tactics used in China's failed Great Leap Forward program, which was blamed for thirty-eight million Chinese deaths. And my father, who was born and raised in Cambodia, worked hard all his life to provide for his family, never dreamt he would not be there to see them grow up. Neither my grandparents nor my father knew of the 1948 Genocide Convention and Universal Declaration of Human Rights, passed with a rallying cry of "Never again" after the world learned of the horrors of the Holocaust. And yet, forty-nine years later, "Never again" had become "Again and again" when it came to Cambodia, Bosnia, and Rwanda.

"Loung." Mark sat down with me on the couch. "I know you don't think I get it. But I really would like to understand. I may never, but I would like to try."

I was silent.

"If you open up to me and let me in a little, maybe I can." Mark caressed my arm.

You wouldn't, I thought.

I was insulted that he even thought he could. His family was safe when the Cold War spread across Europe and North America, when the U.S., the Soviet Union, and China went to battle in Vietnam, Laos, and Cambodia. He never went hungry when the superpowers retreated and left those battered countries in the hands of the communists. Thirty years later, what had changed? Were we as a human race destined to repeat this cycle forever?

"Maybe if you talk to me, you would feel a little less lost here . . ."

"I'm not lost." I cut him off. "I'm in America. People don't get lost in America."

"We're all lost, in one way or another. All the time. Some deal with it by eating or drinking their way through life. But you, you don't do those things. You shut down. You go to a place where no one can reach you. You're not even here right now. I don't know where you are, but you're not here. You disappear right in front of my eyes."

"You've never been lost a day in your life, so don't pretend," I said.

Mark stared at me, his face still. His hand dropped from my arm.

"Don't take your anger out on me. I'm not your punching bag."

He got up and left the room. I watched him leave. My anger softened when he disappeared into the bedroom. On the other side of the wall, I heard him unzipping and opening his travel bag, unpacking his clothes. Or was it the opposite? I knew he didn't deserve my anger, and yet sometimes, those were precisely the reasons I wanted to strike him down. I was envious of his light, of how easy he made everyday living seem. It was the thing I appreciated and disliked about him, the thing that made me feel dark, inferior—damaged. I got up and went into the other room. He was right: The Rwanda news had wounded me. A part of me wanted Mark to be my rescuer, to be the rock I could lean on. But another part wanted him to be my sympathizer, to drown with me in my misery so he could understand my sorrow. But Mark couldn't do this; he wasn't the drowning type.

I crawled into bed next to him. "I'm sorry," I whispered.

When I fell in love, I believed in happily ever after. I thought all I had to do was find the courage to jump into a relationship. No one told me there were other chapters after happily ever after. No one ever told me being with someone whose attributes you admire could show you all the ways you were broken, highlighting all the things you did not want to see in yourself.

"I know we Americans can seem insensitive to you sometimes," said Mark, caressing my hair. "But we're not all like that. For some of us, going on with life is the only way not to let the horrors win."

"I know." I rested my head on his chest, and listened to his heart.

14
Birthdays

Capitol Hill, June 1997

Perhaps my favorite quote of all time is by Albert Einstein in which he said, "There are two ways to live: you can live as if nothing is a miracle; you can live as if everything is a miracle." After my escape from the Khmer Rouge, I made efforts to live as if every day was a miracle and to be grateful for everything I had in my life. However, in the wise words of Lucy from *Peanuts*, everyone is allowed a few crabby days once a year. For me, one of these days was always my birthday.

"Happy birthday to you . . ." the girls sang.

I was with Cassie and new friends Angie, a cool D.C. lawyer, and Erin, a perky economist, at the Capitol Coast, a trendy eatery on Capitol Hill. The room was crowded and noisy, filled with young interns, lawyers, and Hill staffers. Many were dressed in fitted suits and carried briefcases. Outside the window, the Capitol Dome glowed in the evening light.

"Where is that handsome man of yours?" Angie asked.

"In Cleveland, working," I told them.

"I can't believe you guys have been together for—what—seven years?" Erin raised her glass to me. "When are you guys going to tie the knot?"

"Don't know," I said, sipping my wine. "Maybe never."

Erin's eyes widened in disbelief. "Really?"

"I think marriage is great for some people, but my relationship is great the way it is," I assured her. "Besides, I don't really see what the point would be. I don't need anything from Mark; I have my own job, my own place, my own friends. My life is full as is."

Erin looked unconvinced. "But what about Mark—"

"Hey," Angie interjected. "The women's movement was all about giving us choices, so Lulu can choose whatever life she wants!"

"Here, here!" We toasted to that, clunking our glasses.

I was happy when the waitress walked toward us with a small piece of cake and a small flickering candle and the girls sang "Happy Birthday" to me.

"Thank you, ladies," I said when they finished.

Cassie scooped up a bit of frosting with her spoon. "Blow out the candle," Cassie urged, licking her spoon. "I want cake!"

"Make a wish first!" Erin nudged me.

All of a sudden the room shrank. *Today may not be my birthday,* I thought to myself.

Few children in Cambodia knew their birthday, and fewer still celebrated it. Our custom was to save birthday celebrations until we had grown up and lived long enough to have reasons to be honored. As children, we marked the passage of the year with the arrival of the lunar New Year, which occurred sometime in April. On this day, we all turned another year older together.

As a part of this tradition, I had no reason to remember my birth date. And the people who knew it—my parents—were gone, along with whatever records the Khmer Rouge soldiers destroyed when they entered my city. Thus, when we'd arrived at the refugee camp in Thailand, Meng had to pick a birthday for me for the U.N. refugee worker to put on our application. He chose April 17, the day the Khmer Rouge stormed into our city of Phnom Penh. With a few strokes of his pen, Meng made sure I would never forget.

"Make a wish!" the girls commanded me once more.

The candle flickered, creating shadows and shapes that were not there. In the dark, the girls faded, and behind them stood the ghosts of Cambodia's past. They lined up like zombies next to one another, their clothes draped loosely over their thin frames, their arms hanging limply at their sides, and their faces drawn and haggard. But their eyes—their dark, penetrating eyes—never stopped staring at me.

I bent over and blew out the candles as the girls applauded. Cassie reached over and tapped my arm. Yes, you might fool strangers some of the time, yourself most of the time, but you could never, ever fool a good girlfriend.

"I'm okay," I said, answering Cassie's silent question.

Every year on April 17, the war, like an old festering wound, broke open once again. As the date approached, I was reminded of Janie's story in Zora Neale Hurston's *Their Eyes Were Watching God*. In one eye-opening moment, Janie describes her grandmother speaking of

. . . the biggest thing God ever made, the horizon—for no matter how far a person can go the horizon is still way beyond you—and pinched it in to such a little bit of a thing that she could tie it about her granddaughter's neck tight enough to choke her.

April 17 was my choker, a date hidden in a golden locket strapped around my neck. By choosing that date as my birthday, my brother had, in much the same way as Janie's grandmother, pinched my horizon. I was not angry with him, for I knew he did not act out of malice. He did not mean to tie me to the war, but to two thousand years of Cambodian history. He wanted me to be connected to the Cambodia that produced the largest religious temples in the world, five-hundred-pound catfish, and freshwater white dolphins. My brother's Cambodia was fascinating, colorful, vibrant, and musical. It was a nation in which the Khmer Rouge's four-year genocidal rule was merely a blip, not the whole of its history. He wanted me to always remember this Cambodia, and all that belonged to it—our family, our home, our culture, and our land.

But that wasn't my Cambodia, not yet. My Cambodia was still dominated by mass graves and war, by our mother's tears and the soldiers who took our father. And every year, this was the Cambodia I remembered on a day when I only wanted to celebrate with friends, eat good food, slice cake, open presents, and drink myself silly. I knew that on this date, when I was blowing out birthday candles, other Khmers around the world were lighting candles in remembrance of all the lives lost. As each birthday came and went, it became increasingly unbearable for me to celebrate a date that so many associated with death. When I was eighteen, I decided to leave April 17 behind and choose a new day to celebrate my birthday. Every year since, I had chosen a different day. I gave myself complete freedom to choose any day I wanted—another friend's birthday, the solstice, the equinox, the day Punxsutawney Phil didn't see his shadow and predicted a short winter. Any day that wasn't April 17.

This year, I had chosen June 21, the first day of summer. And so as I sat with my friends, people strolled happily outside, relishing the still-mild weather before the D.C. humidity descended. June 21 was a good day to celebrate.

"Happy birthday, Lulu!" Erin cheered.

AFTER DINNER, CASSIE AND I RETURNED to her house to get ready for a night out on the town.

"So are you going to go?" Cassie asked, staring at herself in the full-length mirror hanging on her door and patting powder on her face and nose.

I had just confided to her that Mark had suggested I go to therapy. "I don't think so . . ."

"But all the stuff he said about Rwanda dredging up bad memories for you kinda makes sense . . ."

I picked up a bag of gourmet taro chips off the bed and crunched into them. I was oblivious to the crumbs dropping on Cassie's 600-thread-count sheets until I saw her glare. Cassie looked at me, waiting. I brushed the crumbs off her bed and onto the floor. "Sorry," I told her.

"So seriously, what are you going to do?" she asked, putting lotion on her face.

"I don't know . . ."

"Why not give therapy a try?"

I thought back to the first time I tried to talk to someone, in high school, and it made me sick. Literally. After my session with the counselor was over, I had to run to the bathroom and throw up. I never went back.

I shrugged. "I tried it in high school, and it didn't work."

"What happened?"

"Don't know . . . I just couldn't talk. I sat in the school counselor's office for an hour, rambling on about school and homework." I began munching the chips again.

"Maybe you weren't ready to talk about it then," she said, walking over and snatching the bag of chips from me. Then she returned to her mirror to color her cheeks with pink blush.

"I don't know what's going on—you're not the most forthcoming person with your feelings—but you do seem a little moody and lost lately. Maybe talking to someone will help."

"Cassie, my life is good. I'm living my American dream. Good education, good job, good friends. Jeez, I'm practically the poster child of the American dream. I'm just a little afraid that talking about my past will ruin this dream in some way."

"So you'll dream a different dream."

I considered her words for a moment. "But I like this dream," I said. "I don't want the damn war to define me. All I want is to be happy and light like my American friends."

"I'm sorry to tell you," said Cassie, who stopped brushing her face and looked at me. "But not all of us are light and happy. Only *The Brady Bunch* girls were that way, and they're not real."

"I know that . . ."

"That Mark is a smart guy."

I crossed my arms and sunk into Cassie's plushed pillows.

"You know . . ." Cassie said, admiring her finished face in the mirror. "The American dream I like best is the one where you get to control your own destiny."

"Enough deep thoughts," I announced, jumping off the bed. "Let's go paint the town red!"

And we did exactly that until 3 a.m.

•   •   •

WHEN MONDAY CAME ROUND, I FOUND myself standing in front of the White House. I was with a crowd of more than a hundred activists and protestors calling for a ban on land-mines. A group of students, teachers, writers, nurses, doctors, writers, and former soldiers, we were members of the coalition of more than seventy organizations that made up the U.S. Campaign to Ban Landmines.

This is my therapy, I thought to myself.

Activism was my redemption, a tool to keep the darkness at bay. And a dark period was creeping in; I could sense it. Like a virus, it waited at the edge of my consciousness to make itself known. All this darkness needed was a bad cold, a deep breath, or a moment of stillness to connect the horrors of Rwanda, Bosnia, and Iraq with Cambodia. I had to keep moving, keep focusing on something, anything that was not my war. I had to get out of myself and into a different world, a world where there was still hope, belief, dreams of peace, and the possibility that we could effect change. A world where my actions were more needed than my tears. That was my mission, and if I was healthy and lucky, the darkness would recede, at least for a while.

When the bullhorn was passed to me, I took it. Gone was the girl who hid behind trees and bandanas. Let them see me, let them hear me. I raised it to my mouth.

"What do we want?" I yelled.

"Ban landmines!" the crowd replied.

"When do we want it?!"

"Now!"

I screamed over and over into the bullhorn, my voice rising in pitch and volume. And as I marched and shouted in the rally, the war slowly loosened its grips on my soul.

15

A New Path

"What are you wearing tonight? Mark asked, his voice low.

In the four months since my move to D.C., Mark and I had managed to see each other only three times. As an intern at a nonprofit organization, I had neither the money nor vacation days to make many trips to see him, and at his father's real estate firm, summers were the busiest season. Luckily for us, AT&T had just invented their unlimited calling plans, so we could at least talk to each other every night.

"Well . . ." I looked at the brown coffee stains and bits of dried rice on my old pajamas. "A black, sexy silk nightgown . . ." I purred, scraping rice clumps off my shirt.

"Liar." He called me out.

"I'm wearing nothing and watching *Night of the Living Dead*," I teased.

"Turn that off," he told me. "You'll scare yourself and you won't sleep."

I refused. I appreciated a good scary movie, especially if it gave me nightmares of being attacked by zombies in my sleep. But Mark was right, I slept badly that night.

The next morning I woke up groggy but was able to force myself to show up early for a meeting at the International Campaign to Ban Landmines. I was so early, I was the only one there, but I'd planned it that way. I had once read an article in which Secretary of State Madeleine Albright advised young women that in order to get a seat at the table, they had to show up bright and early. I took a seat at the oblong-shaped table and waited. Madam Secretary also advised women to speak up.

I popped a breath mint into my mouth. *I have prepared my brain, but it doesn't hurt if my words come out smelling minty fresh too!*

Soon, the other members of the task force arrived. They were an impressive group of mostly Caucasian men and women who looked and spoke like they had all graduated from Harvard. One by one, they took a seat at the table. The late arrivers had to rearrange their chairs and form a second row.

"Thank you, Madam Secretary," I said under my breath.

As the room filled, I stilled my nervous hands beneath the table and breathed. A man in a wheelchair was the last to roll in, and everyone rushed to clear a space for him at the table. He was in his fifties, with a shock of white hair and a ruggedly handsome face.

"Hehee, thanks!" He had the most incredible laugh I'd ever heard—a mix between a goose cackle and a horse's neigh.

He rolled over next to me, and I made room for him. For the next few seconds, he just sat there and stared at me. "Do I know you?" he asked pointedly.

"I don't think so," I answered.

"No," he stated. "I know you."

"Well . . . I know we've never met."

He continued to stare. "What are you?" His voice was strong and commanding, his brown eyes piercing. He possessed a zany, crazy energy that reminded me of Gene Wilder in *Willy Wonka and the Chocolate Factory*. The kind of crazy that made you take notice.

"Last I checked, a woman," I said, returning his stare.

He chuckled. "Smart aleck. I mean, where are you from?"

"Cambodia."

"Ahh, I thought so," he said, nodding. "I've been to your country. Beautiful country. Beautiful people. Heartbreaking genocide. I'm sorry for our government's involvement in what happened to your country."

"More bombs were dropped by the U.S. in Cambodia between '68 and '73 than were dropped in Japan during all of World War II—then they left and forgot about us."

"So you know your history."

"Just enough to get angry."

"Well, if you want to do something more about it than get angry, give me a call." He handed me his card. It read: "Bobby Muller. President, Vietnam Veterans of America Foundation."

I'd read about him in my research on the landmines campaign. Bobby cofounded the International Campaign to Ban Landmines with a friend in 1991 that garnered worldwide attention on the issue. Rocker Bruce Springsteen, a friend, whose song "Born in the U.S.A." was said to be inspired by Bobby, called him a hero.

"We run centers in seven countries that make prosthetics, orthotics, wheelchairs, and other stuff," Bobby said. "We give them for free to landmine victims and war survivors."

"Just one question," I asked him.

"Shoot."

"Does your group work in Cambodia?"

"As a matter of fact, it's our flagship project."

"Then I'm in."

"SO YOU'RE TURNING DOWN COLUMBIA?"

"Yep."

It was Saturday, and Cassie and I were leaving our favorite dim sum restaurant, the China Garden. With our stomachs bloated from all the peppers and dumplings, we walked across the George Washington Bridge to the Newseum, the 250,000-square-foot museum about the history of news. I stared at the building in awe—seven levels of galleries that covered five centuries of news history with up-to-the-second technology and hands-on exhibits. We entered the brightly lit gallery and walked through the News History Gallery. The gallery images told the timeless story of the news, of many voices struggling to be heard, and of the people and machines that spread their words. We stopped at the time-line exhibit showcasing the Newseum's extensive collection of historic newspapers and magazines. Encased in glass frames along the wall were newspapers dating back to the early history of written news. I stood in front of the headlines for 1975. One was about the Vietnam War crossing into Cambodia.

"What's this group again?" Cassie asked as we continued our tour.

"The Vietnam Veterans of America Foundation, VVAF."

"What does VVAF do?"

I'd memorized a pamphlet Bobby had given me, and I repeated it verbatim back to Cassie: "They're an international humanitarian organization that addresses the causes, conduct, and consequences of war through programs of service and advocacy."

Cassie stopped, stared at me. "What the hell does that mean?"

"They're working to ban landmines. They make prosthetic limbs and wheelchairs to give free to victims of landmines and war."

We arrived at the Journalists Memorial. We stared at the rows of glass panels etched with the names of more than 1,800 photographers, reporters, and broadcasters who died reporting the news in places all around the world.

"Thirty-seven foreign and Cambodian journalists disappeared or were killed covering the war in Cambodia between 1970 and 1975," I told Cassie, reading the information.

We paid our respects with a moment of silence and moved on. "So what will you do at VVAF?" Cassie asked.

"I'll be their new communications assistant."

She frowned. "What does *that* mean?"

"I'll be the lowly staff-person answering phone calls for the communications director," I replied. "I'll be putting out flyers, folding pamphlets, licking stamps."

"Fun," Cassie said.

I stopped, waiting for her to catch up. "Sounds like it, doesn't it?"

"And you'll be poor."

With my right hand resting on my chest, I turned to her. "Poor in possessions but rich in spirit."

"That's crappy poor-people talk."

"This coming from a public school teacher?" I raised my eyebrow at her.

"Touché," Cassie answered. "So when do you start?"

"Next week."

"What does Mark think?"

I walked ahead of her, taking pictures of the museum's garden. "He's very supportive, of course," I told her.

"Mark's great like that," Cassie agreed. "Now that you're staying here, have you thought about asking him to move to D.C.?"

"I couldn't do that," I said. "His family and job are in Cleveland, and he loves it there. Besides, I don't want him to move here for me."

"Why not?"

"If we don't work out, I don't want to be responsible for uprooting his life."

"After six years together, you're still thinking you won't work out?"

I shrugged. It had become a familiar emotional pattern: the joy of seeing Mark, the anxiety of knowing he would have to leave, and the sadness of his departure. Still, I looked forward to our times together. But . . . "You never know what could happen between now and the next time he visits me," I said. "Each time he leaves, half of me still expects never to see him again and the other half worries that something will happen to him to fulfill this prophesy."

"Goodness, Lulu, that must be exhausting."

I sighed. "It is."

THE NEXT WEEK, I TURNED UP at my new workplace wearing a blue suit and black pumps. I was given a small office on the fourth floor with a window that looked out onto the Dupont neighborhood's busy Connecticut Avenue. If I squinted,

I could make out all my favorite restaurants—Bistro du Coin, La Tomate, and Thaiphoon. I walked from the window to my door, on which a paper sign read "Communications Assistant." I sat down in my rolly chair and spun. When I stopped, Bobby was there. He rolled in.

"How are you doing, kiddo?" Bobby asked.

"Good . . . but . . . I would be better if I knew what my first task is."

"Well, that's easy," Bobby chuckled. "Your first task is to learn as much as you can about Cambodia, the Vietnam War, and its politics."

He spoke very rapidly, as if he were an auctioneer.

"Yes, sir." I saluted.

"You can start by visiting our library." Bobby lightly slapped my hand down, grinning. "And watch the twelve-hour PBS miniseries on the Vietnam War."

"Okay . . ."

"And"—Bobby chortled like a schoolboy—"that's an ugly suit."

"What?" I gasped, flabbergasted.

"It has no shape, and the color is blah!" Bobby told me. "It makes you look matronly."

"Well, I think it's professional looking."

"Look, Loung," Bobby started again, a bit more seriously this time. "I'm going to say something, and I hope you don't sue me for it."

"We'll see."

"You're a good-looking woman, and that's nothing to be ashamed of. I'm not saying you should flaunt it; just don't hide under frumpy and lumpy clothes and old nun's hair."

I was silent. For a moment, I mulled over whether or not I should file a report with HR. I'd never had anyone say these things to me before. I had spent the last three years working at a women's shelter where my stable of clothes consisted mostly of overalls and boots. True, I shopped mostly at the Salvation Army and thrift stores. T.J. Maxx was a splurge for me. I frequented these places partly because, in addition to being frugal, I viewed myself as an environmentalist. I liked the idea of recycling clothes—it was one small way I could help to reduce the massive garbage landfills mucking our earth all over the globe. And Mark never seemed to care or mind my old clothes, and I could make myself presentable for our dates. All these years, I'd actually thought people viewed me as artistic, original, maybe even unique. Did they? Or was Bobby right? Had I been hiding?

"I can see I've scared you," Bobby laughed. "Don't mind me. Just want to welcome you to the team."

I was flustered.

"Have a good day." He wheeled out.

We're off to a good start, I thought, slumping in my chair.

After another cup of coffee, I headed to the vast VVAF library, which was a back room with wall-to-wall shelves filled with books, reports, magazines, and VHS videos on everything pertaining to war and conflicts. I perused the books about the Holocaust, Rwanda, Bosnia, and Palestine. Then I picked up the stack of reports on Cambodia and sat down to read.

"To keep you is no benefit, to destroy you is no loss," a Khmer Rouge slogan stated in one of the reports.

I stared at the pictures of Tuol Sleng, the Khmer Rouge prison in Phnom Penh, and shuddered at the proofs of this statement.

When the soldiers stormed into the city on that April day in 1975, Pol Pot's security forces took over Tuol Svay Prey High

School and turned it into Security Prison 21 (S-21). It soon became the largest prison and torture center in the country, and more than fourteen thousand people were brought in for interrogations. Only twelve lived to tell their stories. The others were tortured, starved, and then trucked to the outskirts of the city where they were killed and their bodies were buried in mass graves. More than a million skulls have been accounted for; many indicate death was caused by a blunt instrument striking the back of the head.

For a moment, I wondered if my father and mother could have been brought there.

"Hey." Bobby poked his head into the room. "How ya doing?"

"Good . . ."

"You know you don't have to go through it all on your first day."

"Okay."

As he rolled away, Bobby cackled. "And when you're finished here, we have another library for you to go through." By the end of the day, I came to realize that I was indeed off to a great start. At VVAF, I'd found a place where I was understood. I'd found people who understood why, even though I tried to stay away from wars, I followed them. I immersed myself in the collection of books, videos, and articles from VVAF's vast library.

It took a month, but I eventually watched the PBS 12-hour miniseries about the Vietnam War, *Hearts and Minds*, *Year Zero*, and other documentaries. And when I was done, "the gumbas," as they called themselves, were always there to discuss them with me.

"You're one of the gumbas now, kiddo," Bobby told me late one night.

I grinned. "Thanks, boss," I said, saluting him.

We were all gumbas: a paraplegic superman, a former Special Forces soldier trying to make amends for his past deeds, and a reporter who shot some of the first horror scenes coming out of Cambodia after the war. At VVAF, we had our own Vietnam Vets A-Team. And Bobby was our Colonel Hannibal, our fearless leader, a brilliant tactician and the most charismatic person I'd ever met.

On April 29, 1969, Robert "Bobby" Olivier Muller was a twenty-three-year-old U.S. Marine Corps first lieutenant leading an infantry platoon in Vietnam. He was eight months into his second tour when a bullet sprayed through his chest. As he collapsed to the ground and felt life ebbing out of his body, he remembered thinking, *I'm dying on this shit piece of ground.*

But the medical helicopter arrived and whisked him away. He was so severely injured that someone had written on his medical chart that had he arrived just one minute later, he would have died.

"When I woke up, there were tubes sticking out all over my body," Bobby told me. "But I was ecstatic. I couldn't believe my luck—I was alive!"

Then the doctor told him he was permanently paralyzed.

"Don't worry about it; that's okay," Bobby shot back in his Long Island accent. "I'm alive!"

The doctors patched him up and sent him home in a wheelchair.

"I don't feel sorry for myself," Bobby told me. "I am here and a lot of my buddies aren't."

In 1978, Bobby founded the Vietnam Veterans of America, and two years later he started the VVAF. In 1981, Bobby led the first delegation of American veterans back to Vietnam since the end of the war in an effort to make peace with America's former enemy. The group's reconciliation work assisted the U.S. government in normalizing relations between the two countries. Then he went about setting up medical centers. In 1992, VVAF opened Veterans International–Cambodia with the mission to provide rehabilitation services to people with disabilities and victims of war and a production center to make prostheses, orthoses, and wheelchairs. The next year, Bobby returned to Vietnam to establish a clinic at Bach Mai Hospital, the place of a December 22, 1972, U.S. bombing campaign that killed twenty-eight Vietnamese hospital staff and many innocent civilians.

"Keep hope alive!" Bobby was fond of saying. He was a man who had chosen to write his own life instead of suffering the hand that fate had dealt him. Every year since the day of the shooting, Bobby celebrated two birthdays: his real one, and the day he came back to life after being sprayed with bullets across his chest.

If Bobby was our Hannibal, Ed was Templeton Peck—aka Faceman. Ed had been a gorgeous blue-eyed army captain and military adviser with the Special Forces. On a hot April day in 1969, Ed stepped on a landmine near the border of Cambodia and lost both his legs above his knees and an eye to infection, as well as suffering severed bone, nerve, and muscle damage to his arm. But he kept his gorgeousness, his brain and heart.

Our B. A. Baracus was John, Mr. Fix-it and executor of VVAF's many programs. The rest of the ragtag crew consisted of Mark, our word-meister; Greg, our in-house historian and scholar; David, adventurer-journalist and filmmaker who first broke the story of the Khmer Rouge with his film *Year Zero*; Gail, the group's female yin to their yang energy; and me, the littlest one in the bunch, whom they called the Tank. Together we dealt with depression, rage, and war. Then we drank, smoked cigars, and ate.

When I left Cambodia, I never would have thought that one day I would come to call these men friends, mentors, and allies. I was more than two decades younger than them, but in some ways, they would always be young men caught in a war. Because of this, I was not afraid of them. They respected that I stood my ground and spoke my mind. In between our rants against the war machine, we talked about God, or gods in my case, and the afterlife. We read and passed around the same books: *On Death and Dying*, *When the War Was Over*, and *Trauma and Recovery*. I was thick as thieves with them, so thick that I would sometimes be asked if I was having an affair with one, or all, of them. We shared a camaraderie that few people could understand, unless they'd seen death. But we also bonded over our gratitude for life and being alive, and over our desire to make every one of our bonus minutes count.

A FEW WEEKS AFTER I'D BEEN THERE, Bobby called me into his office.

"Loung, stick around tonight," he said, his voice booming. "We're going to a reception on the Hill to drum up support for the campaign."

That was how Bobby was. He didn't ask, he told you what he wanted. And if you didn't want to do it, he respected you more if you said so.

"It'll be fun and there'll be free food," he promised.

By then, the gumbas already knew of my affection for food. Especially free, succulent seafood like shrimp cocktails.

"Okay," I answered. At the reception, I was pleasantly surprised at how friendly people were to me.

"Do you say things like that to many men?" Bobby asked after listening in on one of my conversations.

"Things like what?"

Bobby looked at me; his eyes narrowed.

"What?" I kicked his chair, jolting him in his seat.

"It explains why you're so popular with the men."

"What are you talking about?"

"The word is schmooze, not smooch!" He laughed his crazy laugh.

"No!!" I gasped.

The gumbas teased me on a daily basis in ways that most people couldn't get away with without a swift kick to the shin. But they took me in under their collective wing. Still, there were times when I thought, *These were the soldiers sent to destroy my land; they were the soldiers I was told to fear as my destroyers, rapists, and killers.* Perhaps they had killed someone who looked like me, was intimate with and left behind girlfriends like me, or called a bomb strike to demolish a village just like mine. That was our past; something many of us were trying to make amends for. I didn't ask them questions, and they didn't probe into my life during the Khmer Rouge.

16

Cow Teats and Five Hundred High School Boys

Washington, D.C., September 1997

At VVAF, as my days flowed into weeks, the books, articles, and essays about wars and war crimes piled up on my desk. When I finished reading one, another was already there waiting. And soon, I was finding myself in the office six days a week.

But on Sundays, I slept in. On Sundays, I stayed all day in my pajamas, let my hair stay wild and my face go unwashed. On Sundays, I drank freshly brewed coffee and read in bed. It was a luxury I looked forward to all week, so I was annoyed when a knock on the door interrupted me.

"Who is it?" I grumbled, swearing under my breath. But my heart skipped when I opened the door and saw Mark, whom I hadn't seen in a few weeks, standing there. "What are you doing here?" I gasped.

Mark smiled. "I drove six hours to be here so I could surprise you. Are you surprised?"

I flew into his arms. Then, quick as slingshots, my fingers sprung forth and pinched his nipples, my favorite form of physical punishment for him.

"Ouch! Stop that!" He bellowed.

"You know I don't like surprises! You know I like to make plans!" I ran after him, my thumbs and fingers snapping like crab-claws at his nipples as he backed away.

Mark grabbed my hands. "Okay, you win . . ." he said, as I continued to try to pinch him. "The only way to lull you is to feed you."

After lunch, Mark and I biked to the Washington Monument. The sky was cerulean blue with cotton-white clouds, and the place was mobbed with tourists.

"What's work been like these few weeks?" he asked when we stopped. "You haven't said much about it."

Images of bomb explosions, shallow graves, and decomposing dead bodies formed in my head. "I don't want to talk about work," I said, my hands gripping the handlebars. "This is going to sound weird, but I don't like talking to you about it."

I paused, contemplating my words. I didn't mind talking about work with friends and colleagues, but with Mark, it was different. "What I mean is," I said, beginning again, "you are my safe place—sunny, happy."

He looked at me quizzically. "I'm not—"

"You are to me," I told him. "And with you, I can also be

that person too, even if it is only for a moment. With you, I can play and have fun and not think about it."

I stared at the looming monument in front of us. All around it, people were picnicking, flying kites, and taking pictures of each other. It looked like such a safe world.

"Do you understand?" I asked Mark, rolling my bike along. Mark took my hand. "Okay," he said. "Let's have fun."

After that, we biked and played, leaving the world of wars and atrocities behind until Mark returned to Cleveland the next morning.

On Monday, I walked to work listening to my favorite album, Emmylou Harris's *Wrecking Ball*, on my CD player. I was humming along with "Orphan Girl" and licking envelopes when Bobby rolled into my office and stationed himself near my chair.

"We need to talk about something," he stated loudly.

The landmine campaign had recently gained the support of such luminaries as Princess Diana, Queen Noor, Senator Patrick Leahy of Vermont, and singers Emmylou Harris, Sheryl Crow, and Paul McCartney. They were all endorsing the challenge by the Canadian Foreign Minister Lloyd Axworthy to world leaders to come to Ottawa on December 7, 1997, and sign a comprehensive treaty to ban landmines. With this mission in place, it was time for us worker bees to get the word out.

"You're ready to hit the road, Kiddo."

"I'm not!" I stopped in mid-licking process.

"You can do it. You know our message, and you know the rules of public speaking." He waited expectantly for me to fill in.

"Know who you're talking to, know what you're talking about, and know when to shut up."

Bobby chortled. "I'm proud of ya."

The next week, I arrived at an all-boys Jesuit high school at 9 a.m. to speak at the morning assembly. My palms sweated profusely. The weekend before, Cassie had taken me shopping and helped me put together my "presentation outfit": a formfitting red shirt, a black jacket, and black pants. I wiped my hands on my thighs and marched toward Father Mike, my contact. He looked to be in his early forties and wore the black robe of the Jesuits.

"Welcome to our school, Ms. Ung." Father Mike extended his hand.

I shook it with three firm pumps. "Thank you."

"Our students are ready and waiting in the auditorium," Father Mike said, leading me into the school. "We have about five hundred boys in attendance. We've given them your bio to read, but most of them have little or no knowledge of Cambodia or landmines."

As he talked, my mind was still focusing on *five hundred boys*. I'd never spoken to an all-boys school before, let alone *five hundred high school boys*! *Eeekkk!!*

"Father Mike," I asked, attempting to make my voice strong and commanding. "What would you like the boys to leave with after my talk?"

"I want them to want to be involved with social causes, to be inspired."

"Okay . . ."

"Well, here we are."

Father Mike and I were now standing in the auditorium. Surrounding us, sitting body to body on the bleachers, were five hundred rowdy, randy, loud young high school boys. As I stood there, they continued to talk to each other, completely ignoring me. My mouth went dry.

Father Mike quieted them down and introduced me. I walked up the steps to the podium. Images of my feet tripping over each other and me falling off and cracking my skull filled my head. But I somehow made my way up. I opened my mouth, and nothing came out.

It has been said that fear of public speaking ranks number one in the list of phobias, above death, even. Public speaking had not been my number-one fear until I stepped in front of five hundred high school boys. At that moment it exploded like a newly active volcano in my stomach. The noxious gas of the sausage, ham, jalapeño, tomato, onion, and feta omelet I'd had for breakfast pushed back up my esophagus. When I opened my mouth, all that came out were foul-smelling burps.

"So . . . before I begin . . . [*burp*] . . ." I began. "I must apologize because English is not my first language . . . [*burp*] . . . And when I have to speak on things that are near and dear to me . . ."

I took a deep breath, attempting to psych myself up. *I am powerful, hear me roar. I am powerful, hear me roar.*

"When I first arrived in America, I only spoke about three words of English," I began. "America was my safe place. I had just lived through a war in Cambodia, so I brought with me many fears. What I did not anticipate was my fear of your Holstein cows."

The students finally quieted down, sat up. They were interested to know where I was going with this. And so was I. I flipped through the catalog of topics in my mind, from Cambodia to America, Vietnam to the Khmer Rouge, child soldiers to landmines. But somehow, inexplicably, I began talking about cows. And once I landed on cows, I couldn't leave the topic.

"In Cambodia, our cows, like our people, are little, brown, and cute. But in Vermont, they have giant cows. When we were on field trips to visit farms, I was afraid the cows would charge at me and mow me down."

Oh, no! I shrieked in my head. I paused, trying desperately to turn my talk back to landmines and traumas. The crowd was quiet, waiting.

"Come on!!!" a boy heckled me.

Loud laughs erupted from the bleachers and traveled like a wave down the row of students.

Time stopped. The room began to blur, my face heated up to match the red of my shirt. "We Cambodians don't drink milk and, therefore, do not have milk cows," I continued. "With huge teats," I blurted out.

Once I said the word, I knew all the boys had heard it. The priest stared at the floor as if praying for it to open up and swallow me.

"Cows teats here are huge! The first time I saw cows being milked in their stalls, I was afraid. Very, very afraid."

The student body erupted into laughter. I turned and saw Father Mike turning the pale color of his collar, his face grimacing with regret and fear. Under my jacket, my armpits were raining monsoon sweat. I knew what I must do next.

"Class," I began again when they quieted down. "I'm sorry if I seem unprofessional thus far. I have to admit I am very nervous because I've never spoken to such a large group before, and never in front of five hundred high school boys. I am grateful you gathered here today to hear me speak about Cambodia and landmines. I hope you will be kind and patient with me as I gather my thoughts and begin anew."

The students looked up. Some nodded their heads as if giving their approval. I added a fourth rule to public speaking: Be real. This meant admitting I was nervous.

The next thirty minutes, my talk went smoothly. When I

was finished, a few boys came up and shook my hand. They told me they had learned a lot. I left the school learning a lot myself. I knew bad nerves would always be my issue because I cared so much about the subject. I wanted to be a strong representative for VVAF, my family, Cambodia, and the landmine victims whose story I was sharing. And if I tripped in the process, so be it. The story was bigger than me.

When I told Bobby about my day, he threw his head back and laughed loudly. Not with me. But at me. After he stopped rolling his chair around in fits, he suggested that I become Ed's protégé and we go out to speak together. We would tag-team as speakers—with me telling the stories of war and Ed sharing the stories of peace.

Two weeks after that, Ed and I headed out to give a talk at a church. Ed drove.

"Ed, please slow down," I pleaded.

"HA!" Ed laughed. "I'll slow down when I'm dead. And I aim to live." Ed, who had lost his legs in Vietnam, had only one good eye, his right. Because of this, when he turned his head back to look at the road, I half expected it to rotate 360 degrees like Linda Blair in *The Exorcist*. I became his left eye when we drove.

Two hours later, we arrived at the church and found ourselves in front of an audience of five people. I turned to the minister.

"Is this everyone?"

"Yes."

"Well, let's get started then."

Ed fixed his blue eye on the crowd. Enchanted, the three women sat up in their seats. The two men scowled.

"The International Campaign to Ban Landmines works to ban landmines because many survivors of war are in danger of not surviving the peace," I began. "For long after wars are declared over by governments and media, landmines continue to kill and maim people, turn children into orphans . . ."

I reached into a brown bag and pulled out a handful of green wooden landmines of all different shapes and forms.

"Lives devastated. Families ruined. Landmines are the second most painful injuries next to burns. When you step on a mine, everything below you—rocks, dirt, toenails, grass, shoes, socks—become second missiles, shooting up into your limbs, melting your flesh, crushing your bones. To survive, most victims have to have their limbs amputated."

I looked at Ed; he nodded for me to go on.

"All by this little weapon system the size of a boy's hockey puck, a girl's compact powder case, a coffee cup. Landmines are weapons of mass destruction in slow motion, taking one limb, one leg, one life at a time at a rate of 18,000 people every year."

Though I felt better about my speaking than I had at the boy's school, I still slumped in the car as Ed drove us back home.

"Why do we do this when no one cares?" I asked, despondent.

For his service in Vietnam, Ed had received the United States Army Silver Star for bravery, the Bronze Star, the Purple Heart, the Vietnamese Cross of Gallantry, the Vietnamese Campaign Medal, the Air Medal, the Good Conduct Medal, and the Combat Infantryman's Badge. Upon his return to the U.S., Ed joined the antiwar movement and cofounded the Vietnam Veterans Against the War. He marched on Washington and tossed his medals on the steps of the Capitol. A few years later, he returned to Vietnam and Cambodia to help build the rehabilitation clinics there.

"Because it's the right thing to do."

"What makes it the right thing to do?"

"Because there's a need."

LIKE A LOST SOUL WHO HAD FINALLY found a purpose, I dove into the landmine cause the way divers sink into the depths of the ocean. As days turned into nights, I began to stay longer and longer in the office. Late one evening, I returned home to find the red light on my answering machine blinking.

"Hi, sweetie." I listened to Mark's message. "I'm so looking forward to your visit this weekend."

I plopped myself on the couch, grunting. In the past few weeks, I had either missed or cut short our once long nightly conversations. It used to be that we would stay on the phone for hours, sharing the details of our days and philosophizing about the state of our world. As I drifted off to sleep, Mark's deep voice, the last one I heard in my day, would echo in my mind, calming me.

But on this day I dreaded it.

I dialed his number and hoped he would not pick up. For in all my busy-ness, I'd forgotten to let him know I couldn't make the trip. I knew he was going to be disappointed, and I did not want to hear the hurt in his voice.

Mark picked up the call on the third ring. "Hey, sweetie," he said cheerfully. "I've been trying to reach you."

"I know," I replied. "I'm sorry. I've been horribly busy and getting home late."

"I've missed you."

A tinge of annoyance crept into my face, and like watercolor, the red bloomed on my cheeks. "I'm sorry, I've been crashing and going to sleep as soon as I get home."

"Can't wait for you to get here," he reiterated.

"About that." I jumped in. "I'm sorry, but I can't come. I've got a really big meeting I can't miss."

Mark was quiet. In his silence, I found myself fuming.

How could he not understand? I ranted silently. It wasn't as if I were canceling on him to sit on my hands or spin around the room aimlessly. I wasn't going out with other men; I wasn't flying off to Cancún to film *Girls Gone Wild*! I was trying to do something important, like change the world! This was something we both said we wanted in college. I had visions of us traveling the world with our backpacks, working in developing countries, teaching people to read, building shelters, and holding orphaned babies. Instead, he returned home to work in his father's real estate company. If anyone should feel betrayed, it should be me!

"Mark?"

"Okay," he finally replied.

"I'm sorry."

"I know. It's okay."

When we hung up the phone, I knew we were not okay. But I was too exhausted to worry about it and soon fell asleep.

THE NEXT DAY I RETURNED TO work and sunk deeper into it. Each time I went under, I stayed longer and longer beneath the piles and debris of research, news accounts, position papers and all sorts of other materials. And when I came up for air, I did so only to eat and sleep.

When I was not on the road with Ed, shouting at rallies, licking envelopes, or mailing out flyers, I went to the Hill with Bobby and his small army of advocates. Together, we knocked on the doors of senators and representatives, trying to get them to support the treaty to ban landmines. Behind closed doors, Bobby took on the senator while I tried to enlighten his or her aides.

"It's not a cause people feel connected to," one aide told me. "It's not a cause that's even reported in the news, because people don't want to deal with it. It doesn't apply to Americans, to the senator's constituents."

"But you're wrong. It does apply to Americans. This is one world, our world. Are we not all connected, not our brother's keeper?"

I pulled out a wooden mine—it was green, shaped like a butterfly—and fit into the palm of my hand.

"This is called a butterfly mine," I told the aide. "For adults who step on landmines, it's a lifetime of pain and scars. For children, it's a lifetime of pain and scars revisited. Depending on how fast they grow, how well the amputations were made, and how old they are, every eight months, a year, a year and a half, they have to return to a clinic and have their limbs cut and recut again until they stop growing. Because even if their stumps heal, their bones will continue to grow and protrude out of their stump."

The aide listened.

"And with millions of these in the ground in a third of the world's countries, and millions we don't know about, how do you know your next step will be a safe one should you choose to leave the United States?"

Fifteen minutes later, the meeting was over.

I returned to my office and began another task.

"Hey, kiddo." Bobby rolled in moments later. "Good job on the Hill."

"Thanks, but I don't think I got anywhere."

"Sure you did."

I shrugged. "If you say so."

"I do," Bobby said, chuckling. "Hey, what are you doing here so late anyway?"

"Changing the world one staple at a time."

"Fun," Bobby said. "But I have an assignment for you, should you choose to accept it."

"What's the mission, Captain?"

"Be our spokesperson for Cambodia."

"What would I be doing as the spokesperson?"

"Raising money and awareness, talking to the press some. You would be traveling all over the country and the world to do this. But most importantly, you'd tell the world about landmines and the Khmer Rouge."

I lit up, though my throat choked up at the honor. Somewhere in the shadows, I felt the hand of my proud father resting on my shoulder.

It was October by the time I made it to Cleveland to visit Mark. As the plane pulled into the gate, the familiar flutters of butterfly wings returned to my stomach. It had been six weeks since we'd last seen each other.

When Mark picked me up at the Cleveland Hopkins International Airport, his greeting was restrained. He did not say much as he drove me to his family's house for dinner.

"Ready?" Mark asked, squeezing my hand.

"As ready as I ever will be," I replied.

We entered the house to find his family already seated. On the long table sat a brown honey-glazed round ham, baskets of golden bread, red and green salad. Around the table, endless conversations and merriment passed between the twenty-one family members and their significant others. Mark's family bantered back and forth, their words flying like Ping-Pong balls at a dizzying speed over my head. Amidst them all, I felt as heavy as a brick. I thought about Meng and Eang and my nieces in Vermont. I missed them, and felt guilty because I hadn't been home in many months. They were my only family in America and I had no time to see them. I wished I could be in two places at once.

After dinner, Mark and I visited the Rock and Roll Hall of Fame and Museum in Cleveland. Mark stood against the railing facing Lake Erie. Behind him, the Rock Hall, designed by world-famous I. M. Pei, sparkled and shone like a futuristic pyramid. I walked up to Mark and braced against the cold, the lake-effect wind whipping my hair into my face. It was October in Cleveland, and already it felt as if winter had moved in. The days were growing shorter and shorter, and the temperature colder. I looked up, saw no stars in the dark sky. And yet, hidden somewhere behind the mass of heavy, low-hanging clouds, a full moon was shining. Its silver rays were trapped in the atmosphere, but some escaped to be captured by the cottony clouds, giving them a glowing grayish-white tint. In this light, the lake shimmered far into the distance.

I knew I had to come clean about something, and this seemed like my moment. "Hi, there," I touched his arm.

"Hi."

"I'm sorry but . . . I have to cancel our plans for my next visit," I told him.

"I half expected it," he said, his voice was muted, emotionless.

I took his hand, but he pulled away from me. "I'm sorry."

"I know. Lately, even when we're together, I feel like you have one foot already out the door."

"Work is just crazy right now."

"It always takes precedence."

"I wish it could be different, but it can't be," I said. "A big part of me wants to stay here and forget about the world out there. I'm only a small voice in this campaign to rid the world of landmines, so maybe my voice will never be heard and my work doesn't mean anything."

I looked at him, imploring him for understanding, but Mark did not look at me. He started walking.

"Maybe my work doesn't mean anything," I repeated. "But what if it does? What if I can actually make a difference? Even a small difference to just one person?"

I walked beside him, my feet sinking heavier with each step.

"The people who need our helping hands don't get a holiday break from their situation."

Mark turned toward me, finally. "But what about our life together?" he asked.

"I guess it'll have to wait."

"We've been together seven years now, and I've yet to meet your family. They still don't even know that I exist." His words froze in the air. "My friends think I have a phantom girlfriend; my parents are wondering why they can't meet your family."

"You know my family is traditional, and they don't believe in dating."

"What does that even mean?" Mark asked. "Do they expect you to be arranged like them? Do you mean they will expect you to pick someone of your race?"

"No . . . I don't know, I don't think so . . ."

I began to move away from him. I'd just gotten off a plane after a long week at work, had just made pleasantries with his family all evening, and had yet to recover from our big dinner. *Why?* I muttered silently. *Why couldn't he just let well enough be?*

"Sometimes," Mark said softly, "I wonder how long we'll go on like this. Being together but living in separate places, leading separate lives. There are times I wonder if you even want to be with me, if you would rather be alone."

I couldn't tell him he was wrong. For me, being alone was often the path of least resistance. A pull that was always there, always present. And sometimes, I dreamt it had the idyllic landscape of a Norman Rockwell painting, a place where things were completely serene. I knew this place didn't exist, just as the happily-ever-after in fairy tales never came true in real life. Still, I longed for it.

Mark turned and walked ahead of me, his hands in his pockets. In the gray-white cloud-light, I noticed the trail of his footsteps on the grass, and saw how my small steps were dwarfed beside his size-twelve feet. I hurried to catch up to him, walking in his footsteps. I saw then how it must feel for him to be with a woman who is so different from his culture and community. It was the same for me; neither of us had a map of how to proceed. But we kept going nevertheless. I took his hand.

Mark remained silent for many more minutes as we continued walking, but then slowly, he slipped his arm over my shoulders and pulled me in. "Just don't make me wait too long," he said.

"Or what?" I asked, trying to be playful. But my tone was full of challenge.

We stood our ground, staring at each other.

"Well," Mark said quietly. "I guess being with you means accepting that your family comes first, then Cambodia and work, and then me." He paused. "I'm never going to be your first priority."

"I'm sorry." I touched his arm, but again, I couldn't tell him he was wrong. "Why do you put up with me?" I asked.

He stopped walking and turned to face me for a moment that felt like an eternity. Then he walked up to me and cupped his hands around my face.

"Because," he breathed, "you're you. Because I know your heart is good and loyal. And I'd rather be with you than be without you."

He pulled me into his arms and kissed the top of my head. "And I *am* proud of you," he whispered.

THE NEXT MONTH, I WORKED WITH the zeal of someone who'd been given a chance to redeem years of inaction. I stopped for a moment on October 9, 1997, when the Nobel Prize Committee announced the Peace Prize was awarded to the International Campaign to Ban Landmines and its coordinator, Jody Williams, "for their work for the banning and clearing of anti-personnel mines."

After the champagne bottles had been popped and the liquid emptied, Bobby rolled into my office. "You're a part of that voice, kiddo," he said.

I dove deeper into work.

Soon the days and nights blurred into one another, and fall became winter. Still, I worked with the exhilaration of knowing that together, our team was achieving something, that together we were effecting change.

On December 3, 1997, our work was again rewarded when 122 world leaders gathered in Ottawa and signed the Convention on the Prohibition of the Use, Stockpiling, Production, and Transfer of Anti-Personnel Mines and on Their Destruction. The signatory states committed to "put an end to the suffering and casualties caused by antipersonnel landmines" by addressing current landmine problems and preventing future ones.

As one world leader after another approached the podium to put down their names, I stood in the back of the convention hall with my colleagues. We were Cambodians, Americans,

Africans, Europeans, and Latin Americans. The ICBL family had grown to many thousands of people with campaigns in more than seventy countries, and included doctors, lawyers, students, teachers, activists, Christians, Buddhists, Muslims, and Hindus. I clasped hands with John, Meta, and Kosal, the other campaigners from Australia, Norway, and Cambodia. Our faces were bright and cheerful, our eyes shining with tears and hope. We were a diverse group of people who came together to work toward the same goal, to help leave the world a safer place for all.

I gazed beyond the hall and into Cambodia then. In my vision, I saw my sister Chou walking through the fields in our ancestral village, and the land cleared of mines. I saw her daughters safely running after her, chasing butterflies.

17
Never Silent

Spring arrived with the gentleness of a new mother. Day by day, as the daylight hours stretched longer and longer, young green buds pushed out of dormant branches, and gray skies cleared into blue. Life began anew. For many Washingtonians, the light meant more time to play outside, more hours to lounge at their favorite happy-hour establishments, more time to enjoy life. But for me, the longer daylight came without my notice. I was lying in the dark late one night when I realized I did not even know the date. A glance at the calendar told me it was already April 14. My breath caught in my throat for a moment.

When I was young, I thought trauma was something I had to get over. In self-help books, it was described as a brick wall I had to punch my way through, and my healed self would emerge bright and in Technicolor on the other side, like Dorothy in the Land of Oz. Then off I'd go, singing, skipping, and making friends on the yellow brick road until the flying monkeys and the crazy witch attacked. I did battle, but my witch refused to stay dead.

The clock flashed 12:13 a.m. It was now April 15.

I stared at the shadows cast by the desk lamp. On the ceiling, dark shapes hovered and waited. When I blinked, they changed, like inkblots taking form on a psychiatrist's chart. Before my eyes, they spread and expanded. I turned my head, and willed the shadows not to come to life. But the shadows breathed.

"You have a heart arrhythmia," a doctor had told me when I was in college, after she listened to my chest.

"What does that mean?" I asked.

"You have an irregular heartbeat. A normal heart rate is between fifty and a hundred beats per minute. Your heart can beat faster than a hundred twenty beats per minute."

Under my breastplate, my heart flipped.

"A heart palpitation . . ."

Sometimes my heart fluttered, flip-flopped as if it were tripping over itself. I always thought it was just running away. "What caused it?"

"It's genetic," the doctor continued. "You've probably had it for a while but it's gone undiagnosed. Sometimes, something can happen to trigger it."

"Like what?"

"No one really knows. Coronary artery disease, injury from a heart attack, changes in your heart muscles—these are some factors. Other factors include too much caffeine, too little sleep, and stress. But you're healthy and young so I don't think these are the causes. I don't think you have anything to worry about," she soothed. "Your heart is strong. We'll keep an eye on it, do some tests."

Nothing to worry about, only a murmur, a whisper of my heart.

What are you trying to tell me?

My heart did a cartwheel.

The clock read 1 a.m.

I got up to check that the windows and door were locked. I made sure the path from the bedroom to the door was not obstructed in any way, so that if needed, I could make a quick escape. In the dark, my apartment creaked and squeaked. The refrigerator hummed in a language I did not understand. The floorboards seemed to breathe in with each gust of wind, whistling out as if exhaling. In the shadows, the Wicked Witch of the West rose from my floor. Her pointy black hat emerged like an inverted cyclone, her midnight cape spun into a dark storm.

"Well, my pretty!" she cackled from her black lips.

I quickly ran into my bedroom and pulled the door closed.

WHEN I WOKE UP, IT WAS YET another blue-sky spring day. Languidly, I followed my normal work-life routine—shower, eat, get dressed. Twenty minutes later, I arrived at my office without incident. After pouring myself a cup of coffee, I settled into my chair and turned on the radio.

"This just in," a reporter announced. "According to Thai military sources, Pol Pot, the former leader of Cambodia's Khmer Rouge, is dead at age seventy-three."

My hands trembled on my desk.

"Pol Pot, whose real name was Saloth Sar, led the Khmer Rouge from 1975 to 1979 in a regime that was blamed for the deaths of an estimated two million Cambodians . . ."

The words flew out of the radio like gnats and stung my skin. I got up, pushed my door shut, and locked it. Leaning against it, I slid down to the floor. In the hallway, a colleague's booming voice seeped into my office as he passed by. I stared, eyes unblinking, out my window. On the yellow-green trees, a flock of birds sang sweetly as if serenading one another. Above them, the sun traveled slowly over the city as the earth rotated.

Please. A moment of silence for the two million victims . . . I thought. I closed my eyes.

I left work early that day and walked around in a haze. In the street, diners sat in outdoor patios, enjoying their meals and drinks. Their conversations drifted around me as I walked by, but I did not catch their meaning. One foot in front of the other, I made it home as if in a drunken stupor. I dropped my bag at the door and sank into the couch. I did not remember my finger pressing the power button on my remote control, but moments later the television was on.

"Pol Pot left behind his twelve-year-old daughter," the news anchor narrated. "To many, he was described as charismatic, grandfatherly."

I sat catatonic on my couch, staring at the screen. A grainy black-and-white photo of Pol Pot appeared; he was smiling.

I turned from the TV, eyes on my ceiling. My lids began to droop, my body slid to lie on the couch. I believe I fell asleep then, but it was not a rejuvenating rest. And through my thrashing, other reporters came on, their voices a jumble of mixed sounds and accents, reporting:

Pol Pot's name came to symbolize the deaths of two million people under his rule in Cambodia for four horrific years: 1975 to 1979.

Senior Thai military sources told CNN they received a report of Pol Pot's death around midnight—on April 15, 1998.

He was described as a kindly, gentlemanly grandfather.

He called himself the father of our nation, said that everything he did, he did for love.

He was seventy-three years old at his death, and left behind his second wife and a young daughter.

Somewhere in between my state of sleep and waking, my anger slowly pulsed. It was the same anger that sparked to life when I read the interview Pol Pot gave to Nate Thayer, an American journalist for the weekly *Far Eastern Economic Review* in October 1997. In this interview, Pol Pot told the reporter that his conscience was clear, and what he did in the revolution was done for the love of the nation and its people. How dare this man call his actions love, when Cambodia was torn to pieces by him! Two million people perished because him. I had a wish then: to reach my hands into the television screen, wrap them around Pol Pot's neck, and squeeze.

When I opened my eyes again, the room was covered in shadows. I was disoriented, my throat was dry, and my stomach growled from hunger. But there were also other feelings—feelings that entwined tightly around one another like the wires in a power cord.

In the dark, I reached for my journal and pen.

As a girl, I would write because there was no one I could talk to. I wrote because although I could not speak of it; the war was never silent to me. My words were written in the scrawl of a young girl's hand. But when my emotions were fully charged, I printed them in black, blocky letters of different sizes and shapes. The fonts and letters varied as I wrote about deaths, murders, and suicides. My body tensed and pulsed until the stories were captured on paper. Only then was I able to let go.

Now I picked up my pen and journal again.

"How dare Pol Pot die without his due punishment!" I scrawled on the page. "I hope he suffered!"

Black ink lifted off the pages and swirled around me, forming our home in Phnom Penh, the roads of our village, and the thatched-roof huts our family sat huddled under during the Khmer Rouge regime. When I wrote of hunger, my stomach bloated and concaved. I stopped eating, allowed my rice pot to go cold so I could properly write of that pain. But when Monday came, I returned to my American working life and rejoined the effort to ban landmines.

In this way, though my workweek looked normal, each night held a life of its own, and Friday nights bled into weekends. Slowly, I pulled away from my friends and family, and one by one, they began to call.

"Haven't heard from you in a week," Mark said on the answering machine. "You okay? I miss you. Call me back."

I ignored his message and wrote. My hands gripped the pen as if possessed, furious fingers pushed ink onto the pages. The writing was a purging of toxic rage from my body. I vomited out the words.

"Lulu," Angie left a message. "We're going to see the flower blossoms on the Potomac Saturday. Come with us."

Outside my apartment, couples strolled by arm in arm. A young woman leaned in and whispered into her boyfriend's ear. I pulled my shades down.

Maria was the last to call. "Kgo, what are you doing this weekend? Mommy, Daddy, Tori, and I are going to Montreal to visit Grandma and to have dim sum. Just wanted to let you know in case you call and can't reach us."

I unplugged the phone and turned off the answering machine.

April turned into May, bringing more sun and blooming flowers. But as sunlight poured in through windows, I stayed inside my studio apartment and wrote. And when I was not writing, I was reading. My studio was piled with books and black-and-white portraits, all of Cambodian men and women who had lost their lives at Tuol Sleng, the Khmer Rouge prison in Phnom Penh. Of the fourteen thousand people brought there, images of as many as six thousand remained, and many years later, copies found their ways to the VVAF office. And now they were in my home.

I tacked a photo of one of the prisoners, a woman, on my wall. Her name was Chan Kim Srung. Her hair was disheveled, cut short just above the nape of her neck. She wore the regime's black pajama shirt. She stared into the camera, wearing an expression of disorientation, confusion, and fear. In her arms, she held her sleeping newborn.

What do you want to say? I asked her.

But Chan Kim Srung remained silent.

One by one, I tacked more photos on my wall. Their dead eyes stared at me in fear and silence, all of them in black pajama shirts. I looked at them as I wrote; their stories lifted off the pages and came to life. I turned to the photos strewn across the floor. And slowly, the floor seemed to cave into itself, creating a big sinkhole in the middle of the room. I continued my

writing with my head bent over my books until a knock interrupted me. I looked at the clock and saw that it was late.

"Lulu . . ." Cassie called out.

I peeked through the keyhole. Cassie stood there, her hair as
perfectly blond as ever, her hands over her hips in impatience.

"I know you're in there; I can hear you," Cassie said. "And
I'm not going anywhere until you open the door."

I grabbed a rubber band and gathered my hair into a bun,
hoping to hide the fact that I hadn't showered all weekend.
"Hold on a minute."

"Why haven't you been answering my calls?" she asked.

I opened the door and held on to it. "Sorry, I've been busy,"
I answered, staring at her through the slit.

"Not a good excuse." Cassie pushed her way in.

She walked around the room, eyeing the dirty plates in the
sink, the coffee-stained mugs, the crumpled clothes strewn
on the floor. She walked up to the photos on the walls and
scrunched up her face into a grimace.

"Why do you have all these funeral pictures on your wall?"

"I'm doing a bit of writing," I said defensively.

"You didn't say anything about turning your home into a
mass grave."

I paused, searching for the right word. "I was trying to . . ."

"Well, look . . . you need to get out. Come on, let's go.
Fresh air will do you good."

"I can't," I protested. "I'm a mess."

"You look like road kill," Cassie agreed. "Just put on a hat
and a clean sweater."

"I can't—" I resisted.

Cassie opened the door and waited, a determined stance in
her posture. "I'm not taking no for an answer."

Reluctantly, I followed her out.

An hour later, Cassie helped me back into my apartment. She helped me to my bed. "How can you get drunk on two glasses of wine?" she asked.

"I haven't eaten much this weekend," I mumbled.

"Why are you starving yourself?"

"So I can write about it."

"You have to stop all this craziness."

The room spun. When I turned my gaze to the door, the knob jiggled and began to dance. Before my eyes, it multiplied into many round doorknobs that then turned into little munchkins floating before my eyes.

We represent . . . the lollipop guild, the lollipop guild . . . They sang and danced the song from *The Wizard of Oz.* "The doorknobs are dancing."

"No, they're not," Cassie told me.

"Yeah . . . they are," I responded, singing, "We represent the lollipop guild . . ."

"You stay in bed while I make some coffee."

I nudged at Cassie's arm. "Remember at the health club, when that woman said we looked like sisters?"

"She said we looked like twins." Cassie pulled my shoes off.

"Wonder twins power, activate! Form a—a—something-something."

"Form a sleeping, Lu."

"You know, I had three sisters once. People always thought my sister Chou and I were twins. Chou was the good girl. I was the black sheep. She would never have left me the way I left her."

"You never left her, Lu. She is always in your heart."

"That's not true. I left her. I told her she was soft."

"Shhh, don't think about it now. Go to sleep." Cassie soothed me.

But it was too late. The toxic thought made its home in my brain. "My head hurts," I moaned.

"You'll be better in the morning." Cassie pulled the curtains shut.

But I was not better the next morning. My head throbbed.

"Owww," I grunted as I searched my way from my bed to the couch, where an old cup of coffee sat. I slurped it down cold with my eyes still closed. It tasted stale and sour, but I was in too much pain to spit it out.

On my desk, Chan Kim Srung was still there. She was looking at me from the neat pile Cassie had left her on top of. In her arms, her baby was still asleep. The room was rocking as if it were moving through the high seas. I lay down and fell back to sleep on the couch.

Minutes, or perhaps hours, slipped away. I woke up to the phone ringing near my ear. In my grogginess, I heard Mark's voice on the answering machine. I did not reach for it. That moment, I knew it wasn't hard to leave the world. If you shut down your heart, eventually, your body will follow.

18

Lifelines

No one ever told me that if you go deepwater diving, you should make sure to have a lifeline.

In the weeks during which I wrote of my mother's and four-year-old sister Geak's deaths, I dove without a line. In this memory whirlpool, I felt myself falling into a deep abyss. All around me were dark caves and walls, and the water was cold and unforgiving. I looked at the walls and saw that I was surrounded by portraits of the victims of Tuol Sleng. In the middle of them were the faces of my mother and sister. I gasped, trying to swim away.

I jolted up in bed, my hair matted from sweat. My studio

was all of a sudden too small, and its walls too close. The phone had been ringing long before I reached for it. "Hello?" I rasped into it.

"Loung, I'm worried sick," Mark told me. "What's going on? You haven't been returning my calls."

"I'm just crazy busy."

"I'm coming over this weekend to see you."

My hand tightened around the phone. "No. It's not a good time. I'm really busy with work."

"Come to Cleveland. You can work here, too."

"I'm sorry but I can't. Not now."

Mark exhaled deeply before continuing. "If not now, when?"

"Mark . . ." I whispered. "I can't see you anymore."

"Don't say that . . ."

"This isn't the time for us, Mark; I'm sorry," I said and hung up on him.

Before I knew what I was doing, I was on my hands and knees cleaning the floor with a sponge. Crying and cleaning. Cleaning and crying. Two things I seldom did, and never together. But I was unable to stop, even with the thirty-three things on my to-do list pressing on my brain.

Beside me, Death stood. Cloaked in his dark hood, he placed his skeletal hand on my shoulder. And just like that, I fell to the floor. *Dead. They're all dead* . . . I moaned. The thought washed over me. And then the small, frightened voice of a wounded child cried out, *I want to die . . . I want to die . . .* I muted the voice until the only sound was the humming of the room.

When I thought I couldn't take any more of the darkness, I split. Or rather, my spirit split. I didn't know how this happened, but there I was, a carbon image of myself, sitting on the couch, watching the girl on the floor cleaning and crying. I knew that I also was her, the girl on the floor. But I also felt separated from her, as if she were a mirage and not quite real. Only she looked solid, and I was not. I realized then that she could not see my presence.

In this phantom state, the conscious me was joined by another presence. I sensed that I had heard her before, met her before, but never in this form. She was ageless. She had seen the sea grow red, the sky turn black, and magical creatures die. She had seen flowers bloom, communities built, and babies born. Perhaps she was more a sage.

They're all dead . . . they're all dead . . . the girl on the floor moaned.

The sage and I watched her. I did not feel her pain, only the sage's compassion. As the girl on the floor sobbed, her body curled even more into itself, so that she looked like a child. The earth me, the old me, wanted to run to this girl and tried to rescue her, fix her. And if I couldn't, I would have told her to stop crying, to buck up, to get moving. Keep moving. Nothing's ever been solved by the shedding of buckets of tears.

Just be here, the sage whispered, her voice soft and deep.

Infused with the sage spirit, I let those thoughts go. I simply sat on the couch and observed. I sent the girl on the floor my compassion. She continued to cry.

And then, it was as if we all just went to sleep.

LOUNG . . . A SOFT VOICE CALLED out to me in my sleep.

Soft lips touched my forehead. The faint scent of Drakkar washed over me. A bright light flashed across my eyes. I was inside a tropical dome on the last vacation Mark and I took together. In the middle of the dome, a rain forest grew. Cascading waterfalls sprayed mist on my arms and face. Layers of soft, glistening green moss covered the wall, and leafy ferns hung like jungle chandeliers from the ceiling. Across the dome, thick brown, blue, and green vines twisted and draped like party streamers. Jungle leaves detached from the trees and floated downward. Yellow, purple, and red sheaths fluttered and turned into butterfly wings. They hovered and fanned my arms and shoulders, blowing gentle breeze onto my skin. Covered by hundreds of winged friends, I wanted to fly.

You'll be okay. Mark was with me in the dome, aiming his bulky Nikon in my direction. I felt myself transforming from a mortal girl into a wood nymph. Behind the lens, an eye winked, a smile crinkled the corner of his lips. Lithe, light, ethereal, I opened my arms.

Loung. Mark covered my hand with his, and the weight pulled me out of my dream. Inside the dome, my winged friends let go and dispersed into the air. I opened my eyes to see Mark kneeling next to me.

"Hi," he whispered.

I was in my bed. I did not remember how I made it there.

"I drove straight here after I got off the phone with you," Mark told me.

I looked at him, still confused by his presence in my room. The memories were forming again. Yes, I had broken up with Mark. "We're broken up?" I asked, my voice small.

"Not unless you still want to be." Mark took both my hands.

"No."

"I'm never going to leave you."

A choking sound erupted, filling the room. I placed a hand on my chest, surprised that the cry came from me. I closed my eyes, wishing I could go to sleep until the pain subsided.

"Why does it still hurt so much?" I asked him. "How long do I have to live like this?"

As Mark held my hand, I knew I needed him.

I don't need anyone. Even as I whispered this to myself, I knew I was lying.

There was a time when I needed my parents to shelter me, but I soon learned I could survive on my own. As a child, I needed Meng and Eang to provide me with food and shelter, the U.S. government for health care, and our sponsors to teach us about life in America. Then, slowly, one by one, I untied these binds.

"Why do you want to be with me when I'm such a mess?" I asked him. "When I am so broken . . ."

"You're not broken. Not to me. Never to me."

Mark's kindness and compassion were what drew me to him, but his love and his loyalty to his friends and family were why I loved him. At an age when others left home, Mark stayed near his family in the community where he was born and helped to rebuild it. All the years I'd spent running and moving, Mark had taken the best of his family, community, and faith into his life. Because of this, his world was stable and full, and he was secure in it. This, I believed, gave him the ability to love without fear. It is this love that I needed from him.

"Mark . . . I ne—" But I could not say the word. "Thank you."

I knew then that without love, the war and soldiers would win their battles for my heart and mind. I did not want those bastards to win.

Outside, the sun was shining. Warm, bright light flooded my room through my window, landing on all the scattered papers and pictures on the floor. Mark's eyes took them in and filled with worry.

"I'm okay," I said, sitting up.

Mark took my hands. "Writing about your past has brought

up a tremendous amount of emotion and deep feelings," he said. "Sometimes I think you've got to let it all out and cry, and kick and scream if you want to, and I'll be there to hold your hair and rub your back and hug you tight. But that's more about me wanting to be a rescuer and be a part of making you feel better than perhaps what you need to do for you. Other times, I wonder if it isn't better for you to leave it all behind, to not speak about it. I've gone back and forth about how to be there for you."

"Be with me," I told him. "I want to finish this book. I can do this . . . but I don't want you to push me about it, okay? I will share it with you when I can, when I am ready."

Mark's voice was full of concern when he asked, "Are you sure you want to continue this?"

Then I remembered the sage. I did not know what she was, or how she came to be. But I knew that she had helped me mute the sadness enough to allow me to sit with my pain—and then to wake up. I closed my eyes, ran a mental and physical check of her presence. Under the covers, I crossed my fingers and hoped this hadn't been a case of spiritual possession, or something worse. I wiggled my toes; they moved as commanded. I sighed with relief. I was once again the owner of my body and mind.

I looked at Mark and slowly nodded yes in answer to his question.

As Mark hugged me to his chest, I knew I would be all right.

THE NEXT WEEK, I TOOK MARK and went to see Cassie's therapist.

"What would you like to discuss?" the therapist asked.

I pressed my hands on my thighs to keep my knees from

knocking. The room was warm in temperature and in its decor. On the wall framed pictures of bubbling brooks and streams hung neatly next to one another, as well as a whole row of diplomas, recommendations, and licenses. I turned my head here and there, took in the two sitting chairs, coffee tables, wooden desk, boxes of tissues scattered about the room, the shelves filled with books. There was no couch in sight.

I crossed and uncrossed my legs in my nervousness. "What do people usually talk about?" I asked.

"Well, their lives," she replied, removing her glasses and placing them gently on the table. "Sometimes, they share stories of their dates, spouses, or partners. Sometimes, they talk about their parents, friends, and work. We can talk about whatever you want."

I hesitated, and considered the question.

"Let's start with your parents," the therapist suggested.

"Well . . . they're dead . . ."

She looked at me kindly. "I'm sorry," she said. "May I ask how?"

The first time I tried to tell my story aloud, I was a sophomore in high school. I could not get the words out and vomited in the school's bathroom. The second time I tried to share my story, it was to a trusted friend in college. For an hour, she'd interviewed me for her college paper. She promised to change my name to give me anonymity. With her, I shared my story as if it were a dark secret; a secret that I, alone, must bear.

I turned back to my therapist now and saw that she was waiting.

But perhaps it had not been my secret to keep? I wondered. Perhaps this story did not belong to me and needed to be let out because it belonged to the world? And maybe, the more people knew, the lighter my load would be? Through the years, I had shared my story with others, and had even been interviewed and written about in newspapers. However, more often than not, I told the story as if it did not belong to me, did not happen to me, but to that little girl whose name just happened to match mine and whose memory was lodged in my brain and body. The girl who believed she was loved and wanted, even though she came into the world as the sixth of seven siblings, and whose childhood was cut short by the war.

The day I arrived in America, I tried to leave the girl behind and to pretend that she wasn't a part of me. As I sat up straighter in my chair, I began to accept the fact that she was me.

"It was a long time ago . . ." I began.

19

Exorcist of the Writing Kind

D.C. and Cambodia, June 1998–February 1999

For nine months, I revisited my childhood in Cambodia. With Mark and my friends at my side, I poured my love, anger, and hate into the computer. And in the midst of this writing, I traveled back and forth to Cambodia as a spokesperson for VVAF, leading delegations of supporters and public figures to tour our centers. And with each consecutive trip, I learned more and more of the people's lives and Cambodia's history.

Like many Khmers, I was grateful when the Vietnamese came into Cambodia and defeated the Khmer Rouge. Vietnam, once an ancient enemy of Cambodia, allied with the Khmer Rouge from the 1950s to 1975, first against French colonization, then against their common aggressor, the U.S. When Phnom Penh and Saigon fell to the communists in April and May of 1975, the U.S. left and troubles erupted between the two neighboring countries. Soon, decades-old wounds reopened, and the Khmer Rouge began raiding Vietnamese villages and executing Vietnamese captives. For more than three years, the two countries negotiated truces to halt the incursions, but they never lasted and the Khmer Rouge soldiers kept on raiding.

In 1978, Vietnam decided to support the Cambodian resistance forces fighting to topple the Khmer Rouge regime. The People's Army of Vietnam heavily armed its 150,000 troops—along with a group of 20,000 exiled Cambodian soldiers of the Kampuchean United Front for National Salvation—and invaded Cambodia on Christmas Day, 1978. It took them just two weeks to defeat the Khmer Rouge and, on January 7, 1979, take control of Phnom Penh. To honor this, Cambodia declared January 7 a national holiday. The next day, a new Cambodia was formed, the People's Republic of Kampuchea. Many Cambodians cheered.

But the Vietnamese refused to leave. Their occupation of Cambodia turned from weeks into months, and months into years. The cheers turned into jeers. For numerous Cambodians, history was repeating itself with the Vietnamese taking over their land again. They applauded again when Vietnam, suffering from a lack of support and resources at home, withdrew its troops from Cambodia in 1989. Their departure allowed Cambodia to open the door for democracy. Three years later, under the auspices of the United Nations Transitional Authority in Cambodia (UNTAC), Cambodia held its very first national election, thus becoming an emerging democratic nation.

On each of my trips, after my work was complete, I took time to visit my family's village. Through the years, I had traveled many roads in Cambodia that were once dirt, then gravel, and then black tarmac. Season after season, I watched thin, malnourished schoolchildren grow taller and sturdier walking on their way to school. With each trip, I fell more and more in love with the country, but it was not a perfect love. There were cracks and frustrations, heartbreak and anger. I was not blind to the injustices and social ills that still existed there, but I chose to see the positive parts and decided to focus my energy on what I could do to help and, hopefully, effect change. I also spent time with my sister Chou, brother Khouy, my grandmother Amah, and the rest of my uncles, aunties, and cousins.

When we weren't slurping down large bowls of Phnom Penh *katiew* noodle soup and eating mangos picked ripe off the trees, I'd interview family members for my book. And with graciousness and generosity, they bravely remembered, cried, and laughed as they told their stories. When it was time for me to leave Cambodia, my family gathered to bring me to the airport.

One late evening when I was just back from a trip to Cambodia, Bobby found me in my office listening to Cambodian music and translating my family's words from Khmer into English.

Bobby chuckled and wheeled closer to me. "You've been traveling and staying late the last few months. I salute your dedication and I like all the overtime you're doing, but you know I can't pay you for it, right?"

"Understood," I agreed.

"What are you working so hard on?"

I touched the stack of papers and photos on my desk absent-mindedly. "A book, I hope."

"About?"

I looked at him, smiling. "Me."

"Ah, always an interesting topic," he said, grinning widely. "Is Cambodia in it?"

"Of course."

"Hmm. Who is it for?"

"My family. No one. Everyone. Anyone who will listen."

Bobby nodded and spun his chair back and forth in a semi-circle. I knew his mind was racing. "Then it must be published," he said loudly.

I shrugged.

"It's a story that should be told, a message that needs to be heard." Bobby fixed me with his famous stare, his eyes locked onto mine. "You could also use this book as a vehicle to raise awareness about Cambodia, to talk about the larger issues of war and peace. If people read it, it could provide you with opportunities to meet supporters, donors, and policy makers who could help Cambodia."

My eyes brightened at the prospect.

"Anyway, just think about it," Bobby said, rolling himself out. "I have a friend who's an agent. When you're ready, I'll pass it along to him."

"Thank you," I said gratefully.

WHEN I FINISHED THE MANUSCRIPT, I ALLOWED myself a moment of celebration with a glass of wine. But in the quiet of my own home, Guilt was beside me. Like a mud mask, it covered my face and sucked out much of my exuberance.

I had begun the manuscript in anger, an act of revenge against Pol Pot and his soldiers, and ended up writing not a historical book on Cambodia but a memoir of my life and family. Instead of telling my story as a traditional past-tense narrative, as many memoirists did at the time, I wrote from a child's point of view, in the first person, present tense. I wanted readers to be there, to feel my raw anger, my searing pain as a child. I knew others in Cambodia had lived different stories, and yet, despite our differences, I hoped my memoir touched upon some universal truths about love, family, and country. Still, Guilt was there to rain on my parade.

"You can't celebrate this," Guilt accused me. "It isn't right. This story is real and horrible. The respectful thing to do is to be somber and sad."

I couldn't argue.

I sent a copy to Mark. It was time for him to know.

He called a few days later. "It was a hard read."

"It should be," I said defensively. "War isn't easy. It's hell on earth, and people have to realize this. Maybe then people would stop and pay attention."

"It was hard for me because you were so hurt," he said soothingly. "It's hard because this happened to someone I love."

I remained silent.

"I'm sorry you had to go through this," Mark continued. "It must have been horrible reliving it."

I held the phone close to my ear. "I've been reliving it all this time," I told him.

"I have so many questions—"

"Stop," I interrupted him. "I know you have questions, but I'm not ready to discuss the book with you just yet . . . I'm glad you read it . . . but to speak of it still feels too real. Especially with you. And I . . . just . . . can't go there yet."

I waited, hoping he would understand. Writing—no matter how difficult it was at times—was still a process I controlled. But the spoken word, like powerful incantations, would take me back too much. And I wasn't ready to go there, not with Mark. I wanted him to still be my safe place.

"You don't have to explain," Mark told me. "Just know that when you're ready to tell me your story, I'm here."

"Thank you. Now that I've captured it on the page, perhaps I can let some of it go."

I believed this. There was something about writing that allowed me to capture the things that I feared and, in making them tangible, took away some of their power. With my pen, I cut the war and its soldiers down to size. And I named them. There was power in the naming of things: soldiers, guns, Khmer Rouge, war, genocide. They were things men made and brought into the world. They had no divine power, and no control over my mind. The soldiers were no longer evil monsters but men, and as men, they could not cross continents, or space, to hurt me. With each stroke of my pen, in a kind of exorcism, I killed what I need to destroy and kept the people I wished had lived alive. In this way, writing was cathartic and healing.

Still, I was full of anxiety when I gave the pages to Meng to read. I told him very little about what I'd written—only that it was the story of our family during the Khmer Rouge. I let him know he had full veto power to cut, edit, or tell me not to seek publication. I would follow whatever he said. Then I had the same manuscript translated into Khmer and sent it to the family in Cambodia, but I knew their permission all rested on Meng's word. After that, I waited.

Would he like it? I worried. Would he think I'd written authentically of our family, of our struggles? What if he hated it? I woke up in the middle of the night with anxiety. I was prepared to bury my work if Meng asked, but I wasn't ready for the hurt that would come if he told me I'd been careless with our family's memory.

It took two long, agonizing weeks for Meng to call me. "It's good," Meng said. "Go ahead, get it published."

I exhaled a long sigh and thanked him. He handed the phone to my niece Maria, who was now nineteen. There wasn't more for him and me to say. Meng and I had long ago evolved into a brother-sister team who did not discuss the war.

"Hi, Kgo," Maria whispered.

In the background, I could hear her feet pitter-pattering up the stairs and into her room.

"Hi, sweetie pie."

"So," Maria said quietly. "Daddy read it."

"Did he say anything?"

"Not to me, but he told Mom it was good and said he was proud."

There was no need for him to say any more.

WITH MY FAMILY'S BLESSINGS, I SENT MY book to George, Bobby's friend and now my agent. George soon sent my book proposal to twenty-five publishers. But it took just one yes, from HarperCollins Publishers, to change the path of my life yet again.

The day I received my book contract from HarperCollins, I went for a walk in Rock Creek Cemetery. The sky was blue, covered by large brushstrokes of expanding white clouds. When I looked up, a cool fall wind blew through partly bald trees to caress my face. As I walked, I hummed a Cambodian lullaby, pausing long enough to read a few names and dates on the headstones, and to follow Mark with my eyes. He turned to me and waved, then disappeared.

It had been a long journey for me to go from being a child who was afraid of cemeteries to a woman who found them a place to rest. The horizon shimmered and sparkled like a white sequined curtain as snow fell silently on the ground. Darting between trees and headstones, my child-self appeared—shy, strong, and fierce. I beckoned her forth. We were friends now. There were times in our past and possibly times in our future when we would not be. But for the moment, I was happy; happy that we shared the same heart.

Suddenly, strong arms wrapped around me and pulled me in. I leaned my head against Mark's chest.

"Hey, you," he whispered.

"Hi."

"Did you tell them about me this time?" he asked.

"Tell who?" I asked coyly.

Mark rested his chin on my head and squeezed me tighter. "Your family."

"Tell them what?"

"That I exist. It's been nine years for us, how much longer are you planning on keeping me a secret?"

I silenced him with a kiss.

20

Millennium

The day I received the galley copy of my book, I stared at it in disbelief. On the red cover was a photo of me the day I'd arrived at the refugee camp in Thailand. I was small and thin, with dirty matted hair, holding a chalkboard with my name written on it. It felt strange that this should be the face to go out into the world to tell the story of my family and me. But I was also proud of it. For despite the dark shadows under my eyes, there was a determination and rebelliousness to my expression. Immediately, I called Mark.

"I'm so happy for you." His voice was soft and tender. "What's the title going to be?"

"Umm," I paused.

I'd turned the book in to the publisher with a list of working titles, including "Tears of a Daughter," "Eight Grains of Rice," and "The Red Khmers." I was not good with titles. But together, the publisher and I came up with *First They Killed My Father: A Daughter of Cambodia Remembers*. I told Mark.

"Wow."

"Wow, indeed," I agreed. "The publication date is April 2000."

Then the significance of the date hit me. April 2000 was the twenty-fifth anniversary of the Khmer Rouge takeover of Cambodia.

After Mark and I said goodbye, I hugged the galley pages close to my chest. I hoped I'd done some justice in my portrayal of my family's spirit, courage, and love. I hoped people would read my work and understand a small bit more about Cambodia and its people. And I hoped to be a published author, if the world didn't end in four months.

Please . . . don't let the world end! I sent a prayer out to the universe.

Around me, headlines in magazines and newspapers announced the possible end of our world. A possibly cataclysmic event loomed on the horizon. The culprit was a little bug known as Y2K. Created by the powers that be—also known as computer programmers—Y2K was used to free up memory space in our machines by shortening the four-digit year to two digits. As the millennium date approached, rumors, truths, and half-truths spread across the globe that when the clock struck midnight on January 1, 2000, computers all over the world would misinterpret the year "00" as 1900 and crash. And with them, the whole of Western civilization.

For months, the press wrote about this cataclysmic event.

They told stories of computers producing erroneous data and mistakenly releasing criminals from maximum-security jails. They spread horror stories of power grids going black, drinking water turning brown, traffic lights staying red, and nuclear plants accidentally getting the green light to fire off nuclear warheads. The stories had reached such fervor that many of us were very afraid.

In response, President Clinton formed the President's Council on Year 2000 Conversion, Congress passed the Year 2000 Information and Readiness Disclosure Act, and businesses joined together to create the Y2K Information Sharing and Analysis Centers (ISACs). Every other day, one or two or more of the groups held press briefings to assure the public that the best and the brightest in the country were at work to fix the problem.

Even with all that, the questions remained: Would they come up with the solutions in time? Would they be able to get to all the computers in the world in time? It was a race against the clock. Millions and billions of clocks.

All across the world, people made plans to travel home to be with their family, to cook sumptuous last meals, to dance the night away with friends and family, to make slow and sensual love into the New Year.

Mark and I went to Disney World.

I RAN AHEAD OF MARK TOWARD THE square at the Magic Kingdom. When we arrived, it was only five minutes to midnight, the dawn of a millennium.

"Come on," I urged Mark, pulling him along by his hand. "We don't want to miss the fireworks."

By the time we arrived, the square was already crowded with cartoon characters and furry creatures gathered in cliques. In one area stood the clowns: Goofy, Donald Duck, Mickey and Minnie Mouse. In another, the princesses—Ariel, Pocahontas, Sleeping Beauty, Snow White, and Cinderella—smiling prettily, dancing, and twirling. Circling around them, the princes in their tights.

"Hey, if the world is going to end, which heaven do you think we'll end up in? Buddhist or Christian? I wonder if we can cross back and forth between the two?"

"The world is not going to end." Mark tightened his grip on my hand.

"Thank you," I whispered. "This has been the best day."

"Ten . . . nine . . . eight . . . seven . . ." The crowd counted down to the end of year.

Mark folded his arms around my waist. In my bag, a turkey leg, a loaf of bread, and a jar of peanut butter nestled next to my map of the Animal Kingdom and my Swiss Army knife. If the world did end, I would not go hungry. The stars winked at me.

"Three . . . two . . . one . . . " the crowd chanted.

The sky exploded in electrifying fireworks. The blossoms crackled and turned from white to red, blue, white, and gold. The crowd cheered, their hands clapping in appreciation. I joined in.

"I love you," Mark whispered in my ear. "Marry me."

I breathed in, elated, and closed my eyes. Somewhere in the imaginary world inside my head, a handsome blond knight chose a dark warrioress over all others. I inhaled luxuriously and traveled still deeper inward. It was there that I found my two selves waiting.

My dark half—dressed in a black skin-tight leather suit and high platform heels—turned to me and hissed, "You don't want to get married. What's getting married going to prove?"

"But he proposed!" My light half—in a flowing white dress—appeared. "You should be so grateful he isn't afraid to show his feelings."

I opened my eyes and I was back in the real world. Mark's arms constricted me in his embrace. I began to squirm, but Mark held me tighter.

"We've been together for ten years now." He turned me around to look at him. "I think it's time we make this commitment to each other. Marry me, baby."

I shook my head. "I'm sorry," I said.

Mark released me slowly and walked away.

When our vacation ended the next day, so did our relationship. The decision was mutual. There were no arguments, tears, or screams. We spent the morning packing in silence, Mark in his corner of the room and me in mine. We said goodbye at the airport and boarded two planes that took us to our separate geographic locations.

A week later, I fled to Cambodia, to my sanctuary, my family, my grandmother.

Part Three:
Double Happiness

'mothers'

21

Srok Khmer

"Loung," Amah called, pulling me out of my revelry.

I opened my eyes to see that I was back in my family village in Kompong Speu, back at grandmother's house. In the yard, a mango tree stood tall, its branches heavy with green fruits. In another four months, the sour fruits would turn deep yellow and ripen into sweet, delectable meats. My lips curved upward. *They're his favorite fruit.*

I had been in the village more than two weeks and hadn't spoken to Mark. In that time, I had adapted to living without running water, sit-down toilets, or electricity. In a way, I'd enjoyed this. The world was quieter and slower without these

modern amenities. But without electricity, there were no telephones, and there was no way for Mark to reach me.

Amah must have heard my sigh, because she lifted her hand
to my face and caressed my cheek. "Granddaughter, did you
know that your Ma married your Pa even when we refused to
give them our blessings?" she asked. "I'm glad she did, because
now we have you and your brothers and sisters."

A gust of wind rustled the leaves on Amah's thatched walls.
I drew closer to my grandmother's side. Next to us, a flock
of ducks waddled out of her pond. It was a large family, the
mother duck leading a row of ducklings. They quacked and
nudged at each other, picking at grass and trash. And wherever
the mother duck went, the ducklings followed.

I pressed Amah's hand to my face. For a moment, her eyes
clouded over. Her back, bent almost ninety degrees by scolio-
sis, curved even more into the chair.

"You are so much like your mother," Amah said, smiling.
"You talk to her."

"I will," I told her.

"Ay Chourng . . ." Amah called my mother's name, reaching for my hand.

It was happening more and more now—the periods when
Amah was caught between the past and the present—and in
her reality, I was my mother. Perhaps our language was lost
in translation, because Amah and I were conversing in my
broken Chinese and her limited Khmer. Or perhaps Amah's
mind was confused again, and she did not remember that her
daughter died twenty-two years ago.

"Daughter, you've been gone a long time." Amah took both
my hands in hers.

I did not know why Amah confused me with our mother
and not my sister Chou. Perhaps it was because Chou lived in

the village and visited with her every day, so Amah knew her voice. Perhaps it was because my voice resonated with a tone and vibration similar to my mother, Amah's first-born daughter. For whatever reasons, Amah sometimes heard my mother's voice when I spoke, a voice I had long forgotten the sound of. I was happy that in her confusion, my mother was alive with her somewhere.

"I've missed you, daughter," she told my mother.

"I miss you, too," I replied.

I placed Amah's hand in my palm, where it curled into the size of a child's fist. Amah looked at me, her eyes growing sad. "Daughter, I've had a hard life," she said.

Amah slowly told her story to me.

As a young woman, Amah made her home with Akoang, my grandfather, in Swatow, China, a rural coastal village located on the South China Sea. On the day my mother came into the world in 1937, Amah summoned the spirit of her grandmother, great-grandmother, great-grandaunts, and all the women who'd come before her, asking them to help guide her firstborn daughter safely into the world. They came all at once. Their spirits hovered over Amah; invisible hands cradled her body in a protective embrace, giving her their strength and courage. Once my mother was born, the women touched her forehead one by one, gave their blessings, and disappeared.

As Amah nursed my mother inside her small, one-room concrete home, a few miles from her green rice fields, more Japanese soldiers arrived on the island of Formosa, a short boat ride from the motherland. Generals and commanders gathered at Formosa, occupied since 1895 by Japan and used as a base, to draw up plans for war. While they plotted, Amah brought my mother's hands to her lips, kissed her wrinkled newborn skin, and vowed to keep her safe. The Second Sino-Japanese war began in 1937, and at its height in 1942, Amah kept her promise to my mother and left China with her husband, my five-year-old mother, and my eight-year-old uncle Heang.

The day their boat chugged out to the South China Sea, Amah scanned the port. It was empty. She closed her eyes and saw the faces of her father, mother, brothers, sisters, cousins, and friends. They all pleaded for her not to go when she told them she was leaving China. They warned that she and her family would drown at sea, their bodies lost. And without proper burials, their spirits would be trapped at the bottom of the sea. There they would stay, in their murky graves with the fish and bottom-crawlers, damned for all of eternity in the dark.

"If you leave, you cut out my heart." The words of great-grandmother, Amah's mother, landed on her face like a slap to her cheek.

Amah dropped to her knees, her head touching the floor. "Mother, please forgive me."

Once at sea, Amah held my five-year-old mother close to her chest. Above her, seagulls followed and squawked. Four days later, they arrived in Cambodia. Amah had never been out of her province, spoke no Khmer, and was thin with hunger when she stepped off the boat.

"What is this place?" she asked the captain.

"The weeping Chinese village," he told her.

Amah wept.

When she finally stopped, she saw a Chinese woman approaching her. The woman was one of approximately three hundred thousand Chinese merchants, fishermen, farmers, and contract laborers who now lived in Cambodia. She took Amah and her family to her village and showed them the best fields in which to catch crabs, the types of poisonous snakes to avoid, and which crops grew best in the new land. With these kind people's help, Amah and her family settled into Cambodia, or Srok Khmer, as the natives called the country.

As time passed, Amah gave birth to two more sons and another daughter. She did not imagine that thirty-three years later, the war she'd risked so much to escape would follow her to Cambodia, along with the soldiers and their communist fervor.

I SAT SILENTLY AS MY GRANDMOTHER RECOUNTED her time during the Khmer Rouge. She described how she'd been living with my uncle and his family when the soldiers came into her village in the northern town of Battambang. They were able to live and work for a while, until the day the soldiers came for my uncle. Amah had bowed her head to the ground, feeling grit and rocks digging into her skin as she begged them not to take her son. The soldiers did not relent. Amah's eyes were full of dirt and tears as she watched her son disappear into the fields, leaving her to survive with his young wife and daughter.

When she was finished telling her story, Amah slumped back into her chair, exhausted. I motioned a cousin over, and together we lifted Amah and transferred her to bed. I propped a pillow under her knees and smoothed out her silk pants.

"Daughter," she said to my mother, "I was lucky to come back to the village after the war."

"You are safe now." I soothed her as she closed her eyes, her breath becoming even and rhythmic.

While Amah slept, the sun lowered in the sky and hid behind a patch of thick white clouds. I brushed back stray white hairs resting on her forehead, and tugged her sleeves down to cover more of her arms. As I held her hand, I felt grateful for the years of conversations that had allowed me to piece together her story.

Suddenly Amah stirred in her sleep, her feet kicking under the blanket. "I didn't want to leave them . . ." she murmured in her sleep.

"You did what you had to do . . ." I whispered, thinking of her earlier words to me. "You trusted your heart."

I wished I could do the same.

THE LAST TIME I LISTENED TO my heart, I was eight years old. It was also the day my mother sent me away.

As I marched off, my body ached to run back into her arms and bury my face in her chest. I knew she was there, standing at the door of the thatched-roof home my father had built, her body leaning against the frame. My four-year-old sister Geak was beside her. I did not look back. But I knew that if I had, my mother would be gone.

I had seen my mother disappear before, when I was seven, the night the soldiers came for my father. The sky was ablaze with the colors of the gods. Gold, burnt sienna, and red swathed across the horizon in majestic strokes. I turned my eyes from it. But my mother stood outside our hut watching the earth eat up the sun, her eyes focused on the path down which the soldiers had led my father. At first her body stood erect and strong in the waning light, but by the fading of the sun's last glow, she was bent and hollowed. When she walked back into the hut, her steps were so heavy her bare feet dragged in the dirt. She appeared a hundred years old. And weak.

That night, I began to worry about her. I feared she would be slow at work the next morning, that she would fall and hurt herself, that the soldiers would beat her for crying. I had witnessed them doing this to others. Only the strong survive, I told myself.

When my mother turned toward me, I stared at her eyes. Before the war came into our lives, my mother's eyes were beautiful, the shape of perfectly formed almonds. After the soldiers came, I had seen her cry many times. But on the night my father was taken, tears gathered in the rims of her lids and spilled over like spring brooks. They slid down her cheeks and left two trails on her mud-stained face. And when she tucked us children in to sleep that night, the wetness transferred from her cheeks to ours, and the sadness soaked us in our sleep until we woke up shivering in its dampness.

Three days after my father's disappearance, we heard rumors that he had been executed. A part of my mother died that day. Gone was the laughing mother on whose lap I bounced on our way to the market, gone was the beautiful woman who filled up a room with her energy and spirit. All that was left was a shell of the woman. Three months later, she woke us children up from our dreams to tell us that we had to leave her.

"Tell them your ma is dead already," she instructed.

When I refused, my mother pushed me out the door and swatted my bottom. "Go! I don't want you!" she yelled.

I glared at her, gritting down on my teeth. *She does not love me*, I told myself. The words pricked my skin like sharp, poisonous thorns. All my young life, I had believed that my mother loved me. Even when I fought loudly with my sisters and made my mother scream, I believed this. My father had loved me and fought to keep our family together, to keep me with him. And now that he was gone, my mother told me to leave. In that moment, the trust in my heart cracked. Slowly, I dug my toes into the dirt and marched away.

22

Khsae Family Line

Kompong Speu, January 2000

Out of the shimmering haze, my sister Chou materialized, walking toward Amah's house, where I was waiting.

Chou and I were separated when Meng took me to America. This explained my spinsterhood at age thirty, and Chou's life as a wife and mother of five at thirty-two. Married at eighteen and living in the village where my mother spent her childhood, surrounded by aunts, uncles, cousins, and grandmothers, Chou had found her peace. She was connected to our mother through her daughters, to our father through her sons. In a world where people believed in spirits, gods, and goddesses, Chou had never been separated from our parents, who were always a prayer away when there was a thought to share or a hug for the children. Chou's kindness and compassion had never allowed her to blame Ma for sending us away. Or to question how Ma let herself get caught by the soldiers.

As Chou walked, the soles of her feet connected fully with the red dirt road before pushing her off on another step. She was only two years older than me, but in appearance and characteristics, we were opposites. Chou was dark-skinned, I was light. Her hair, when let down, curled into shiny ringlets, whereas mine frizzed and waved, never able to decide which it wanted to be. Chou's heart was secure in her family and herself, at peace with the land and its history. And I—caught between two worlds, three cultures, and four languages—could not hold one thought in my head without my many schizophrenic selves trying to speak at the same time. As I watched Chou approach, I wondered what it would be like to fully connect to the earth before I took off again.

As Chou came nearer, I saw that she was followed by her four-year-old daughter Ching-ching.

"Mama!" Ching-ching called. "Wait for me." Ching-ching hurried toward her mom, her feet slapping against her too-big flip-flops. "Auntie!" Ching-ching called out when she saw me, waving.

"Loung, why is your face so dark?" Chou asked as mother and child arrived together. "How will you find a husband if your face is so angry?"

I smiled.

"That's better!" Chou exclaimed. "Now we are ready to go find your husband."

Like all my family, Chou did not know of Mark's existence. "Is Amah still sleeping?" Chou asked.

"Yes."

"How much Hennessy did you give her?"

"Not a drop!"

Chou shook head. "Watch her, she's wily," she said affectionately. "Sometimes she tricks us to give her two shots a day instead of one!"

"She says it warms her blood and—" I began to argue but Chou stopped me with a glare.

"It makes her drunk and chatty."

As we argued, I spied Ching-ching climbing onto the bed to give Amah a kiss on her cheek. "I like her stories," I said, winking at Ching-ching.

"Amah is a great talker, but all her stories are mixed up!"

"Not if you listen to them closely enough."

Chou walked over to Amah's sleeping body and pulled the blanket up to her chin. "Amah, Loung's shift is over," Chou whispered, caressing Amah's arm. "We're going home now. But do not worry; Cousin Hong is here to stay with you. You sleep well. All your family loves you. We will be back. Please do not leave before we get back."

As we left, Chou turned and looked at Amah once more.

"We never leave her alone," Chou let me know. "Someone is with her around the clock. This way, when her time comes to pass, she will not be alone. Whoever is with her will alert everyone and we will all be there for her."

Unlike Ma, Geak, Pa, and Keav, I thought. Each time the soldiers came for them, they'd been taken away alone. How afraid they must have been, surrounded by soldiers instead of family as they passed from this world to the next. In our family, this would never happen again.

"Let's go home," Chou pulled my hand.

As we walked the five minutes from Amah's house to Chou's, she hooked her arm in mine, as she used to do when we were children. We passed by an abandoned concrete one-story house overtaken by shrubs and weeds at the edge of the village. I stared at the black mildewed walls and roofs covered in thick nets of spider webs.

"That house is haunted," Chou whispered, pulling me near. My eyes flew open. "Really?"

Chou cackled loudly and hit my arm. "Are you still afraid of ghosts?" she asked.

When we were children, Chou often protected me from my own worst enemy—my mind. Knowing that I had an active imagination, our brother Kim would jump out of closets, from behind trees, and into the dark hallways of our home to scare me. And when he had me cornered, he filled my mind with stories of ghosts and ghouls.

"Ghosts are spiteful and jealous," Kim whispered one night. "Given a chance, they will steal human children."

Seeing me cowering with fright, Chou leaned over and wrapped her arms around my shoulders. "Why?" I asked.

"Because they have a spirit but not a body," Kim said. "We humans have spirits and bodies. The ghosts want that. When they have a spirit and a body, they can live human lives and do things we do."

"Why would they steal children?"

"Because it's easy to do. They can possess a kid's body with no one knowing. Adults don't pay attention to kids, so they don't know if ghosts have occupied their kids unless they really look. No one knows how many children have been taken. How many of them—us—are walking around as living ghosts."

As Kim talked, I pushed both my clenched fists against my mouth to keep from squealing.

"The way to tell a possessed child from a normal child is

by his unblinking, bulging eyes," he continued. "Ghosts are greedy and want to see everything. When they take a child, the child cannot blink and their nostrils flare and—"

Kim paused, his eyes rounded like a night owl, unblinking. "And—" He leaned closer to me, his bugged-out eyes glaring, his nostrils flaring like a bull's.

"Don't listen to him," Chou told me with all the infinite wisdom of an eight-year-old. "If you ever see a ghost, grab it by the neck and don't let go until it gives you the winning lottery numbers."

Back at her village, Chou and I walked quickly past the haunted house. "Her husband stepped on a landmine and died many years ago," Chou said quietly. "They brought his body to the village and she screamed so loud everyone here heard it."

I grabbed Chou's arm as we hurried along. We sauntered by the outdoor market, the noodle shop, and the stall selling gallon bottles of petrol. Everywhere Chou went, I imagined a bamboo thread that stretched and wrapped around her and the village. In Cambodia, this familial bond is known as *khsae*, literally a cord or rope that connects people to their families. We walked by the village school, an old, one-floor rectangular yellow and white concrete building. It was Saturday evening, and all was quiet at the school ground. Chou's children were somewhere playing with their cousins and friends. She wasn't worried about them, because in the village, every adult was a parent, and every parent helped raise the children. Thus, when Chou's nine-year-old daughter, Chang, had been hit by a motorcycle, it was the goldsmith who stopped traffic, the noodle seller who scooped her off the road, the watchmaker who chased after the culprit, and the seamstress who ran to fetch Chou and the family. They all arrived at once to tend to

Chang, and like a fallen bird, she was cared for, healing so that only a small scar was left on her ankle from the accident.

"Chou, did you always know you wanted to get married and have children?" I asked, missing Mark suddenly.

"What a silly question! Everyone wants to marry and have children."

"Not everyone . . ." I said. "Not me."

"You talk crazy."

"I'm not crazy. I'm choosing not to marry and not to have children."

Chou stared at me, her eyes narrowing. This notion was too strange for her to comprehend.

"Why are you so firm against this?" she asked.

I had many answers, but none would please her. "Did you love Pheng when you married him?" I asked.

"How could I?" she shrugged. "I'd known him since we were kids. I thought of him like a brother."

"But why didn't you say no?"

Chou looked confused. It was as if the thought had never occurred to her. In the village, no "good" girls rejected their elders' choice of a husband for them. It was unthinkable. A rejection said to the community that you did not trust your elders' choice, or trust that they knew what was best for you. A "good" girl would never disrespect and shame her elders in such a way.

"But Chou, you were seventeen."

Aunt Keang, the wise wife of my Uncle Leang, the second brother of our mother, arranged Chou's marriage. Chou was lucky that she learned to love her husband the moment their first child was born.

"Aunt Keang is very wise," Chou said, her voice sounding confident. "She looked upon me as her own daughter. She only wanted what was best for me. She picked the best husband she could for a girl of my stature with no money or family."

Being poor and orphaned with no land or titles to offer a husband meant the pickings were slim for Chou. But times were different now. So different that a girl like me could choose her own destiny. If only she dared.

I looked at Chou, grateful that Aunt Keang had chosen well. Many other Khmer women I knew were not so fortunate. "Chou, weren't you afraid?"

"Of what?"

Of the neighbor's horse running over your husband; of your child being killed by mosquito bites; of your husband being murdered by bandits; of war erupting once again in Cambodia; of the risk that your heart would shatter into so many pieces you would never be able to put them together again. My breath caught in my throat from fear. But I did not tell Chou those things. Instead, I asked, "Of something bad happening to your family?"

"Of course I worry. But you cannot protect them from bad things. You do your best. The rest is up to the gods. You can't worry your life away. If you do, you'll make yourself crazy."

I matched my steps to Chou, wishing I had her faith.

"Like the grandmother down the road," Chou continued, pointing to a hut in the woods. "She worries so much she sees the ghosts of people who haven't even died yet!" Chou grabbed my arm and guffawed. "When you start seeing ghosts of living people, then you should be afraid."

23

Fear of Landing

I knew it was more than a dream. As I lay in my bed in the village, my eyes moved back and forth rapidly under my eyelids, bringing forth a memory of my first vacation getaway with Mark.

We were riding in a roofless Jeep in Venezuela, dodging waves as they crashed under us. Mark was driving; I was smiling at him, my hair whipping across my face. He reached over and pulled me in for a kiss but I pushed him back.

"Keep your hands on the steering wheel!" I hollered.

He reached for me again, grabbing my arm to pull me in. I resisted, laughing. And then, our Jeep went suddenly dead.

"What happened?" I asked.

"I think the waves flooded the engine," he said.

We were in the middle of nowhere, but not too far from the sign that read "Beach closed." In the dark sky, the moon was full, and beneath our jeep, the water was rising.

"I'll go find help," he told me.

"You stay with the Jeep and try to get it started," I said, my voice rising with anger. "I know nothing about cars. I'll find help."

Before he could answer, I was gone. I ran toward the light shining far in the distance. My lungs were burning when I got to the beach house. I jumped onto the five-foot-high concrete wall and swung my legs over, ripping the back of my form-fitting dress. When I landed, I saw a pair of big guard dogs growling at me. I froze.

"Help!" I hollered when two middle-aged men stepped out of the compound. "Aqua, auto!" *Water, car*, I said in Spanish, miming the sound of a car engine and water crashing.

They motioned for me to get into their truck, and as I climbed in, I realized my bottom was exposed. I thanked the Buddha for my granny underwear, and moments later, the men and I rescued Mark and pulled the jeep out of the ocean.

After the men left, Mark turned to me. "You should not have run off like that," he said. "By the time I grabbed the keys and ran after you, you were gone." He exhaled deeply. "I was worried sick. It was incredibly stupid for you to go, and stupid for me to let you go."

I said nothing, and finally he began to relax.

"You know how you are always asking why I love you?" he asked.

I shook my head.

"It's because you're fearless," he said, embracing me.

I'm not fearless, I told him in my sleep. *But long ago I decided that I would rescue myself first instead of waiting for others to do it.*

I WOKE UP EARLY IN THE VILLAGE. I was shivering, although the room I was staying in was hot and humid. Outside, the world was still dark and asleep, and all was silent except for a few loud pigs grunting in a nearby pen. The sound, unfiltered by the clutters of dense buildings, cement walls, and double-pane glass windows, soared from the field as clearly as an orchestra cymbal up the three floors to my room. Life in the Cambodian countryside was lived with an open-door policy, meaning friends did not have to call days in advance to arrange a visit. And when you stepped outside your home, you arrived in a community where your neighbors knew your name.

Grrr-oiinnkk. The pig's half-groan, half-oink woke me.

I had been in Cambodia for a month, in the sanctuary of friends and family. They had opened their lives and homes to me, believing I was there on a three-month-long work assignment to interview survivors of the Khmer Rouge for our agency's newsletter. They did not know who or what I was running from. In our remote village, there was no directory assistance, registered names, road signs, post office, banks, or town hall, so the outside world could not invade us. In truth, it was the perfect place if you wanted not to be found. But I could not stop my mind from traveling to where Mark was.

Behind my closed lids flickered images of him. Like catching fireflies in a jar, I captured a jarful of memories, each illuminating a special moment in our courtship. There was Mark throwing me, clothes and all, into the water in North Beach, Mark pressing his palm against my forehead to feel if I was sick, Mark's smiling face inches from mine as fireworks sounded around us.

I want us to commit to each other, in front of our family and friends.

Why is it important to you? I asked the Mark in my head.

I want to celebrate what we have, connect our two families, two cultures, two worlds.

But our families have never met, I said.

Mark reached for my hand. *That would be a good place to start. We need to arrange that before we get married.*

You never listen, I said, turning away. *I don't want to get married. I don't want to lose my independence. I have fought hard to gain my voice. I do not want a leash around my neck.*

You don't have to lose yourself to be with me, Mark argued.

I just want to wait until I'm a better person . . . I looked imploringly at him. *Until I like who I am.*

I love you just the way you are.

I closed my eyes. *You will break my heart, you won't love me if you know what a mess I really am, what I've done . . . You will leave.*

I will stay, I won't leave.

You will when you die, I whispered. *I don't know when or where or how, but you will die on me and I can't handle that.*

Nothing will happen to me.

I can't take another person dying on me.

Nothing will happen to me.

I turned and stared out my window. *Why can't you understand? Why can't anyone understand?*

Mark was with me now, he leaned in, his forehead touching mine. Then I opened the jar and let the images fly away.

Outside my room, the sun rose.

I WALKED OUT ONTO THE BALCONY, careful to avoid tripping over the many potted flowers and plants. For many years, Chou, her husband Pheng, and their five children had lived in a one-bedroom thatched wood home. Whenever I visited, against my fervent protestation, Chou insisted I take the family bed. Now my sister and her family lived in a three-story dream home. Gone were the wooden walls, outhouse, and dirt floor. In its place were stone walls, squat toilets, tiled floors, and ten rooms. My room was on the top floor. It was connected to a spacious patio that overlooked the village. On this trip, I had the whole floor to myself, away from Chou's ever-growing family and unending stream of visitors.

"Pa, you would be proud of her," I told the empty space around me.

Even without formal schooling, Chou turned out to be a resourceful businesswoman. With a small investment of capital from her family, she and Pheng opened a produce market, and then they bought the land beneath it. I pulled a chair to the edge of the balcony and sat with my chin resting on the railing. Chou's house was located in the middle of the village, and from her rooftop I could see the bustle of life below. The sky was brightening and the air was crisp and cool. I looked around and surveyed the land.

Like our family, the village had grown much since my first return five years before. Then, there was no electricity, running water, or flushing toilets. Now we still had no running water or flushing toilets, but electricity hummed on from 6:00 p.m. to 9:00 p.m. daily. Or at least that was supposed to be the schedule. Like many things scheduled in Cambodia, it was not to be trusted. One night we could have light for the full three hours, but then another night for only half an hour. Either way, the Cambodians adapted. One night when this happened, we were still in the middle of watching *The Terminator* and for the next ten minutes we made up our own ending.

"He could come back during the Khmer Rouge time and fight them," a nephew had suggested.

"Yes!" the others agreed.

"He could take them all in one fight. The movie would be over in ten minutes!"

I laughed at this memory as a new movie played in my mind. In it, the Terminator arrived in Cambodia. "Chmom mol veng hei," *I'm back*, he said in Khmer. Then he went out and kicked some Khmer Rouge ass.

I moved my chair closer to Chou's deck railing and watched the market come to life.

Below, the fishermen and their wives were the first to arrive on their motos, or motorbikes. Behind them they dragged wooden carts filled with large buckets of live freshwater fish and black eels. The men dumped the fish on the ground while the women set up their stools and weight scales. Next came the wave of food vendors selling *nombachuk* (Cambodian noodles), *mi cha* fried noodles, rice porridge, and other meals. As the vendors set up their stalls, the fishermen and their wives became the first customers. Before they finished their bowls of soup, the fruit, vegetable, and clothes sellers arrived, spreading their products on plastic sheets on the floor. As life burst from all around, the sun rose above the trees and bathed the village in soft, golden light.

My morning was interrupted, as usual, by one of my nieces. This morning, it was four-year-old Ching-ching who approached me. "Auntie," Ching-ching called, rubbing sleep out of her eyes. "Good morning."

Of my eight nieces, Ching-ching was the shiest one, and the one who looked the most like my little sister Geak.

"Good morning, Ching-ching. You don't have school today?"

"No . . ." She paused. "I go to the afternoon classes today."

Like our parents, Chou made all her children go to school, three times a day, six days a week. As soon as they could toddle after their bigger siblings, they were sent out. "Good," I said as she climbed onto my lap.

"Auntie, are you lonely to be up here all by yourself?"

"No."

From where I sat, I could see Uncle Heang's, Uncle Leang's, and Aunt Takea's houses. Across from them, I saw the home where my brother Khouy, his wife Mum, and their six children lived. And to their right lived cousins Hong, Kheng, Chen, Hang, Eung, and Amah in their respective houses. Longtime friends and neighbors whom I'd met and gotten to know in my ten trips back to Cambodia and the village occupied the houses in between my family's homes.

"No, I'm not lonely up here," I told Ching-ching. "I'm never alone in Cambodia."

Ching-ching climbed onto my lap and pointed to her Khmer and Chinese schools in the distance. Beyond them, the rice fields gave way to a small patch of land next to a manmade pond. It was our family burial land, where we buried Grandfather Akoang. Next to him, a plot was already planted with palm trees and flowers for Amah.

"Ching-ching, do you see the cows and farmers over there?" I redirected her gaze.

"Yes."

I felt the spirit of my teacher father guiding me. "Well, many Cambodians, eighty-five percent at least, are farmers and still live on what they grow on their land or fish they catch in our rivers."

"Uh-huh."

"They've lived this way for over a thousand years! Their stories and lives are carved on the stone walls of temples in Angkor."

Ching-ching squiggled out of my arms and sauntered over to the railing.

I looked up at the sky. "I lost her, Pa," I said to my father.

She is too young for history lessons, I imagined Pa replying. *But don't give up.*

"Ma!" Ching-ching called out to Chou, who was just returning from the market, her arms heavy with two live, squawking brown and black chickens, carried upside down. As she walked, the chicken heads swung to and fro, fighting to right themselves.

"Ching-ching," Chou waved to her. "Don't wake your auntie up."

"I didn't. She was up already!" Ching-ching yelled back, as if annoyed that her mother should think such a thing of her.

"Loung," Chou called. "Come down and meet Ree."

I scooted Ching-ching off my lap and trotted downstairs. There, standing next to Chou, was a beautiful young Khmer girl. "Chump reap sur Bang Loung," *Hello Sister Loung,* Ree greeted me in Khmer.

Ree was the daughter of Chou's neighbor, and a soon-to-be bride. She handed me the wedding invitation, her bright, white teeth shining against dark chocolate skin.

"Bang Loung, I'm sorry I didn't come sooner to invite you to my wedding. I didn't know you were back. I was visiting my betrothed's village and just returned."

"Don't worry about it," I said, touching her arm.

"Bang Loung, please say you'll come to my wedding!"

"When is it?"

"Tomorrow."

I took her hands in mine. "I will be there," I said.

"I'm so happy!" Ree gushed, gliding away with the sure steps of one who was loved by both her parents, her feet light and untroubled by the weight of an unhappy childhood.

For unlike in other Khmer Rouge forced marriages, Ree's

parents grew to have tender feelings for each other and elected to stay together after the war had ended. Ree believed her parents' marriage was blessed by the gods. And like many other little girls who grew up witnessing this, Ree went to sleep on most nights dreaming of her own special day.

I thought about how lucky Ree was to be born in a country in which falling in love was not a crime. Under the Khmer Rouge, the government demanded that its citizens be loyal only to the government. Having a child out of wedlock was a crime punishable by death or imprisonment. During its reign, the Angkar, the Khmer Rouge government, dictated whom you married and when. Many people were not told the names of their future spouses or what he or she looked like until their appointed wedding day, part of a mass ceremony that may have included three to one hundred other couples. And on these supposedly happy days, family members were not allowed to attend, and traditional clothes, singing, dancing, and religious rituals were prohibited. Those who dared to refuse such arrangements risked torture, hard labor, and imprisonment. For some women, the only escape was suicide. But this did not deter the government from forcing couples to marry because the main focus of their weddings was not to protect women but to produce children for the nation. Thus, when making their marriage decision, love was not part of their equation. The selection was made purely on the basis of what would benefit the Angkar and support the revolution.

A government-forced marriage would have been my fate if the war had not ended. As a child during the revolution, I was supposed to be pure and loyal only to the Angkar, but I never was. I hated the soldiers with a passion that overwhelmed my small body, filling me with such rage I imagined I would self-combust if I stood still long enough. So I was never quiet—I knocked my knees and tapped my feet.

When the war ended on January 7, 1979, many Cambodian women and men went back to falling in love, and to marrying husbands and wives their elders picked for them. For some, the person they loved and the person they married were one and the same. For others, they entered their wedding day knowing that from then on, their hearts and bodies would belong to different people. But even these unlucky ones could be grateful knowing their mates were chosen for them with care and compassion. For according to our Khmer Buddhist belief, it is the duty of the parents to arrange a wife or husband for their son or daughters. In these arrangements, dowry, possessions, gifts, obligations, and both individual and family histories are carefully considered to ensure the happiness of the union and growth of the family.

Chou came up and stood next to me. "Ree is a very lucky girl," she said, looking at the wedding invitation. "Hers is a love match. Still, it doesn't hurt that her future husband owns many cows as well."

"I don't want cows," I teased her. "I want bulls!"

"Sister," Chou replied, snickering at my naughty remark. "When you get married, I will give you two giant bulls! When you get married . . ."

"Stop!" I pleaded, moving away from her.

Chou came after me, her hand pinching my arm and back playfully. "What are you afraid of?"

"I'm not afraid of anything!" I screamed, running away.

In four years of living under the Khmer Rouge regime, I had become good at running. I ran from the sadness, the soldiers, and the bombs. Two decades after the war I was still running, only now the war had less power over me than before. I had faced it and come out standing, and yet, I ran.

24

Khmer Inheritance

Oudong, February 2000

"If you walk any slower, we will miss all the wedding ceremonies," Chou said, pulling my arm along.

"Okay, okay!" I followed her. Behind me, Ching-ching pushed at my behind.

The dusty, red road was transformed by a bright red tent into an outdoor party space when we arrived in Oudong, a town about ten miles from my family's village. Next to the tent, a two-foot-tall spirit house stood. Black smoke floated into the air from the large red ceramic bowl filled with hundreds of burning incense sticks. Inside the tent, the wedding band played Cambodian and English songs under the makeshift, glaring stage light. Guests walked through a golden temple entrance guarded by giant foam elephants and Hanuman monkey kings.

According to the ancient book of Khmer wedding rules, a Cambodian wedding should consist of many ceremonies and last as long as three days. And a bride should wear as many as twelve different dresses on her wedding day.

"Twelve?!" I'd exclaimed when Chou told me.

"Yes," she'd answered matter-of-factly, shrugging off my shock.

At the gate, we were greeted by the young bride and groom, dressed as a Khmer princess and prince, and a court of similarly attired bridesmaids and groomsmen. The bride wore a gold *sbai*, a shawl that wrapped over her left shoulder and under her right armpit, and a *sarong*, a wrap skirt, both richly embroidered with exquisite small beads and sequins. On her head, arms, and feet, a gold crown, bangles, and anklets sparkled and gleamed. Beside the princess bride, the groom stood in his gold shirt and pants.

"She's beautiful," I whispered to Chou.

"On her wedding day, a woman is a princess," Chou told me. *And the man, a prince.* I smiled, thinking of how Mark would look dressed up like a Khmer prince. Of course, the sleeves and pant legs of Khmer men's clothes would be too short for his six-foot-two-inch frame. I had the opposite problem in America, a country where few things were built for my height— from too-big clothes to too-tall bathroom sinks that left wet stains across my stomach every time I used a public restroom.

"Come, come!" Chou grabbed my arm as we entered the wedding tent.

We scanned the room for our cousins but could not immediately find them. For inside the wedding tent, more than six hundred guests were seated at round tables and already eating noisily. Unlike the Western weddings I'd been to, guests were served food as soon as their table of eight was filled. And as servers hurried to bring food from one table to another, those who had finished eating got up to leave. In this way, the room was constantly in a state of movement with people coming and going. I looked around, amused at how all the women were glamorously dressed, while the men showed up in plain shirts and dark pants.

As there was no designated seating at a Khmer wedding, I sat at my cousins' table, underneath which was a small pile of used tissues, banana leaves, bamboo sticks, and plastic wraps piled on top of cans and bottles. Red dust already filled the creases of my toes. Flies circled and buzzed around the food on the tables. On the other side of the transparent, cloth temple walls, dogs barked, vendors sold their fresh fish, and villagers gathered to watch the wedding procession.

We spotted our family sitting at a table in the back of the tent, and slowly made our way there, careful to avoid bumping into other people's tables and chairs. When we arrived, I saw that the table was populated by the other female cousins of our generation—Eng, Hong, Cheung, Moy, Hoa, and Hoong— all daughters of my uncles. Like Chou, they were beautifully dressed and dripping with their best jewels, their faces painted and their blue-black hair decorated with flowers, extensions, fake braids, and clip-on curls. Eng motioned to the three empty seats next to her.

"Chou," Eng said, eyeing me. "How did you get your sister to do her hair?"

At the village, I was notorious for being a slob. Or the Cambodian version of a slob, which was to say that I rarely dressed up, styled my hair, or put on makeup. Not even for special occasions. But on this day, I was made up like a doll, complete with a stem of purple orchid flowers in my hair, bright red lipstick, and half-inch-long fake eyelashes.

Chou chuckled, caressing her daughter's hair. "I paid Ching-ching one thousand riel to pester her to do it," Chou said. I mocked offense at Ching-ching for being bought for the equivalent of twenty-five U.S. cents.

"Ching-ching, give me the money!" I demanded of my little niece as she giggled, showing her missing two front teeth.

"You look good with makeup!" Eng said. "And what a beautiful shirt!"

"Chou bought it for me," I told her.

Perhaps it was because I left the country at such an impressionable age, but my color preferences tended toward the muted side and my clothing leaned toward the understated. For whatever reason, this was not the sensibility in Cambodia, where the more color and design the better. Thus, my shirt for the wedding, the one everyone complimented, was shiny and bloodred in color, with black polka dots and ruffles along the neck, front, cuffs, and shoulders.

Hong reached across the table to pull at my ringlets. "Let's eat," I said, leaning away from her.

And eat we did. A Cambodian wedding was so much about eating that it seemed appropriate that the Khmer word for wedding was *see-ka*—literally meaning eat-work. The servers brought plates of spring rolls, fried squid, steamed fish, sour soup, roast duck, fried rice, fried noodles, sautéed vegetables, and barbecued pork to our table. Twelve dishes in all.

"Loung," Chou cajoled me as I shoved a piece of juicy, crispy duck into my mouth. "When are you going to give us a nephew or niece?"

The cousins looked at each other. I knew immediately they were all working together.

"Loung," Hong urged. "You birth one for us."

"Loung," Eng pressed. "I'll raise your child while you go on with your traveling and work. You can pick the child back up in five years."

With my mouth full of crispy duck, I asked, "Easy as that? I give you a child and take him or her back in five years? Who's going to take care of the little spoiled brat after that?"

"By then the child will be potty-trained, able to feed and dress himself," Chou said, looking at the cousins. "And if you want us to, we all will keep the child for the rest of his or her life."

The cousins all nodded, grinning.

"Cousins," I said. "My life is very busy. I have no time for pet cats or dogs. Right now, I have five plants that I cannot keep alive."

Quiet for a moment, Chou picked up a fatty piece of barbecued pork and dropped it in my small rice bowl. The other women followed, each choosing the best morsel of food on their plate and plopping it into my bowl until there was no room for more. I stopped them by placing a hand over my bowl.

"Thank you." I acknowledged their signs of friendship.

With each bite, lumps of guilt slid down my stomach with clumps of mashed-up pork and chicken. My sister and cousins generously shared their family and their lives with me, and yet, I was not truthful with them. As each took me aside to tell me their secrets, I had not breathed a word of Mark to them. Instead, I let them believe I was an overworked, lonely old spinster and caused them to worry.

"You are too thin," Chou said, putting more crispy duck into my bowl. "We have to fatten you up so a man will find you healthy and want to marry you."

I ignored her, and continued my eating.

•   •   •

AN HOUR LATER, WHEN WE'D EATEN OUR fill, the ladies got up to leave. I looked at my watch and it was only six o'clock. The band hadn't even started playing yet. All around us, new wedding guests were still arriving and being seated. This was yet another Khmer custom I valued: wedding guests were permitted to come and go as they pleased, and it was not considered rude.

"That was delicious," Cousin Moy said. "But we must leave to drive back to our village."

"Lia suhn hao-y." Chou and I bid them goodbye, standing up and bringing our hands to our chests in a prayer, a traditional Khmer gesture called *sompeah*.

"Please come see us," the cousins said, walking away.

I waved and wished them safe travels to their villages. When Chou and I sat back down I saw that as soon as my cousins had vacated their seats, they were immediately filled. I watched in surprise as a tiny girl took the seat next to me. She was small, looked to be around seven or eight years in age, and wore a tattered shirt and shorts. She trained her big brown eyes on the leftovers on the table. Next to her, more poor-looking children filled the empty seats. Without asking for permission, the children picked up our used chopsticks and began eating our leftovers. No one shooed or chased these kids away.

"Chou, do you know these kids?" I asked.

"I don't know their families, but I've seen them around the village," she said. "Mostly likely, their parents are poor rice farmers."

"I am amazed the bride and groom's families do not mind the children's presence among their dressed up guests."

For a moment Chou looked at me as if I'd said something completely bewildering. "Why should they?" she answered.

"We've eaten our fill, so why shouldn't the children enjoy the delicious leftovers?"

I turned to the girl, who was in the midst of smacking her lips loudly and nodding at Chou's words. "Is the food good?" I asked.

"Very good," she replied shyly.

"Loung," Chou pinched my arm. "We have to go."

"Ouch!" I pulled away from her. "Why are you all such big pinchers?"

"Because it's the best way to hurt you," Chou said as the girl laughed. "Especially when you keep going into your head!"

By the time we got up to leave, there were five street kids at our table, with thirty more milling around the wedding tent. They scurried from table to table, collecting empty bottles and cans to sell to vendors and farmers who would use them to sell petrol or collect palm syrup. In this process, everyone was part of Cambodia's larger recycling programs.

The little girl next to me looked up shyly. I gave her a can of Coca-Cola. She took it. As our group walked away, throngs of kids clamored around our table and began to eat our leftovers. I turned back in time to see the bride's mother, dressed as a golden queen, passing out plastic garbage bags to the kids. I walked up to her.

"Auntie," I said. "That was very generous and kind of you."

Auntie poured more leftover food into another plastic bag. "They are poor but good kids," she replied, calling more of them over. "It's good karma to give."

I nodded.

"During Pol Pot time, I had nothing to eat so I know what hunger feels like."

Yes, I thought. We were a nation in which more than half our people understood hunger.

"I'm happy to let them take the food home to their families," Auntie said. "This way, everyone in the village helps to celebrate the joyous union of my daughter and new son-in-law."

As she spoke, she handed her food bags to the kids. They thanked her and hurriedly poured more table scraps into the bags. Once their bags were full, they hopped merrily home to their families, able to thwart poverty for one more day.

After dinner, I sat alone at an empty table. The *ocheh*, the band, was playing Khmer pop songs as guests gyrated to the music. When a slow song came on, the young people returned to their seats as married couples took to the floor and danced. I watched them sway together, their bodies at arm's length from each other. And suddenly, I was missing Mark again and wishing he were there. He would have enjoyed the commotion and the food. Especially the food.

"I can't believe you can't cook," he harrumphed when I first moved in with him in Cleveland after college.

In college I had served him Eang's gourmet meals with a little white lie that I'd helped make it.

"So I fudged a little lie . . . big deal," I said, hugging him tighter as he made our dinner. "Hey, I can make Jif—."

"Adding spoonfuls of Jif peanut butter to spaghetti is not what I call cooking," he said, turning around.

Lost in thought, I did not notice Eldest Aunt and Second Aunt—both wives of my uncles—approaching until they stood at my table.

"Loung," Eldest Aunt called, sitting in a chair next to me. "Sitting like that you look very much like your mother."

Second Aunt pulled a chair over, sat down, and crossed her legs. "Yes, you have her eyes," she told me. "I am still so sad about your mother. I still miss her very much."

"Stop," Eldest Aunt said, chiding her as other aunties joined us. "Stop remembering sad stories. Tell the girl happy stories about her mother instead."

I sat up in my seat. "Please, Aunties," I said. "Tell me about the happier times."

The aunties gathered around me, some sitting on chairs and others squatting on the ground. I glanced at their faces, brown and wrinkled; they told of a lifetime of hard work toiling in the sun. Had my mother lived, she would have been the aunties' age, in her sixties.

"I was your mother's friend when we were girls," Auntie Takea mused. "Your ma was very funny."

This I never knew. What details I knew of my mother I could count on one hand. That she was my father's wife, my mother, a stern disciplinarian. That she loved pork dumplings and her red ruby earrings. But in all my memories of her, I could not recount her being funny.

"And she loved to ride her bike down hills very fast!" Auntie Takea chuckled.

"She was a bad girl," Eldest Aunt laughed, prompting Grandmother Soy Sauce to slap her arm lightly.

Like many other grandmothers in the village, Grandmother Soy Sauce was not related to us. We inherited her because she had no other family. She got her name because she sold our family soy sauce in Phnom Penh and began a twenty-five-year family friendship.

Auntie Takea pointed to a road just beyond the village. "See that road?"

"Yes," I followed her finger.

"Your ma used to jump on her bicycle and just fly down that road," she said, her eyes gazing into the distance as if she were seeing this again.

"We would follow," Eldest Aunt said, chuckling. "But we couldn't catch her. Your ma would ride so fast her hair was flying everywhere! And her long pants would lift up past her knees."

"And all the young men would stare at her naked legs!" Second Aunt cackled. "She would throw her arms up in the air and fly, steering the bicycle with her knees."

Eldest Aunt tried to stop cackling and ended up coughing so hard her eyes teared up. "Your ma used to get into a lot of trouble with your amah and akoang," she said, wiping her eyes. "They argued a lot, but your ma was a fighter!"

"She had a lot of fire in her," Auntie Takea remembered. "She was very protective; she would fight anyone who picked on her friends."

"And anyone who picked on her brothers and sisters," Eldest Aunt chimed in.

I did not know any of this.

"And her marriage was a love match," Second Aunt said, her voice wistful.

I faced Second Aunt and hesitated before asking. "Did my parents love each other very much?"

"Their love was as unending as the river," Grandmother Soy Sauce answered.

I sighed with relief.

"I dreamt about them last night," Eldest Aunt said. "In my dream, your pa and ma, now old like us, sat in matching chairs next to each other on our balcony in Phnom Penh. They looked out at the city, their hands touching."

25

Somewhere in Time

Kompong Speu, February 2000

I rode my bicycle furiously away from the village, pumping my legs faster and faster, passing men and young boys tossing their long fishing lines into the rice fields. One man jerked his line, yanking it high into the air. Following behind it, a brown frog twirled. The boys laughed, their eyes looking toward the sky, their arms holding an open net. The frog spun in the air, round and round and round, its short legs and arms rotating like a propeller until it landed in one of the boy's nets.

"Hellloooo!!! Hellooo!!! Helloooo!!" the boys yelled, waving at me.

"Helllooooo!" I hollered back as I passed by.

In my trips to Cambodia, I have watched the country change in its many seasons: from dry, when the earth cracks like red clay, to rainy, when I'm forced to check for leeches between my toes whenever I step into a puddle of water. But the season I love best is the rice-harvesting season. During those weeks, if the sun shines at just the right angle, and the breeze blows with just the right force, the yellow rice stalks shimmer and sparkle like fields of gold. It was during the rice harvest that I rode my bike so fast down the road.

I raced forward, navigating my way around a herd of cows, passing a large pond where brown, naked children dove and dunked each other under the water. I cared little about being unladylike. Once, I may have been ashamed that I was not more proper, or embarrassed for speaking up the way I couldn't help myself from doing. I remembered how, when I was a child, my mother paid much attention to our chi, or life force. She sought out fortunetellers to teach her about feminine and masculine energy, or yin and yang. She learned that the yin, the feminine, included attributes such as intuition, giving, empathy, forgiveness, nurturing, and sweetness. The yang, the masculine, was described as quick to anger, confrontational, strong, rational, aggressive, and achievement-oriented. When she returned home from one such session, my mother shook her head and said I was born with too much yang. Thus my interest in burning wings off flies, catching frogs, and climbing trees. I remembered her sadness at this discovery, how my face fell with shame from not living up to her vision of me. But now, flying by the countryside on my bicycle, I realized how I was just like my mother.

My time in the village had shown me that she herself possessed much yang in her spirit, something that she had passed on to me, and for which I was grateful. Had she lived, I believe we could have celebrated this together—that a strong girl-child could grow up to be a strong woman, and be valued for it.

Beneath my tires, pebbles crunched and red dirt plumed. I peddled faster. On either side of the road, green rice paddies covered the ground. In one paddy, a woman bent over, pulling rice seedlings out of the shallow water. Beside her in the shade, her three children sat on a straw mat playing with long grass leaves. The children laughed and waved. I waved back. As I pedaled farther and farther away, I saw my parents in my mind and heard the words and stories of the aunties and grandmothers.

IN 1953, TWELVE YEARS AFTER MY young amah and her family arrived in Cambodia, my mother, Chourng, turned eighteen. In the blush of maidenhood, she saw a poor monk at a pond as she was swimming one day. My mother swam quietly near, hidden by white and pink lotus blossoms. She was still a teenage girl, and he a worldly, twenty-four-year-old nomad monk. She spied his reflection on the surface of the pond. She was in the same spot where she had swum many times to pick lotus flowers to sell at the market. She swam around the webs of watery grass veins. When a small splash of water disturbed his concentration, my father turned. Quickly, my mother ducked behind an uprooted tree, which fanned over the water like a giant shredded umbrella. From there, she watched him, her heart beating so fast she feared it would escape from its cage.

Unaware that he was being watched, my father did not turn around completely. He stood with his back to my mother, balanced on a fallen log that extended many feet into the pond. He stood tall and straight, his body like a young willow tree drinking from the earth. My mother stared at his profile, at his large head and smooth, shaven skull.

There was nothing unusual about the monk. His body was wrapped in a swath of dark, saffron robes that fluttered in the breeze. He stared into the horizon, seemingly lost in deep meditation. To my young mother, a sheltered village girl, there was something very soulful and wise about his presence.

The monk stood with his hands clasped behind his back, his gaze looking past the village and ponds. Without realizing why, my mother dove down into the water, making a big splash. When she came back up again, she was standing in the shallows. The monk turned and stared at her.

I knew I wanted to marry her, I heard my father's voice echo over the fields.

For many days and weeks after that, they met secretly by the pond. He was educated at the monastery and well read; he had access to books and stories she had only dreamt about. As she listened, my father showed her the world beyond the village, a world of gods and goddesses, of powerful kings and compassionate queens, and of monkey kings and flying cows. In his stories, he took her out of the doldrums of life as a peasant girl. It was as if the horizon was the canvas on which he drew pictures of the world for her to see, of lives lived outside her village.

Then one day my father took off his monk's robe, put on the borrowed white shirt and black pants belonging to his best friend, and went to my mother's thatched-roof hut in the village. There he stood in front of my grandmother and grandfather.

"Kind mother," my father said, his voice low to show his respect. "I love your daughter, and ask for your permission to marry her."

"No." Amah balked.

"Ma, please . . ." my mother begged. "Please, let us marry. We love each other."

"You ungrateful girl!" Amah cried. "What do you know of love? This poor boy is not good enough for you. He has no land and no father. His father left them. His mother has two husbands, and more children than she can feed."

My father stepped forward. "My father died," he interjected. "He didn't leave us."

"Be quiet!" Amah ordered, turning to face my mother. "Do you want this to happen to you? We can find you a husband who has more value, who has land."

My mother shook her head. "Pa, Ma, please . . . let us marry," she pleaded.

"What did I do to deserve this?" Amah asked, her hand massaging her chest. "How can you disgrace me? How can you disgrace the family and blacken our faces with shame?"

Watching my grandmother cry, my mother turned to my father. "Please leave," she told him, her eyes cast down. "Please leave."

My father reached for her but she moved away from him. Reluctantly, my father left, his feet dragging in the dirt.

But the next day, my mother and father met again in secret. This time, they ran to a monastery in another village. There they married without the presence of family or friends. They tied a red string around each of their wrists for health and prosperity. When my mother's parents were told, they stopped speaking to her. My father became a farmer, a shopkeeper, and a military police officer. A year later, my mother gave birth to their first son, my brother Meng. Six more babies followed. Somewhere between the first son and the last daughter, Amah and Akoang took them back into the family. But still, their marriage was spoken of in hushed tones, as if it were a black magic incantation not to be recited. The fear was that like a spell, if released, their story could spread evil.

I STOPPED MY BIKE IN FRONT of our family burial land. *Their love was as unending as the river,* Grandmother Soy Sauce had said.

The circumstances of my parents' deaths were shrouded in mystery and horror. I did not know what they saw or suffered the last moments of their lives. All I knew was that soldiers came to our village and took away my father, my mother, and my oldest and baby sisters. None of them were ever seen or heard from again. Of their fate, this much I knew was true: They were dead. But not one of my surviving siblings or I had witnessed my parents' or sisters' deaths. Thus, Chou continued to harbor dreams that perhaps my parents were still alive and living somewhere without their memories. Perhaps they were so traumatized they'd forgotten about their former lives and family, and could not find their ways back to us. But I knew they were dead. I was ten when I realized this, two years after the war had ended. For even amidst all the chaos, confusion, and rage, I never doubted my father's love. I knew that had he been alive, no soldiers, war, landmines, or oceans would have stopped him from coming back for his family.

But sometimes, I questioned my mother's love.

I gazed at the same lush green fields and palm trees my mother stared at many years before; the same ponds my father drank from. The mound of dirt that was my grandfather's grave was cleared of shrubs and trash. But my parents' markers were not there because their bodies were never found.

I stared at the horizon that spanned across Cambodia's green fields and knew that somewhere out there were my parent's graves, unmarked and uncared for. And according to our beliefs, without proper burials for their bodies, their souls were lost to each other.

I stood on my bike, concentrating on the rushing wind blowing up my hair, the sound of air being inhaled and exhaled through my nostrils. I pumped the bike's pedals faster and faster. Then I lifted my arms, flying down the hill, the wind lifting up my wide pant legs past my shins and knees.

26

The Hills of the Poisonous Trees

Phnom Penh, February 2000

There is a Khmer fable that the city of Phnom Penh was founded in the fourteenth century by an old woman named Penh, whom everyone called grandmother, or *daun* in Khmer. One rainy season, Daun Penh visited the Mekong River and found a great big log floating by in the current. When she fished it out, she discovered four bronze and one stone Buddha statues inside. With the help of other villagers, Daun Penh built a temple on a hill to house the five statues. The temple became known as Wat Phnom Daun Penh, the hill temple of

Grandma Penh. This was later shortened to Wat Phnom, the temple hill. Wat Phnom became so famous that people from all over the land came to visit it, and once there, many became settlers and made their lives around or near the temple.

In 1432, a Khmer king moved to the city and found it so lovely he named it *Krong Chaktomuk Mongkol Sakal Kampuchea Thipadei Sereythor Inthabot Borei Roth Reach Seima Maha Nokor*, or The Place of Four Rivers That Give Happiness and Success of Kambuja. As this was quite a mouthful, the people called it Phnom Penh.

AFTER A MONTH IN THE VILLAGE, I returned to Phnom Penh to work at the Veterans International Rehabilitation Center. I was scheduled to be in the city for three weeks before returning to the village. Already, I missed the country. There, we could admire the green fields and trees without the nests and webs of electrical wires and power lines blocking our views. But then my eyes took in the tall poles jutting up above the city. *Telephones*, I thought, as perspiration formed on my face and hairline.

In Cleveland, it would be freezing. February was still the middle of the winter, when temperatures often dropped below zero and snow fell so heavily the city sometimes had to close. I wondered how Mark was keeping himself warm, or with whom. For a moment, my eyes fogged over with jealousy, but I blinked it away. I knew Mark. And even though we were broken up and had not spoken in over a month, he would not seek company in another woman's arms. Of this, I was certain.

As Pheng drove, I sat in the front passenger seat staring out the window. In the backseat, Chou, little Ching-ching, and Auntie Takea sat snug in their seats, eating pumpkin seeds. Slowly, we passed Tuol Sleng Genocide Museum. The rows of nondescript buildings were brown-beige, with a splattering of black mildew and mold. Surrounding the buildings, concrete walls rose twenty feet or so, the tops of them covered with spiraling razor wire.

I watched a group of children run out of the compound, laughing and chasing each other.

"Is that the famous Khmer Rouge prison?" Chou asked.

My eyes followed the children. "Yes," I told her. "But it's a museum now. When the Vietnamese entered the city, they turned it into a genocide museum."

"Have you been in there?" Auntie Takea tapped my shoulder.

"Yes."

"Is it horrible?" she asked.

"Very horrible."

In Khmer, *tuol* meant "hill," and *sleng* was the name of a poisonous tree. Visiting there always reminded me of what Robert Frost said: "In three words I can sum up everything I've learned about life: it goes on." But for the fourteen thousand or more people who were brought to Tuol Sleng, life stopped.

"We've never been in there," Auntie Takea said somberly. "Nobody from the village has ever been in there, except for you."

I looked away, and kept my eyes hidden.

"What is it? Mama?" Ching-ching peered out the window. "Can I see?"

Chou pulled Ching-ching down onto her seat. "Nothing," she said. "Nothing to see, sit down."

I returned my gaze to the city. On the large sidewalk, a few feet away from the road, stores and small shops crowded the ground floors of most of the buildings. Above the doors, bright and colorful panels, banners, paintings, and pictures advertised their products: car motors, spirit houses, dried squids, and snake wines. Whatever your pleasure, you could find it in Phnom Penh. This was not the Phnom Penh of Khmer Rouge times, the black-and-white images of war and suffering that many Westerners perceived to be representative of Cambodia. Back then only a few thousand people had lived in this "Pearl of Asia," doing the government's work. Now Phnom Penh was vibrant, colorful, lively, and a chaotic mass of 1.5 million people.

"Which hotel are you staying at?" Pheng asked suddenly.

I paused before answering. "Le Royal," I replied, feeling guilty just naming the five-star hotel.

Twenty years after the Khmer Rouge's defeat, Cambodia still ranked among the poorest countries in the world, with an average annual income as low as $264 per year and over a third of its population living below the poverty level of one dollar per day. And because the Khmer Rouge especially targeted doctors, lawyers, architects, singers, weavers, musicians, and other builders of the community, Cambodia was unable to pass many of its skills and talents on to the next generation. Thus, poverty continued.

I had explained to my family that my job in Cambodia included showing people the rehabilitation centers where we made wheelchairs, prosthetic limbs, and other orthotic devices to help victims of war and landmines. And that these people included journalists, politicians, and wealthy donors. I'd told them that a delegation of wealthy donors was arriving in a few days and they required nice hotels. But try as I did to explain, Auntie Takea could not understand the waste.

"That's a very big hotel!" Auntie Takea exclaimed. "How much are you paying again?"

"I think the room is $220 a night."

"That expensive?!" Auntie Takea gasped. "That's almost as much as some people make in a year!"

I focused my eyes on the road. "I'm only staying there for work because I have to be close to the Americans who are coming to visit the center," I said. "After they leave, it's back to sleeping on my friend's couch and eating Chou's food in the village."

"It is still very crazy," Auntie Takea whispered, "to spend that much money on a room for one night when the same amount could feed our entire village."

I said nothing else about the hotel as our car inched forward in the traffic. Instead, I watched a pedicab cyclo piled high with two adults and three kids stop next to us at a red light. The pedaler's leg veins bulged out of his skin as he pushed his load forward in the crowded street. He stopped when a motorbike whizzed by with a hundred-pound, upside-down pig strapped securely to the backseat. The pig squealed, its cries rising above the traffic as its feet kicked the air. The biker drove on, passing a group of women on the sidewalk who balanced baskets of grilled eels, crispy crickets, and fried tarantulas on top of their heads. My family watched all these scenes with the glazed look of boredom. But suddenly, they broke out in loud laughter.

"What?" I asked.

"That man is red!" They pointed at a Caucasian man on a bike, the skin of his arms, legs, and bald head burnt pink by our hot sun. Immediately, I thought of Mark, whose white skin rivaled the bicycle man's. In Cambodia, he would turn just as pink. I wondered if my family would laugh and point him out too, and if he could ever fit into this part of my world.

"Hellooo . . ." Ching-ching leaned her head out the open window and hollered.

"Hellooo . . ." the man waved. "Chump reap sur!" He repeated his hello in Khmer.

Along with her daughter, Chou stuck her head out and waved. "Heheheh . . . his Khmer isn't bad!" she exclaimed.

This was a different Chou from the one I'd met on my first return visit to Cambodia in 1995. Then, our Cambodian family was distrustful of foreigners, especially Americans. The Khmer Rouge soldiers claimed, as they'd stormed into Phnom Penh, that America was going to bomb the city. It had been only two years since Cambodia's first national election, and three years since the U.S. had normalized diplomatic relations with the country.

"Brother, what is America like?" Chou had asked Meng on that first trip.

To answer, Meng pulled out his video camera and played tapes of our lives in America. Our family had gawked at all the luxuries—large houses and big cars, paved roads and garbage-free land, and markets lined with aisles upon aisles of food.

"Brother," Chou asked. "If America has so much food, why do they eat rotten milk?"

"It's called cheese," Meng said, smiling. "There are many different types. The worst is Parmesan cheese. It smells very bad."

"I feel bad for you, Eldest Brother!" Cousin Lee said.

"And they eat this *yogurt*," I piped in. "They eat this by the bucketful! It's white and globby, and smells like baby's burp!"

"Disgusting!" Lee laughed. "But I guess if you're hungry enough, you'll eat anything."

Chou suddenly pulled my arm. "Loung, remember when we were so hungry we ate dirt?" she asked, demonstrating by extending her cupped hand. "We would scoop up a handful of fine dirt, shake our hands to toss the big grains to the top, pick out the big rocks, and swallow the fine dust."

The family guffawed loudly.

"Here are our friends," Meng pointed to the screen, where Chou could see our American friends wearing big grins and waving at the camera as if they were greeting longtime friends.

"They look like nice people," she said, smiling at us.

"They are," I said, smiling at her.

Back in the city, traffic had slowed and cars turned into snails. It was midday in Phnom Penh when we arrived at the hotel. Pheng pulled into the driveway of the opulent hotel.

"It's so beautiful!" Auntie Takea exclaimed.

"The garden is so pretty and clean," Ching-ching said, staring at the manicured lawn and greenery. "The stairs and windows are pretty, too."

"Even their dirt is clean." Chou pulled Ching-ching away from the window.

Ching-ching looked at me. "Auntie, is it very beautiful inside?"

"Yes," I told her, but stopped short of inviting them in.

Once, on an earlier trip, I had pushed Chou to stay in the hotel with me. I thought it would be great fun to treat my sister to time away from her kids and husband, and to a weekend of eating at nice restaurants and sleeping in late. I wanted her to enjoy a long shower and soak in a hot bath, something she had never experienced. But Chou felt out of place the moment she stepped in. She was uncomfortable with "the white shirt" doorman opening and closing the door for her, she wanted to take off her shoes before she entered the clean hall, the air-conditioning gave her headaches, and hot baths and showers seemed unnecessary and wasteful. We left that same night to stay at a cousin's cramped apartment. Since then, instead of asking her to visit my world, I went to hers.

When Pheng brought his old Camry to a stop in front of the grand colonial entrance, I quickly opened the door and hopped out. Then, with a quick goodbye, my family left. And as I walked up the steps into the luxury hotel, I turned and saw Chou pull Ching-ching into her embrace.

THAT NIGHT, IN THE DARKNESS OF sleep, my memory retrieved a morsel of another life. In it, I dreamt that I inhabited my mother's body.

Little mouse . . . Through my mother's eyes, I watched my child-self sleeping on a wooden plank bed. I stirred, but instead of opening my eyes, I turned to my side, drawing my knees up to my chin in a tight fetal position.

Little mouse, wake up, my mother whispered. *It's time to go.*

I could feel my mother's heartbeat then as she leaned in, bringing her face an inch away from mine. When I exhaled, she breathed me in, filling her own body with my breath. *Daughter, it's time to wake up,* she said, her fingers parting my hair, brushing loose strands off my face.

No, I protested. *I don't want to go.*

You have to, my mother urged, and slid her hand behind my head to pull me up.

I woke up, yawning and stretching my arms into the sky. Next to me, my mother gathered my brother and sisters together before morning broke, and prepared to send us away from her. She stumbled in the dark, walking into doors and walls, her feet and arms as heavy as lead. One by one, she told us to leave. When my child-self refused, my mother turned me by the shoulders and pushed me out the door. I left feeling unloved and bitterly angry, feelings I held on to for many years.

And now, in my sleep, I cried my mother's tears, felt her arms wrap around her stomach as she collapsed to her knees. In my mind, I heard her wails, the banging of her fists and head, the muffled sound of her choking into her scarf. She was full of fear, her heart a piece of stained glass shattered on the concrete floor. She did trust her body to go on; she did not trust her courage to be strong.

My mother hung her head and sobbed, a river of suffering flowing deep in her veins. *I had to do it.* The river overflowed my mother's body and flooded the room around her. Everywhere it went, it soaked everything in its path with my mother's pain. I felt my mother's anguish.

I looked at her. Behind a layer of glistening tears, I saw something else I had never seen before—the pure whiteness of my mother's love. It was brighter than starbursts and more intricate than a snowflake. It was a generous love filled with so much hope that I was left in awe. My mother sat up, strengthened in her resolve to keep us from the grasp of the soldiers. She walked out the door and began her day working in the rice field. As she worked, she did not let on about her broken heart. When the sun burnt her back, when her hands bled from pulling weeds, as her knees buckled from exhaustion, she smiled. When the soldiers berated her for letting her children run away, and her loneliness consumed her, she smiled. She did not know if they would live or die, be killed or tortured, or if she would ever see them again, but she smiled all the same, knowing she had given them a fighting chance. It was all she had to give me. It was a sacrifice she was willing to make.

In my dream I ran back into my mother's arms. She caught me and rocked me like she did when I was her baby, before my conscious mind could form a memory. But my body remembered, and I curled up in her arms as she hummed a lullaby.

Ma, I blamed you for getting caught by the soldiers. I was angry at you for not surviving and leaving me.

I never left . . .

What I once mistook as her weakness was in fact her strength. I never before imagined the strength it took for her to send us away. But she did it to give us a chance to survive. And because of her courage, five of her seven children made it out of the war alive. My mother was the strongest woman I'd ever known.

I'm sorry, I told my mother finally. *Please forgive me.*

You have always been forgiven, my mother sang. *You need to forgive yourself. You were a child . . . forgive yourself . . .*

I breathed.

A weight lifted off me. In my new lightness, I saw a coppery rope extend from my mother's aura. It was faded, a silk hair that, if I did not concentrate my gaze, would disappear into the color of the earth. Her *khsae* rope circled me, pulling me in. And with that, the world righted on its axis. I was finally free.

I opened my eyes to find myself in my bed in the hotel. In the dark, I reached for the phone and made a long-distance call.

27

A White Giant Barang in the Village

Phnom Penh, March 2000

I waited nervously at Phnom Penh's Pochentong Airport with Pheng for Mark's flight to arrive. The heat was oppressive, like stepping into a sauna. I released my long hair from its bun, let it flow down my back. Instantly, the back of my neck began to sweat, but I told myself to endure it. *He likes my hair down,* I reminded myself silently, peering at the gate as people began to exit, my hands sticky and my face shiny.

"The plane just landed," Pheng told me.

The arrival terminal was crowded with many other Cambodians and foreigners. It was the norm in Cambodia that for every arriving or departing person or family, twenty or thirty people would greet or send them off. My family had wanted to do the same for Mark, but I convinced them not to, telling them he would be exhausted and overwhelmed because he was not of our culture and did not speak our language.

"How do you know this man?"

"He's a friend," I chattered nervously. "We went to school together."

Wait . . . I second-guessed myself. *Was this what I told him before? Or did I say we were colleagues?* I couldn't remember and was grateful when Pheng did not ask a follow-up question.

"Pou! Ming!" *Uncle, Aunt,* an overseas Khmer woman called as she rushed out of the gate and into the arms of her family.

"Kmoy!" *Niece,* her family greeted back. And soon twenty pairs of other arms wove a net around her.

I tore my eyes away from the reunion in time to see Mark's head bobbing above the crowd. My stomach knotted and twisted as if someone were wringing it like a wet towel. I watched him search the crowd, wondering if having him visit was such a good idea after all.

When I telephoned him two weeks before, Mark was confused, sad, worried, and more than a little bit angry at me. I fought the urge to hang up, but instead pressed the mouthpiece closer to my mouth.

I thought over my words, hoping to find the right ones. "I don't want us to be over," I told him. "I'm sorry I disappeared. I just . . . needed to . . . go away."

He didn't say anything back.

I bit my lower lip to keep it from trembling. "Will you come to see me in Cambodia?" I asked, my heart pole-vaulting in my chest.

After a long pause, he finally answered. "Why do you want me to come?" he asked. His voice was freezing, like the winter he was in.

"I want to show you Cambodia . . ." *Show you who I am* . . .

He exhaled deeply into the phone. "Yes," he said. Silence. Somewhere between the twelve thousand miles that separated us, his voice broke into static. Then our call was cut short when the line died.

And now he was here. He walked slowly out of the airport, his gym bag slung over his shoulders. His face lit up when he saw me, and he waved back. And just like that, the tension and anxiety of the past nine weeks melted away.

"Mark! Mark!" I waved, my voice yelping from excitement. Pheng looked quizzically at me. "There he is," I said, my voice calmer now, pointing Mark out to him.

"He's a head taller than everyone!" Pheng exclaimed.

But I wasn't listening to him. My knees shook slightly as I rushed over to him. Mark walked toward me, and when we were in front of each other, before he could hug me, I extended my right hand.

"Take it; shake it," I said quickly in English.

Mark took the cue and shook my hands with three firm pumps. Blood rushed to my face, stretching my grin from ear to ear.

"My brother-in-law Pheng doesn't speak English, so we can talk," I said, explaining quickly. "My Cambodian family are even more old-school than my American family. As far as they know, we're work friends. So please don't look at me with loving eyes." I stole a glance out of the corner of my eye at Pheng, who was watching us intently.

"Hi," he said, not letting go of my hand. "It's so nice to see you, too . . ."

I gazed at him. Where our hands connected, the skin was slippery.

"I've missed you." He squeezed my hand.

"I've missed you, too." I said, pulling it out of his grasp. "And don't reach for my hands beyond this, or touch me with any kind of affection in front of my family."

After I introduced the men to each other, we walked to the parking lot, my arms stiff as wood planks by my side. I did not trust myself to look at Mark. When we found our car, Pheng insisted that Mark sit in the front, in the passenger-side seat, so he could have more legroom. I interpreted the gesture as we piled in. Pheng squinted when he saw Mark's knees touching the dashboard.

Mark turned to me.

"Please don't look at me for too long," I said anxiously. "As far as my family is concerned, you are a friend."

"How was his flight?" Pheng asked.

I began to interpret back and forth.

"Good," Mark said. "But a toddler in the next row cried all night."

"At least it wasn't a goat," Pheng told him, chuckling. "The last time I rode a Cambodian bus, a goat drooled all over me."

It was Mark's turn to laugh. "Tell him I'm sorry I don't speak Khmer," he said.

"No," Pheng replied. "Tell him I'm sorry I don't speak English."

I marveled at how even without their words, the two men struck an easy camaraderie. After a few more questions, the men fell silent. Pheng turned on the radio and focused on the road.

"Hang on," I said to Mark. "The road's about to get bumpy." I sat up in my seat and grabbed hold of the overhead handle bar.

"The last time we talked, you didn't want me to come," Mark said, turning to look at me. "What changed your mind?"

"I don't know . . . lots of things."

"I'm glad you called."

"Me, too," I whispered.

I stared into his blue eyes. "I'm sorry we have to go to the village on your first day here," I told him, feeling guilty I wasn't giving him time to acclimate to Cambodia before introducing him to my large family. "A neighbor is having a baby's coming-out party today and my sister Chou is making me go with her."

"What?"

"In Cambodia, when a baby is born, mother and child are kept quarantined inside the house for thirty days. I think this is done to keep them safe and protected from diseases and germs. And after thirty days, the family hosts a coming-out party, inviting all the friends and family to come view the baby."

"Makes sense," Mark said.

I shrugged, smiling. "Chou is rather baby crazy," I told him. "She insisted that I go with her."

"No worries," he said, grinning. "I'm excited to meet them."

After turning back around, Mark reached his right hand toward me between the shoulder harness and the door. I looked at Pheng and saw that his eyes were concentrated on the rough road. I sat forward and took Mark's hand. His fingers massaged the top of my hand, his thumb caressed my palm. A current of electricity ran through me, causing my face to warm.

As I stared out onto Cambodia's green countryside, I thought of my mother. I saw her sneaking out of her village to see my father, saw his face light up and hers break into a mischievous grin. For the next hour, Mark and I held hands in secret, like two high school kids.

THE CAR STOPPED AT THE VILLAGE SQUARE in front of a crowd of family and villagers who gathered in front of Chou's home to see Mark. When he exited the car, they swarmed around him. He put his hands together in front of his chest and bowed slightly, using the Khmer gesture I taught him long before. "Chump reap sur," he greeted them.

"Very nice," Auntie Takea said, chuckling. "He knows our Khmer greeting."

"He's very tall." Eldest Aunt stated, and the other aunties nodded in agreement. "And white."

I grinned. That was the Khmer way, to comment on the obvious.

"His eyes are very blue," Second Aunt told them. "They are as blue as the ocean."

Grandmother Soy Sauce peered up at them. "Niece, ask him if they hurt when he looks at the sun."

I interpreted all this to Mark in rapid succession. He smiled and continued to greet all the family with the Khmer gesture. "Chump reap sur, chump reap sur," he repeated, butchering the Khmer words I'd taught his American tongue.

The aunties laughed as more family and villagers gathered around him. And soon he was surrounded by a crowd of more than fifty people. They'd all come to see the white giant *barang*, a Khmer word used to describe a foreigner. For many in our rural village, it was the first time they'd seen a white person.

"He's so tall!" a village child exclaimed.

"*Chomp rrriip sour!!!*" another child yelled, making fun of Mark's pronunciation and laughing as the aunties shushed him.

"Bery nice to meet," Eldest Aunt said in English, shaking his hand.

When the aunties saw how friendly he was, they hovered even more. Like mother hens, they circled him. Eldest Aunt held on to his elbow and guided him into the house. Grandmother Soy Sauce barked for someone to bring his bag into the house. Second Aunt took Mark's other hand and led him upstairs to the living room. Auntie Takea followed, giggling like a schoolgirl.

"His hands are very big," Auntie Takea said to another auntie. "If they hit you, it would hurt very much."

My face fell at her words, and I was crushed at their implications. In many communities in Cambodia, domestic violence was rampant and widespread. It was so common that Auntie Takea's sentiment elicited no surprise from the crowd.

Grandmother Soy Sauce took his hand. "But he has a lot of good flesh," she said, staring up at him.

At six-foot-two, Mark was the tallest person in the village, and at 180 pounds, he was also the biggest. "Toat manne," *very fat*, Auntie Takea said, pinching the flesh of his forearm. The other aunties nodded in approval.

"What are they saying?" Mark asked.

I told him.

He stared at me, his eyes widened slightly. Like many other Americans, he didn't like hearing this. "Tell them that where I come from, I'm skinny."

"It's a compliment here," I told him, chuckling. "Fat is good here. It means you're healthy and wealthy. Here, they want to be fat, not skinny."

As we talked, the aunties walked around him. "Fat legs and arms too," they told each other.

"Just smile and nod at whatever they say," I instructed Mark.

We walked into the house to find Chou emerging from the kitchen with a tray that held a coffee pot, cups, and cookies. "Hellooo," she greeted him, using the only English word she knew.

"Chump reap sur." Mark bowed.

"He'll never get lost in the market," Chou told the aunties. "If he does, all we have to do is look up to find his head!" Her words elicited another round of laughter.

"Sit, sit," Chou instructed Mark, motioning him to the wooden table and chairs as the aunties lowered themselves to the floor. Chou saw his eyes following them. "Loung," she said. "Tell him to sit in the chair, and not to follow those silly old women. They complained when we were poor and didn't have chairs, and now that now we have them, they still only sit on the floor."

"The floor is cooler," the aunties chuckled. "We like the floor better."

Chou smirked at them. "What's his name?" she asked me even though I'd told her many times. Because it was a strange-sounding name to her, she had a hard time remembering it.

"Mark," I told her again.

But to Chou and the aunties' ears, the r in his name had disappeared. "Mak, Mak," the aunties repeated.

"Mak," Chou said.

So Mark became Mak.

"He has an open smile," an auntie cooed.

"Yes, yes, and very big teeth," another concurred.

Mark looked around, suddenly noticing that he was the only man in a room full of women, aunties, and children. "Where are all the men?" he asked, looking around.

"I don't know," I shrugged. "They're out there somewhere

doing men things . . . probably drinking beers and eating noodles or something."

"I'm inside with all the ladies."

"Yep."

As we talked, I saw Chou watching me. When I returned
her stare, she laughed. "We better be extra careful around
her," I told Mark. "She's a suspicious one."

The next hour, I was careful to lean my body away from
him, to not look at his face for more than three seconds each
time. Around us, the aunties grinned and hovered. When
Chou left to prepare our tea, she lurked in and out of the kitch-
en. And when I caught her, she changed her tactic and sent her
spies, her sons and daughters, to watch us instead. I felt like we
were living in Big Brother's house.

"Loung, why don't you go visit the uncles before we go to
the temple," Chou suggested after she realized that I was not
going to admit to anything more than the fact that Mark was
a friend.

"Okay."

After he finished his coffee, Mark and I paid our respects
by visiting my uncles' houses. First we went to Uncle Heang's,
my mother's older brother's house. He greeted Mark as a friend
in his modest house. Eldest Aunt brought out three bowls of a
sweet dessert for us to eat.

"Your aunt made this," Uncle Heang told me. "She's famous for it."

"Nom ur-urgh," *tapioca sweet balls*, I said out loud, my sweat
glands overheating.

It is a popular Cambodian dessert made of tapioca sweet
flour, filled with beans, molded into balls the size of a small
child's fist, and boiled in a pot of water until cooked. The
sticky sweet balls are then served in a bowl of warm sugarcane

syrup and creamy coconut milk, with roasted sesame seeds sprinkled on top.

I watched Mark scoop up a ball with his spoon, and the Khmer *nom ur-urgh* song leapt into my head: *Nom ur-urgh, laip mer pleugh, jeung throng plurng.* This translated approximately to: Sweet tapioca balls, swallow one too quick, your legs go straight. As children, we were told this was a dangerous dessert because if you took too big of a bite and swallowed too quickly, the sticky tapioca could get stuck in your throat and choke you to death. The song was to scare us into taking small bites and chewing before we swallowed.

"Mark, be careful," I urged. "If one gets stuck in your throat, your legs will go straight."

He looked at me, his eyes squinted in confusion. "What are you talking about?"

"You know . . . your legs go straight, as in stiff like a plank, a board. Dead."

Mark grinned. "Your mind works in a very mysterious way," he said, scooping up one of the golf-ball-sized desserts and plopping the whole thing in his mouth. He chewed quickly and swallowed. His legs did not go straight. I sighed with relief.

"That was delicious," Mark told Eldest Aunt, who promptly scooped more sweet balls into his bowl. On the wall, large portraits of our family smiled at us. Near the ceiling, in the highest position, Grandfather Akoang, Pa, Ma, and my sisters looked down at us.

Next we walked the short distance to visit Uncle Leang, my mother's younger brother. Uncle Leang took us out to his garden and pointed at his ripe papayas and green coconuts. Mark's eyes lit up.

"I used to only drink coconut milk when I was in living in the refugee camp in the Philippines," he said. "It was delicious and you didn't have to worry that it was contaminated by some amoeba or bacteria."

When I told Uncle Leang this, he picked a long stick up off the ground and began whacking at the fruits. After a few minutes, the sky was raining soccer-ball-sized green coconuts. After we had our fill, Uncle Leang sent Mark and me back to Chou's house with two large bags of fruit.

"Your family is very kind," Mark said, his hands heavy with the bags.

"I am very lucky," I replied, waving to my uncle.

We arrived back at Chou's house to find her waiting for me, grinning widely. "Mak," Chou said, pulling him up the stairs to his room on the top floor, which was conveniently down the hall from mine. "You rest while we go to a party." She stopped, looked at me with her question.

"No." I shook my head. "He would not like to go to a baby coming-out party."

Mark stifled a yawn. "Tell her next time," he said, teasing her. "But today, I will stay here and take a quick nap."

Chou shrugged and pulled me away.

For the next hour, I suffered through a procession of aunties and cousins putting their babies and toddlers into my arms to hold. "Smell that baby's head," a cousin told me, shoving her baby into my face. "Doesn't she smell good?"

Another thrust her infant in front of me. "Baby, tell Auntie Loung you want a little cousin to play with," she said, as if her daughter didn't already have fifty cousins to play with.

By now, I had learned that it was easier not to argue, to just sit, smile, and nod at whatever they said. All the while, I was counting down the minutes, waiting to return to Mark. But when we got back, I found him snoring in his room, exhausted from his twenty-eight-hour flight and jetlagged.

• • •

THE NEXT MORNING, MARK WOKE TO find me propped up on my elbow next to him, with one eye on him and another on the door. Downstairs, pots and pans clinked and clanged noisily, waking the children.

"Hi," he said groggily.

"Morning." I wanted to reach out and touch his face. But I kept my hand to myself. It was too early for that.

"How long was I out?"

I looked at my watch. It was 6 a.m. "Fourteen hours?"

"I needed that . . ." he said, rubbing his face. "It's so hot here . . ."

"It's our hot season. That's why my family has decided to drive to the beach, so we can swim in the ocean."

Mark sat up, stretched his legs. "When was this decided?"

"Last night." I was about to say more when I spied little Ching-ching at the door.

"Auntie," she said. "Ma said to come down . . ."

I sighed, knowing my alone time with Mark would have to come after we left the village.

A few minutes later, the family was packed up and ready to go. Mark watched in amazement as the aunties, cousins, nieces, and nephews climbed into the back of a truck. "Twenty-eight, twenty-nine, thirty people in one car and two pickup trucks," Mark said. "Wow."

"We never go anywhere alone in Cambodia," I explained. "We like to go everywhere as a family here. We really believe the more the merrier."

"Wow."

"Wow, wow, la holt!" Ching-ching and her cousin Moy-moy screeched at Mark, then ran and hid behind their mothers' skirts.

"What did they say?" Mark asked as they stuck out their tongues at him.

"They're making fun of you for saying wow all the time," I said, pretending to glare at my nieces. "*La holt* means always."

Mark stared at the girls. "Woowww," he repeated at them, prompting the girls to dash behind their mothers even more.

FOUR HOURS LATER, WE ARRIVED AT Sihanoukville.

Located 143 miles from the city of Phnom Penh, Sihanoukville was founded in 1960 as a port city. Since then, it had grown to be Cambodia's premiere coastal destination because of its miles and miles of white-sand beaches, where tourists and locals went to swim, snorkel, dive, and eat freshly steamed crabs. And like many other Khmers, our family was especially interested in the crabs. We found a quieter beach slightly off the beaten path, away from overcrowded and popular spots frequented by Western expatriates. As soon as Pheng pushed the truck gear into park, the kids scrambled off and spread out straw mats on sparkly white sand under a big tree. Not far behind them, Chou and the women began negotiating with vendors on the price for five kilos of steamed crabs and grilled corn. The food was delivered to our station thirty minutes later. When the first batch of food ran out, we bought more. All day, this went on. The men played cards and drank beer. The women cooked, told stories, and napped. Mark shot marbles with the little boys.

"He's getting beat," my brother Khouy told me, laughing.

"Having fun?" I yelled out to Mark, who was turning red from the heat and sun. But no one made fun of him or even seemed to notice.

"They beat me every game!" Mark flicked at a brown marble but it went astray and didn't hit any other. "These boys are just too good."

The boys rushed up to me and said something very fast. Mark looked confused. "They said you could buy back your marbles for one thousand riels." I told him.

"Scoundrels!" He mocked them. "I bought mine from these same boys for five hundred riels five minutes ago!"

The boys beamed at me proudly. "Yes, Khmer boys are very resourceful and clever that way," I said. "You better buy now if you want to keep playing, because their next offer will be fifteen hundred riels."

Hearing this, Khouy walked over and offered to teach Mark how to shoot marbles. But even after his lesson, Mark could not win. "I give up!" He threw up his arms and ran into the sea. I joined him, followed by Chou and the aunties, all of us ladies modestly covered in loose-fitting T-shirts and long wrap skirts. The only ones to expose their skin in bathing suits were the little girls. I dunked my head into the water to cool down, too constricted in my Khmer swimwear to swim anywhere far. When I came back up, I watched the little children surrounding Mark. As he swam, they tried to dunk him, but he ended up tossing them into the water instead. When he came out of the ocean, they followed.

"Loung," Chou called me, her voice full of concern. "Your friend is getting too red. Tell him to get out of the water."

I did as I was instructed. As we came out of the water, I spied Ching-ching and Moy-moy quickly running up behind him. Their arms, like fly-swatters, shot up. A second later, the hands came back down. Whap! Whap! They slapped Mark hard on his butt, one after another. I gasped. Mark looked down, and the girls giggled and scurried away.

"Little ones," I asked them. "Why are you slapping his bottom?"

"Because it is very big!" They covered their mouths, hooting.

"When he's in the water," four-year-old Moy-moy chortled, "his bottom does not sink! Like a swollen dead fish!"

"What'd they say?" Mark asked.

I told him, and he laughed. "They are tiny but their slaps are hard," he said, looking at me. "I thought it was just you— tiny and violent—but you are all like that."

The girls stealthily snuck up near him and raised their hands. I stopped them with a glare and they scurried away like little mice. "If they ever hit you anywhere near your head, tell me." I said to him. "They should know better because the head is a sacred part of the body, so the kids are not allowed to touch it. Especially the head of an elder. But it's okay for them to slap your butt."

"What about us?" Mark teased.

"Adult men and women cannot touch each other."

From the mat, the women interrupted us. "Mak, Mak," they called him. "Come eat with us."

"Mak." The men raised their beer cans to him. "Have a beer with us."

Mark looked at the men, then at the women. "Thank you," he said, waving to the men and following me to the women's corner. "I feel like a girl sitting with the ladies all the time," he lamented, as one by one, the old aunties beckoned him to sit by them, their wrinkled faces beaming.

I was happy that my family took to Mark. They showed it by teasing him relentlessly when a wandering pig snuggled up next to him on the beach. When they learned he could not eat raw vegetables for fear of stomach sickness, they fried everything in hot, bubbling oil for him. And every time he left our company, a slew of kids was sent to accompany him. Even to the outdoor toilet.

"Your mother would like him," Auntie Takea told me, walking over to Mark carrying her wriggling granddaughter and handing her to him.

"Uhh, I don't really—" Mark hesitated.

But before he could protest, the kid was in his arms. Around him, the grandmothers and aunties watched as if he were being tested. The child cooed and kicked.

"La awe, la awe," *good, good*, they cooed.

Chou scratched my arm as we were eating. "Mak is very nice. The uncles and aunts all like him. The kids like him, I like him."

I grinned. I knew if Mark had Chou's approval, then he had our family's approval in Cambodia.

"You should keep him," she stated.

"He's not a dog," I cracked. "We're just friends . . ."

"We may not speak English," Chou said, pinching my arm. "But we're not blind."

WHEN WE ALL MADE IT BACK TO the village, it was late at night. We all stumbled to our bed tired and hot. In my room, I lay in my bed and stared at the stars out the window, waiting for the rest of the house to fall asleep so I could sneak into Mark's room. But soon, my eyes closed and I was transported to another realm.

I was driving on a long stretch of road. The land before me was wide open and dotted with palm trees. In the distance, over the green rice paddies and a herd of brown cows, a truck barreled toward me. It was going too fast to take the horseshoe turn and drifted into my lane. It came at me, its headlights grinning like metallic teeth. My knuckles white, my finger bones pushing out of my skin, I yanked the steering wheel sharply to the right. The car skidded. Behind, four black lines sidled like snakes all over the road, chasing me. The engine roared, the tires slid on the gravel, and the car flipped over. Twice. Then a third time.

The windshield cracked. The moon, stars, and trees spun like stained glass in a kaleidoscope. A razor-sized shard dislodged from the pane and flew toward me, cutting my arm. Red tendrils spread out in every direction on my skin. The car slammed to the ground, and finally, my kaleidoscopic world came to a stop, crushing shrubs, branches, and twigs. Shattered glass showered over me, lashing my scalp.

Oh, no . . . I moaned, blood sliding down my throat.

The seat belt held my body up. Above, the stars twinkled, the moon hid behind gray clouds. My fingers shook in defiance, snaking their way to my abdomen. I gasped, opened my mouth, and fought for breath. The burn spread outward, setting my body on fire. On the small round mound protruding out of my shirt, my belly button had popped. It was a perfect outie. I cradled my belly, tears mixing with rage in my mouth. My womb opened and spilled blood onto the seat.

Don't leave me. Come back.

I was dying.

No . . .

I didn't fight.

And then there was only blackness.

I woke up trembling in my bed, my fingers spread out over my stomach. It was still flat. I was not with child, but the pain of the dream lingered. Like a starburst, it spread all over my body, spiraling outward to my limbs, chest, and lungs. Even though it was a dream, I could not bear the feeling of losing a child I loved.

The house was quiet when I snuck into Mark's room, touched his arm.

He stirred. "What is it?"

Hugging my knees to my chest, I said quietly, "I don't want to have a baby."

"That's fine," he soothed, reaching for me.

"No," I looked at him. "You say that now, but you might change your mind. I know I don't want to have a child."

I paused. "In America, everyone thinks you get over your traumas . . ." I continued. "But what if you don't? What if this is as good as I'm going to get?"

"Is that what you're most afraid of?" Mark asked.

"That," I said, looking at him, "and losing someone I love. The thought of it paralyzes me. I cannot live in constant fear."

He held me.

"Mark," I said softly. "I'm not sad about this. I'm at peace with it. I'm happy with my life and my work . . . and you. If we are to make a life together, you have to know this."

"Are you saying yes then?" he asked, hugging me tighter.

Staring into his eyes, I smiled. "I'm not saying no."

THE NEXT DAY, I TOOK MARK to visit my grandmother. She sat up in her wheelchair when she heard my voice calling her, and she reached out for my hand. "Daughter," she asked. "Did you bring me grandchildren?"

"No, Amah." I took her hands. "But I want you to meet a friend."

"Who is he?" Amah squinted.

"A friend from school in America."

She pulled my hand toward her, moving me in closer. "How does he like Cambodia?"

I looked at Mark, who was smiling at my grandmother. "He says he likes it very much."

"Good, good. Bring him here so I can see him."

Mark pulled up a chair next to her.

"Tell him I'm from China, but I also love Cambodia." Amah's voice trailed off.

Since she'd left China sixty years before, Amah had never returned. But when she spoke of her homeland, her voice still filled with longing and homesickness. This, I understood. Cambodia was the country that gave me many of my first loves—food, country, culture, colors, music, friends, and family—and would always be home to me.

"Daughter," Amah chuckled. "Is he pretty?"

"Yes," I answered, in awe of her humor, courage, and her generosity of spirit and hope. I took Mark and Amah's hands, and brought them together.

Amah sat up in her chair and turned Mark's hands over so she could examine his palms. "His has good, big hands," she commented. "Soft. I can feel very few lines. He has not lived through hard times." She turned his hands over and stroked his fingers, knuckles. "They are good to carry babies with, good to take care of you with."

"No—" I started to challenge her, but stopped in mid-thought and decided to let Amah be Amah, a matriarch and baby hoarder. "Amah, I have to leave for a few days, but I will be back."

"Daughter." She pulled my arm. "Talk to your mother."

"I will."

When it was time for Mark and me to leave the village three days later, the aunties, grandmother, nieces, and cousins gathered in the town square to see us off. Chou held Ching-ching's hand and stood near the car, waving as Mark and I climbed in.

"I'll be back," I assured my sister.

"We know," she answered. "But we don't know when our new friend Mak will be back. Tell Mak to come visit us again soon!"

As we drove off, my eyes drifted to the old tamarind in front of Chou's house. Its branches swayed and danced in the breeze; its trunk was gnarled with age and stress. I saw that my family was like the tamarind tree, each person a new branch growing, in spite of war and poverty. And within each branch, new leaves would sprout with each coming year, and through them our family line would go on. Even without my contribution.

28

A Gathering to Heal Lost Souls

Siem Reap, March 2000

Mark and I spent a few days exploring Phnom Penh, eating our way through my favorite restaurants and walking hand in hand along the Mekong River. When our time there ended, Mark and I woke up at the crack of dawn and boarded a boat for a five-hour ride from Phnom Penh to Siem Reap, the land of Cambodia's famous temples. The boat was crowded, filled with both Cambodian and foreign tourists. But while many Khmers sat inside, enjoying the shade and karaoke, Mark and I sat with other foreigners on top of the boat, exposed to the sun and to the magnificent view. With Mark's arms around me, I watched the river widen and narrow. Along the boat's route, life sprouted and grew, fishermen threw open nets, children attended school in boats, and mothers bathed in the water.

We arrived at Siem Reap and made our way on a rented motorbike to Phnom Kulen, the sacred mountain where King Jayavarman II proclaimed independence from Java, marking the birth of modern Cambodia in 802. From the main road, we drove the twenty-kilometer ascent to the temple summit, where a large reclining Buddha was carved into the sandstone boulder. As we climbed up the road, we gazed at lush giant palm leaves, their old vines shading the path. I stared at the ancient shrubbery, half expecting a pterodactyl to fly over our heads.

The sun climbed high in the sky as we rode. It was becoming too hot to go temple trekking, especially for Mark, whose white skin was turning the shade of a cooked lobster. We decided to wait for the sun to lower before climbing up the mountain. To stay cool, we veered off the path to a nearby waterfall. We rented a thatched-roof hut built above a rushing stream and equipped with hammocks and mats, and we lay down to rest. In the tranquility of moving water and singing insects, I swung on my hammock.

"It's so restful here," Mark said from his hammock. I turned to see Mark was watching me with a peculiar look on his face. "Are you okay?" he asked.

There was something different about me. I'd felt a shift in myself throughout my stay in Cambodia, a subtle change unlike others I'd experienced in my previous visits.

"I'm fine," I said, inhaling and exhaling deeply.

And there and then, for the first time in the years I'd known him, I told Mark all about my life during the war. Many of the details he'd read in my manuscript, so he knew my story, but he'd never heard it told from my lips. I had not discussed with him the nightmares of my parents' and sisters' deaths that continued to haunt me, or the Vietnamese soldier who sometimes still invaded my sleep. Or the scars that I continued to carry these many years after the war. I confessed the decades-old battles I'd waged against the Khmer Rouge soldiers, and how they'd fought me the hardest when I was in my teens. And every month, as my body changed, the soldiers seemed to gain strength. Many times, I wanted to give up the fight. I told him of the times when I wallowed in despair, wanting to end my life. I told him how, during numerous returns to Cambodia, I stood at the edge of a mass grave—from which more than fourteen thousand bodies had been unearthed—and prayed. A majority of those who had been buried there—fathers, mothers, brothers, sisters, uncles, aunts, and grandmothers—had had their lives silenced by a blunt instrument to the backs of their heads. But they were not silent to me, I told him. They were never silent to me.

Somewhere downstream, a mother and child bathed in the cool water, and their laughter echoed in the air. Imbued with this spirit, I told Mark about my dream of my mother's courage, strength, and love, and the confusion I had over my guilt and shame. I opened up to him about my two decades of episodic depression, which continued to occasionally take over my body in tsunami waves, threatening to pull me under. In these moments, dreams turned into nightmares, and light into darkness.

After I told him all that was in my heart, I sat numb and still in my hammock. A part of me waited for Mark to get up and leave. But he did not leave. "You know I'm crazy, don't you?" I asked.

"Only the good parts," he said, holding my hand.

"Mark," I whispered, "I don't want you to see the genocide museum or the killing fields or any of the mass grave sites."

"Why?"

"I need you to stay clean—to be my safe place."

Mark looked at me. "If that's what you need," he said.

My legs were light as I pushed myself back and forth in the hammock. When I stopped, for the first time, no muscle in my body twitched. Nothing jerked, jumped, or wanted to run away. In that moment, I felt more at peace than I ever had before.

THE NEXT WEEK, MARK AND I returned to Phnom Penh for his departure back to America. When we arrived in the city, I left Mark in the hotel and went out by myself. A short while later, I arrived at the entrance of a small, worn-down temple and walked in. Inside, a young monk offered me a handful of incense sticks.

"Maybe you would like to pray? Light incense in the temple?"

I nodded and put a few dollars in the collection box.

Inside the temple, I fell on my knees, staring at the burning incense and golden Buddha. The monk lit three sticks of incense. Once the flames caught, he walked over and handed the incense to me.

"Thank you," I whispered as he left.

I held the incense sticks in my hand, pressed between my palms. I prayed to my mother's spirit. I asked the gods to take care of my family and always keep them together, wherever they were. Then I placed my incense in the large golden bowl to burn with the hundreds of others. At the door, I brought my hands against my chest and bowed to the smiling Buddha at his altar.

Outside, I sat on a bench under a tree. And in the quietness of the temple ground, I pulled my notebook out of my backpack. Slowly, I rewrote my parents' last days of life on earth.

To do this, I reached back into time to find my parents sitting together in the rice fields. First, I whited-out from the scene the soldiers and their guns. Next, I erased the years of suffering etched on my parents' faces. I plumped up their cheeks, brightened their skin, put glints of laughter in my father's eyes, and covered my mother's lips with pink lipstick. Then I dressed my parents in new clothes: a silk blue shirt and silver sarong for my mother, a cool khaki shirt and green pants for my father. Finally, I painted their world with tall green palm trees, a perfect blue sky, and a warm round sun that covered everything in gold. I connected their hands so that their fingers clasped. Though in another world—they died apart, both in time and distance, in this world—they were together. Since it was my creation, I could imagine anything I wanted. So I superimposed all their children into the picture. I painted us fat, happy, and grown. We sang and danced in the village square as they watched. My parents closed their eyes, at peace at last to leave the world of the living, knowing that we were well, that we could take care of ourselves, and that we would take care of one another. I completed this picture by painting flocks of white pigeons to carry their souls into the heavens. And there they stayed, growing old together in perfect harmony. A love to last for all of eternity.

When the incense sticks burnt out, I met Mark by the riverfront. He was sitting on a baluster, staring into the Mekong River. I walked toward him, to a spot where perhaps my father and mother once sat and watched the sun set. In the sky, the sun gently lowered into the horizon and bathed the city in shimmering red light.

"You know, sunsets used to kill me," I said, sitting next to him. "The night the soldiers took my father, the gods had painted the sky like silken swaths of red, pink, and gold. How I hated the gods then for giving us such a perfect sunset." I paused. "But it's actually beautiful, isn't it?"

I watched the river swallow the sun. And in the distance, on the dark, sparkling surface of the water, a fishtail flipped and splashed ever so gracefully.

I ARRIVED BACK HOME IN WASHINGTON, D.C., to find the red light of my answering machine blinking. I pressed the play button.

"Loung." Meng's voice came on. "Your sister-in-law wants to say something to you. Call us."

Meng always had Eang talk to me when the news was bad. I picked up the phone and dialed their number.

"Loung," Eang demanded. "Chou and Khouy have already called twice. They drove two hours from the village to Phnom Penh to make the calls after you left. They said we should tell you to marry Mak. Who is this Mak?"

I was caught.

"He's my fiancé," I blurted out.

29

Double Happiness

Vermont, August 2002

In Cambodia, when it rained, it was a monsoon. Soon after the first raindrop, everything was flooded. In America, my engagement to Mark followed the same weather pattern.

"Loung, I had nice talk with Mark," Eang said, leaving a message on my answering machine. "Mark say you have church wedding; so we decided you have Chinese-Cambodian weddings, too. Okay. Mark will tell you more."

"Oy," I whispered.

Beep.

"Hi, sweetie," Mark's voice came on. "Your sister-in-law is a riot. Anyway, she . . . um, *we* decided on two wedding dates. Call me."

Beep.

"Loung." Eang was on again. "Your brother and me talked. We decided your Chinese-Cambodian party will be barbecue in backyard. We think, maybe we have two hundred fifty people . . . how many on Mark's side?"

It was supposed to be zero. It was going to be a romantic elopement. But at a July 4th party with his family in Cleveland, Mark told his mother. After that, there were tears, loud words, and more tears. We left the party with our elopement canceled.

Beep.

"Loung." Eang again. "Mark say August 22 for American wedding, and August 24 for Chinese and Cambodian ceremonies.

So it was decided. I went from no wedding to three ceremonies on two separate days.

Chou chuckled when I reached her on the phone that night. "Brother Meng told me you're engaged!" She hollered into the earpiece.

"Because you told on me!" I chided her. "You got me in trouble."

"I told you to keep him," she cackled.

"And I told you we were just friends."

"I told on you the way you used to tell on all of us when we were children!"

Here we are, I thought. Old women, and still telling on each other like children. But I wouldn't have it any other way.

SOON THE BIG EVENT—OR, RATHER, EVENTS—ARRIVED.

After much planning between Mark and Eang, it was decided that we would marry in Burlington, Vermont, with the church wedding to take place at Saint Michael's College Church, and the Khmer blessing and Chinese tea ceremonies to be held at Meng and Eang's house. For our ceremonies, Mark and Eang had planned three days of festivities. My brother Kim, who was living in Vermont with his family at this time and was a trained pastry chef, would make our wedding cake. Nieces Maria and Tori would serve as my makeup artists, stylists, and cheerleaders. And because it was an Asian wedding, children were invited. To entertain the guests, we put together CDs of the best '80s music to play on our two large boom boxes, bought a box of Hacky Sacks and Frisbees, and set up the Ping-Pong table in the basement. For the little ones, a trampoline would be erected in the backyard.

On August 17, 2002, Mark and I flew to Vermont. From there, Mark, Meng, Eang, and I drove an hour and a half to Montreal to rent my Cambodian dresses. The whole ride there, they attempted to convince me to pick three dresses, but I bartered them down to two. I chose a gold princess costume dress, complete with a gold tiara, necklace, bracelet, and anklets; and a sparkly orange outfit with a scallop-scale pattern that made me look like a mermaid.

A few days later, our family and friends arrived from Canada and all over New England. The Asian contingent converged at Meng and Eang's house, the aunties and grandmothers went to work cooking our wedding feast of pork barbecue, egg rolls, fried noodles, roast duck, grilled quails, sausage fried rice, and beef shish kebobs, and the men figured out the mechanics of setting up three large tents on a very small plot of land in the backyard. In each room, young nieces and nephews decorated the walls with red paper cutouts of the Chinese wedding symbol. Composed of two duplicating Chinese characters for happiness written next to each other, this symbol formed the word double happiness—a blessing for the new couple to find happiness together.

Mark's family checked into the Inn at Essex, where we would hold our American reception. Later that evening, Mark and his family came to Meng and Eang's home for a family-and-friends meet-and-greet before our wedding the next day. At the appointed time, I came down the stairs to find Mark's family—all his seven siblings and their wives, partners, children, and friends—in the living room mingling with our Asian family and friends. In our open kitchen, Eang rolled her famous egg rolls and waved. She and the aunties had filled one table with steamed dumplings, crispy chive cakes, golden roasted pheasants, and other Asian finger foods. On another table, they had carefully arranged plates of cheese cubes, deviled eggs, and cold cuts for the Americans.

"Hello, Saw." Mark greeted Eang as sister-in-law in Chinese. "I brought something for dinner." He handed Eang the cheesecake from the Inn's famous restaurant.

"Thank you," Eang said, smiling.

"Oops," I muttered. I'd forgotten to tell Mark that, like many other Asians, our family was lactose intolerant. Without mentioning this, Eang put the cake in the refrigerator.

Throughout the night, Mark and I moved around from one group to another, keeping a close ear on the conversations, making sure everyone was having a good time. I stopped for a moment when I heard our family friend Lang, a young man Mark's brother's age, say to him, "That's a nice shirt. How much you spend on it?"

"I don't know," Mark's brother answered.

"Whatever you paid, I'm sure it's too much." Lang told him. "See my shirt? I bought it at JCPenney on double discount day and paid seven dollars for it."

Somewhere in the room, Eang's friend Mai's ears perked up. In an Asian household, discussing discounted deals was like sharing insider-trading secrets with Wall Street stockbro-kers. Mai walked over to join them.

"Feel this shirt," she said, lifting her arm so the others could touch the cloth. "See, very soft. I got this on my last trip in Cambodia for three dollars."

But Mai's bragging rights were cut short when another family friend joined them. "That was nothing," Uncle Po said, gently pushing Mai's arm away. "Now look at this shirt." He raised his arm to everyone's eye level, rolling the material be-tween his thumb and finger. "I bought this shirt for one dollar in China and they gave me another one free!"

The group applauded loudly.

From there, I continued to dash around the room, making sure to say hi to everyone. I headed to the food table when I saw Meng talking to Mark's sister as she was staring at the plate of golden deep-fried pheasant. "So you like to eat baby birds?" he asked.

Oh no, I groaned to myself.

"Loung's favorite food is unhatched duck eggs."

Mark's sister took the bait. "What are those?"

"It's when farmers take duck eggs and let the mother duck sit on them for nine to sixteen days. Then the farmers take the eggs away and boil them. When you crack it open, the baby ducks are in there, with head, body, intestines, and feather wings already formed. It's delicious." Meng chuckled. "You eat it with lime juice, salt, and pepper."

Mark's sister turned a shade whiter as Meng continued to describe other Cambodian delicacies to her. But my worry turned to relief when she began to laugh and ate a pheasant.

As the evening wore on, Mark's clan and the Ungs appeared to be getting along. "See, they like each other," Mark whis-pered when he caught up with me.

"I wasn't worried." I smiled.

• • •

ON OUR AMERICAN WEDDING DAY, MARK POKED his head into our room at the Inn where I was getting ready. "Are you ready?" he asked, smiling.

I stared at myself in the mirror and exhaled deeply. "I guess."

"You look beautiful."

"Have they all left for the church?"

"Yes." Mark extended his hand out to me. "Let's go get married, baby."

Shaking my head frantically, I looked at him. "There's one more thing we have to do before that," I said, sitting down on the bed.

"What?"

"We have to write down our will."

"Now?"

"Yes, yes, yes. We have to do it now."

"Now?" Mark repeated.

I glared at him. "Okay, okay," he said, walking over to the desk and picking up a sheet of paper and a pen.

"Okay, write this down," I instructed. "I, Mark Priemer, promise not to die first."

"Wait a minute. I can't do that—okay." He wrote it down.

"When I, Loung Ung, die, I want to be cremated, with half my ashes scattered in Cambodia in my family's village, and half buried with you. I want to be cremated in the cheapest casket there is. No funeral, no wake."

"The family will need something to bring people together."

I considered his request. "Okay, they can throw a party if they want. But no open-casket wake, no funeral."

"If I die first, I'll want a wake and a funeral," he said, scribbing down what I had just said.

"You die last," I reminded him, squinting.

"I mean, hypothetically, if I die first."

My hands on my hips, I tapped my feet on the floor with annoyance. "Fine," I scowled. "But I won't be there."

Mark stopped writing and looked at me. "You have to be."

"Why?"

"Because it would be good for you to say goodbye to me . . ."

"No, it won't," I said, shaking my head. "I hate goodbyes. Besides, I have a plan."

"Okay, let's hear it."

"If you go first," I told him. "I will take ten thousand dollars and move to Cambodia to work at an orphanage for a year. I mean, what better place to grieve than in a place where I would be surrounded by new life?"

"Hmmm, that's actually a good idea."

Still, he insisted on a funeral and a wake for himself. He assured me his family could make all the arrangements so I wouldn't have to.

Next we moved to dividing up our assets. I wrote two things on the list: my mother's blue silk shirt and her green jade ring. The total value was $250, but both were kept in a bombproof, fireproof, and waterproof safe deposit box in Meng and Eang's house.

"Okay." I reread the contract. "That's good for now."

We both signed it.

"Are we ready now?" Mark asked.

"Okay," I said, smiling.

When we finally arrived at Saint Michael's Church, my heart was thumping as if it were a horse at a race waiting for the gate to open. Mark pulled the car door open and extended his hand. I took it, knowing that he could not promise he would not die on me. But until such time of our departure from each other, we had many chapters and pages to fill. Life would be what we made it. And we could color it with all the razzle-dazzle, razzmatazz, cosmic cobalt, and sienna red we wanted, because the world was full of all those shades and more. In the darkness, there was light, and in war, there was also love. As a daughter of Cambodia, I had witnessed the worst of man's inhumanity to man, but in the love of my mother, the bravery of my father, the kinship of my siblings, the pride of my countrymen and women, the work of my colleagues, and the grace and beauty of my friends and family, I had also seen the very best of man's humanity to man.

"Ready?" Mark asked, and I nodded.

Together, we walked down the aisle to see the happy faces of our family and friends surrounding us. "We would like to invite our family to come up and form a circle around us," Mark said.

Mark and I held hands and opened our circle to our family, our eyes sparkling as we gazed at each other. Our friends and families came up to the altar and encircled us. I felt the presence of Pa, Ma, Keav, and Geak in our circle. And somewhere in Cambodia, I knew Amah, Chou, Khouy, the aunties, and the cousins were cheering and choosing the fattest pig in the village to roast in my honor.

"Do you, Loung, take Mark . . ." the priest began.

"I do."

Acknowledgments

I am deeply indebted to my family, whose numbers are too large for me to list them all, for their continuous support and love. I owe much to the friends who've lived many of the stories in this book with me. They are a fine, funny, and good group of people, so it was with great regret that I squished their brilliant 3-D selves in order to fit them onto these pages. In many instances this meant I had to miniaturize their bodies, flatten their features, and rewrite their dialogue from my memory. I wish I had a photographic memory, but I don't. So, dear friends, you know who you are. I've tried my best to stay true to your character and our conversations.

A special thank-you goes to my grandmother; my sister Chou; brothers Meng, Khouy, and Kim; and sisters-in-law Eang, Mum, and Huy Eng. I am fortunate to be able to say that even if they were not my family, I would still call them good and decent people.

I am blessed also to have in my life wonderful groups of friends whose support made my writing life a little less crazy and lonely. Thank you to the PenGals Writers Group—Sarah Willis, Thrity Umrigar, Paula McClain, Sara Holbrook, Kris Olsen, and Karen Sandstrom—for their invaluable advice; the White Rice & Spice Sisters—Mala Yin, Angie Lau, Brenda Kim, Lea Yin, Sopheap Barrett, and Chul-In Park—for food and laughter; and the Cleveland Yoga Ladies—Sindy Warren, Jen Gorman, Tami Schneider, and Parker Bean—for stretching my body out after a long day of sitting in a chair.

My gratitude extends to Heidi Randall, Putsata Reang, Chivy Sok, Youk Chhang, Ronnie Yimsut, Roberta Baskin, Vanessa Trengrove, Chelsea Trengrove, Joanne Moore, Pam Putney, Beth Poole, Jeannie Bremer, Angie Pitha, Susan Bachurski, Gail Griffith, Elizabeth Taylor, and Barrett Thornton for their readings and words of encouragement. And to the tremendously talented Jenna Free at Girl Friday Productions, thank you for helping me with story development. I am also grateful to my extraordinary editors at HarperCollins Publishers, Gail Winston and Maya Ziv, and to my super-agent Gail Ross at Ross Yoon Literary Agency.

To my friends at Omega Institute for Holistic Studies—Elizabeth Lesser, Carla Goldstein, Gail Straub, Sarah Peters, and Ellen Wingard—thank you for the Phoenix. And to Isabel Allende, thank you for *Paula*. You inspired me to write this book for my mother.

In addition to my phenomenal women friends, I am lucky to have many remarkable men in my life. I'd like to give a shout-out to these good men: Chet Akins, Michael Thornton, Robert Smith, Michael Augoustidis, Sam McNulty, Scott Kim,

Ed Miles, Mark Perry, John Shore, George Greenfield, Dith Pran, and Dan Warren. To my heroes Vermont Senator Patrick Leahy and Tim Rieser, thank you for making this world a safer place for all. And to my mentor and friend Bobby Muller, and to the "gumbas": You are the finest of men.

Of course, this book would not exist without my husband, Mark Priemer. Thank you to all the Priemers, especially to the lovely Lynn and Gordon, who started them all.

Bibliography and Sources

I've included much more history in *Lulu in the Sky* than in my previous books. This was done because (1) I find Cambodian history fascinating, and (2) I wished to give readers a fuller picture of the country and its people. From its creation myth and ancient temples, to its winding rivers and lush green land, to its periods of truces and wars, Cambodia is a nation rich in story and heritage. In addition, Cambodia's political history is long and complicated, and historians continue to disagree on the exact numbers of survivors, victims, and military campaigns and operations that took place in Cambodia. Thirty years later, much of this information is still classified, hidden, or lost.

Admittedly, I am not a Cambodian scholar or historian and this book is not meant to be read as a definitive book on

Cambodian history or culture. I've written a memoir, so to keep the story moving, I've had to simplify and truncate the history. In order to add vibrancy and authenticity to a time I was not there to witness, I relied heavily on field research, documentary films, articles, papers, and books. Below is a list of resources I found extremely helpful. In many instances, I pulled from them morsels of information and facts and incorporated them into this book. I am indebted to these writers, producers, and filmmakers. Thank you all.

Informative Documentaries

"Angkor," *National Geographic* special, http://ngm
.nationalgeographic.com/2009/07/angkor/stone-text.

Bombhunters, Bombhunters.com.

Enemies of the People, EnemiesofthePeopleMovie.com.

New Year Baby, NewYearBaby.net, Broken English Productions.

Pol Pot Biography, www.biography.com/people/pol-pot-9443888.

S21: The Khmer Rouge Killing Machine, directed by Rithy Panh.

Articles

Fifield, Adam, "A Cruel Past Lingers: Echoes of the Killing Fields" (*Philadelphia Inquirer*, December 12, 2004).

Gourevitch, Philip, "Pol Pot's Children" (*The New Yorker*, August 10, 1998).

Huy, Ratana C., "Khmer Rouge Wedding" (*Magazine of the Documentation Center of Cambodia*, January 2002).

Siegelaub, Marc, "A Man Reborn" (*Newsday*, October 17, 2001).

Wilkinson, Alec, "A Changed Vision of God" (*The New Yorker*, January 24, 1994).

Books

Becker, Elizabeth, *When the War Was Over* (New York: Simon & Schuster, 1986).

Chanda, Nayan, *Brother Enemy: The War After the War* (San Diego, CA: Harcourt Brace Jovanovich, 1986).

Chandler, David, *A History of Cambodia* (Boulder, CO: Westview Press, 2000).

Chhang, Youk, Daryn Reicherter, and Beth Van Schaack, editors, *Cambodia's Hidden Scars: Trauma Psychology in the Wake of The Khmer Rouge* (Phnom Penh, Cambodia, Documentation Center of Cambodia, 2011).

Dy, Khamboly, *A History of Kampuchea (1975–1979)* (Phnom Penh, Cambodia: Documentation Center of Cambodia, 2007).

Ebihara, May M., Carol A. Mortland, and Judy Ledgerwood, editors, *Cambodian Culture since 1975: Homeland and Exile* (Ithaca, NY: Cornell University Press, 1994).

Gottesman, Evan, *Cambodia After the Khmer Rouge: Inside the Politics of Nation Building* (New Haven, CT: Yale University Press, 2004).

Ibbitson Jessup, Helen and Thierry Zephir, editors, *Sculpture of Angkor and Ancient Cambodia: Millennium of Glory* (London: Thames and Hudson, 1997).

Jacobsen, Trudy, *Lost Goddesses: The Denial of Female Power in Cambodian History* (Copenhagen: NIAS Press, 2008).

Kamm, Henry, *Cambodia: Report from a Stricken Land* (New York: Arcade, 1998).

Kiernan, Ben, *How Pol Pot Came to Power: A History of Communism in Kampuchea, 1930–1975* (London: Verso, 1985).

Paskin Carrison, Muriel, and the Venerable Kong Chhean, *Cambodian Stories from the Gatiloke* (Boston: Tuttle Publishing, 1987).

Pran, Dith, *Children of Cambodia's Killing Fields: Memoirs by Survivors*, edited by Kim DePaul (New Haven, CT: Yale University Press, 1997).

Power, Samantha, *"A Problem from Hell": America and the Age of Genocide* (New York: HarperCollins, 2003).

Roveda, Vittorio, *Sacred Angkor: The Carved Reliefs of Angkor Wat* (Bangkok: River Books Press, 2007).

Schanberg, Sydney H., *The Death and Life of Dith Pran* (New York: Viking Press, 1985).

Shawcross, William, *Sideshow: Kissinger, Nixon and the Destruction of Cambodia* (New York: Simon & Schuster, 1979).

Willmott, William E., *The Chinese in Cambodia* (Vancouver: University of British Columbia Press, 1967).

Helpful Websites

Cambodian League for the Promotion and Defense of Human Rights, www.licadho-cambodia.org.

Cambodian Women's Crisis Center, www.cwcc.org.kh.

Documentation Center of Cambodia, www.dccam.org.

International Campaign to Ban Landmines, www.icbl.org.

National Coalition Against Domestic Violence, www.ncadv.org.

For more information, visit www.LoungUng.com.

About the author

About the book

Read on

Insights,
Interviews
& More...

A Conversation about Writing and Healing with Loung Ung

Interview with Marianne Schnall, July 2, 2008.

Marianne Schnall: *You have said that when you first started writing, you wrote to save your life. How did it do this for you? How did the experience of writing help you?*

Loung Ung: Writing is very cathartic, a great therapy for me. But on a psychological level, it changed who I am. There was one scene in particular I had such a hard time writing. The scene where the Vietnamese soldiers tried to rape me. There was so much shame surrounding that. I had never told my brothers. My sister knew, who was there, but we didn't talk about it after that. There was so much shame that I was nine years old. Why did I go into the woods with him? Why was I picked?

When I was writing that scene, there was a moment after I finished it, I thought, "I didn't escape a rape, I fought my way out of a rape!" That is very much the seed of my power. To go from being a victim to a fighter, a survivor! I fought off a would-be rapist! I was nine, I was pushing him and I kicked him, and somehow, some way, my foot landed in his groin, and he clutched his balls and he went down and

I ran away. I thought at that point, like, wow—I was lucky. But now I look back and I go, wow—I fought my way out of rape. And that changed my focus. That changed who I am. I'm a fighter.

MS: *What do you think is the power of the memoir?*

LU: Memoirs bring the numbers of casualties to a human face. We often hear about how many hundred thousands killed in Darfur, and two million in Cambodia. All these big numbers. A memoir brings it down to a family, a face, a story, a brother, a father . . . it breaks down that barrier of what is Cambodia, Vietnam, Sierra Leone, Darfur—to a father, a mother, a brother, a sister. How I missed my mother—is that very different from how your children miss you? How I long for my father's touch on top of my head is not different from any other child's longing. A memoir connects the humanity in us.

MS: *As a survivor yourself, what advice would you give to people who have survived violence and other atrocities?*

LU: Each person's healing path is unique. Don't let other people hurry you, the path is different for everybody.
I do believe, however, that it is not enough to go deep in your healing but you have to go wide as well. For me, talk therapy and writing goes deep. In the West, I think we often go deep, but ▶

66 How I long for my father's touch on top of my head is not different from any other child's longing. 99

A Conversation about Writing and Healing with Loung Ung *(continued)*

rarely are we ever told to go wide. When you go deep, you can get stuck in the thought that "this" is all about you. But it's not. I survived the Khmer Rouge genocide . . . but so did 5 million other Cambodians, and 120 million others of other wars in the last century. What happened to me was not only a crime against Cambodians, but a crime against humanity. I have to keep this in mind, spread out the pain a little, or I'll drown in it. So I get involved with causes, become an activist, and cast my nets for like-minded friends and helping hands everywhere. Because going deep without a safety line to pull you out when you're in the dark, you can get lost in it. It's important to keep a foot in the world as you are going inside your heart.

MS: *What advice would you give to people on making a difference?*

LU: Start by learning about a cause or program that causes your heartstrings to vibrate. Go to the computer and read up on it. On their websites, they'll have a page telling you how you can take action, help out. If the program doesn't have one, help them build a site. Or raise that $500 to help them build a site. Do what you can, however you're able. Just do something. There are over a million registered charitable organizations in the U.S. A lot of people are doing a lot of good work. Join them.

66 It's important to keep a foot in the world as you are going inside your heart. 99

4

Activism is like a muscle—the more you use it, the stronger it gets.

MS: *How do you create balance and keep yourself centered in your own life?*

LU: I eat really well. [Laughs.] I love food. I write, play, and ride my tandem bike with my hubby. I try to good care of myself. I have a wonderful group of friends who love me and support me. There are times when I overcommit, or find myself in that dark place of my survivor's guilt, ashamed for the food I stole, people I hurt, lies I told to survive. I reach out to my friends. I'm not afraid to ask for help, food, a movie night, a good joke. Sometimes, when I am in that dark place and feel bad about myself, I think—I can't dishonor my friends by thinking so badly of myself. My friends are good people, and if they love me, I can't be that bad. That actually helps me. I am very blessed in that I'm surrounded by good people, good human beings.

MS: *What is the one message you would most want to convey to the world today?*

LU: That as a people, we have more courage, more worth, and more strength than we realize.

We women are told everywhere we turn—in newspapers, radio, televisions, magazines, books—that we are imperfect in so many ways. Be it our ▶

66 As a people, we have more courage, more worth, and more strength than we realize. 99

A Conversation about Writing and Healing with Loung Ung *(continued)*

appearance, relationships, personalities, there seem to be so many things terribly wrong with us. But how can there be that many things wrong with us and yet here we are? We've got to sit down sometimes and look at what's right. And know that what's right is not anything that the world out there can dissect. It is wholly what is in you. ∽

To read the full interview, visit www.feminist.com.

Marianne Schnall is a writer and author, and the founder and executive director of Feminist.com. Her interviews appear at Feminist.com; *O, The Oprah Magazine*; *Glamour*; *The Huffington Post*; and others. Marianne's new book, which features Loung Ung, is *Daring to Be Ourselves: Influential Women Share Insights on Courage, Happiness and Finding Your Own Voice.*

The Inspiration for *Lulu in the Sky*

FIRST THEY KILLED MY FATHER: *A Daughter of Cambodia Remembers* (2000) was born out of my need to tell the world about the Cambodian genocide, and *Lucky Child: A Daughter of Cambodia Reunites with the Sister She Left Behind* (2005) came out of my desire to share my sister's story and my own transformative journey from victim to survivor in the aftermath of war. In my latest, *Lulu in the Sky: A Daughter of Cambodia finds Love, Healing, and Double Happiness*, I wanted to share the story of the love that binds my family and me together, the love of a child for her mother, and of a woman and her partner.

Lulu in the Sky jumped into my mind on my thirty-eight birthday as I was blowing out the candles on my cake. As my friends cheered, I was focused on one singular thought: In one year I would outlive my mother. Suddenly, instead of laughing, I felt myself sinking into a depression.

My mother died when I was eight. But with each passing year, as long as I knew she was alive at my age, I could feel her presence. Throughout my childhood and metamorphosis into a woman, I continued to talk to my mother as if she were near. There were days when I could even see us walking side by side, sharing our lives, and having intimate mother-daughter conversations just like my friends ▶

had with their mothers. And sometimes, when I was particularly creative, I imagined my mother living out her life in a parallel world. But not that day.

In one year, my life would move past my mother's, and our roles as mother and daughter would reverse. Wrapping my mind around this thought made the room sway. I had spent my life thinking about my mother and speaking to her as an elder, but soon I would be the elder. It was then that I was hit with another fear that forced me to sit down. *What if, when I outlived my mother, I stopped feeling her presence?* The room darkened as the anxiety of losing my mother all over again crept into my consciousness. The cells in my body screamed for me not to let this happen.

As my birthday candles went out, I was reminded of the time, a few years back, when I went to see a psychic to try to communicate with my mother. I had resisted visiting one until then out of fear that this could open a portal to the other side and I'd be stuck with all kinds of spirits following me around. But I was desperate to speak with my mother so I pushed away my trepidation. I found a reputable medium through a friend and arrived early for my reading.

The medium was a man in his early fifties, with a face that reminded me of Mr. Rogers. I scanned the room; it was decorated like an old farm cottage and smelled of burnt incense and potpourri.

❝ In one year, my life would move past my mother's, and our roles as mother and daughter would reverse. ❞

"Please sit down." The medium beckoned me.

I took a seat in the stiff-backed chair across from him.

"I sense you have written something . . ." he began.

I nodded.

"I sense it would make a good movie," he said. "You should ask Cecil B. DeMille to help. He would like this movie."

"Oh . . . okay . . ." *Cecil B. DeMille?* I asked silently. I was an avid fan of the American Movie Classic channel and knew Mr. DeMille's most famous works (*The Ten Commandments, Cleopatra,* etc).

"I sense a lot of spirits around you," the medium said. "Your parents and sisters are here with you. Your sister Geak—"

"Geak! What . . . what does she say?"

He gazed over my head, stared at my right shoulder, and said, "They say they forgive you. They love you. They say you don't need to say you're sorry."

"Love means never having to say you're sorry," I muttered the line from *Love Story.*

The medium breathed deeply, as if in a trance. He looked at me for a very long moment, crossing and uncrossing his legs. "I'm sorry," he said. "But this session is over."

"What?" We were barely fifteen minutes into my supposedly one-hour reading. ▶

The Inspiration for *Lulu in the Sky*
(continued)

"They're speaking a language I do not understand."

"Wait," I said, incredulous. "You can't understand them? Isn't there a universal language of the dead or something? Is my mother in the Buddhist Heaven? Is she with my father and sisters? Wha—"

The medium ushered me out the door without answering my questions. I returned home that afternoon bluer than when I'd left it.

After my birthday I became obsessed with learning more about my mother, who she was, her dreams and desires. Exploring these questions made me realize how little I knew about her beyond her roles as a wife to my father and a mother to my siblings and me. It was then, as I lay on my bed fuming about the medium, staring at the pens and papers on my bedside table, that I knew the portal to my mother was in me all along. It was that night that I began to write about her.

The next few months, in between visits with family, friends, and my therapist, I spent ten to twelve hours a day talking to my mother, dreaming up her thoughts, and reliving her life. At first I could only write about how much I missed her, how I wished she had been there to watch me grow up, graduate from schools, and travel back to Cambodia. But the more I wrote, the more I saw that a story about my mother would not be complete without the stories of her family. And soon I was

❝ As I lay on my bed fuming about the medium, staring at the pens and papers on my bedside table, I knew the portal to my mother was in me all along. ❞

writing about the lives that have grown from her line, weaving in the threads of my own life as well as those of my grandmother, sister, brothers, and friends. Writing my mother's story also made me realize that she had always been with me. She was beside me when I reunited with my sister and family, she was watching when I fell in love, and she stood next to me when I married Mark. Even in the times I could not feel her presence, I believed she was there in all the big and small moments in my life. *Lulu in the Sky* is a story about those moments.

I wrote this book in honor of my mother, grandmothers, and other aunties and mothers around the world. As an aunt and great-aunt, I want my mother's descendants to know her, at least as much as I could gather of a woman who was vibrant, beautiful, and full of light. As a daughter, I wanted to say thank you to my mother, and to let her know— wherever she may be—that I am proud to be her daughter. ❧

> **❝** I wrote this book in honor of my mother, grandmothers, and other aunties and mothers around the world. **❞**

Have You Read?
More by Loung Ung

LUCKY CHILD

After enduring years of hunger, deprivation, and devastating loss at the hands of the Khmer Rouge, ten-year-old Loung Ung became the "lucky child," the sibling chosen to accompany her eldest brother to America while her one surviving sister and two brothers remained behind. In this poignant and elegiac memoir, Loung recalls how she assimilated into an unfamiliar new culture while struggling to overcome dogged memories of violence and the deep scars of war. In alternating chapters, she gives voice to Chou, her beloved older sister whose life in war-torn Cambodia so easily could have been hers. Highlighting the harsh realities of chance and circumstance in times of war as well as in times of peace, *Lucky Child* is ultimately a testament to the resilience of the human spirit and to the salvaging strength of family bonds.

"Remarkable. . . . *Lucky Child* is part adventure, part history, and, in large part, a love story about family. The Ungs' tenacity and enduring kindness testify to the very best of human nature. After surviving 'the worst kind of inhumanity,' the Ungs remain human."

—*Cleveland Plain Dealer*

FIRST THEY KILLED MY FATHER

Loung Ung's *First They Killed My Father* is an unforgettable narrative of war crimes and desperate actions, the remarkable strength of a small girl and her family, and a triumph of human spirit over oppression. Loung Ung, one of seven children of a high-ranking government official, lived in Phnom Penh until the age of five. She was a precocious child who loved the open city markets, fried crickets, chicken fights, and sassing her parents. When Pol Pot's Khmer Rouge army stormed into Phnom Penh in April 1975, Ung's family fled their home and moved from village to village—hiding their identity, their education, and their former life of privilege. Eventually the family dispersed in order to survive. Loung was trained as a child soldier in a work camp for orphans, while other siblings were sent to labor camps. As the Vietnamese penetrated Cambodia and destroyed the Khmer Rouge, Loung and her surviving siblings were slowly reunited. Bolstered by the bravery of one brother, the vision of the others, and the gentle kindness of her sister, Loung forged on to create for herself a courageous new life.

Have You Read? *(continued)*

"There can be absolutely no question about the innate power of [Ung's] story, the passion with which she tells it, or its enduring importance."
—*Washington Post Book World*

Don't miss the next book by your favorite author. Sign up now for AuthorTracker by visiting www.AuthorTracker.com.